Mendini

Mendini

**ALESSANDRO MENDINI:
IMAGINATION TAKES COMMAND**

Stefano Casciani

All works and drawings throughout, unless otherwise indicated, are by Alessandro Mendini. Collaborators and working groups are detailed in the extended picture captions and credits section at the back of the book.

LETTER TO A FRIEND TRAVELLING THROUGH SPACE AND TIME	7
CHAPTER 1 IN SEARCH OF LOST TIME AND SPACE: THE ORIGINS	13
CHAPTER 2 RADICAL DESIGN: THE GHOST IN THE MACHINE	35
CHAPTER 3 PROUST: A KITSCH REVOLUTION FOR THE COMMON MAN	65
CHAPTER 4 FROM POSTMODERN TO NEOMODERN: THE ALESSI AND DOMUS YEARS	83
CHAPTER 5 ENDLESS EPHEMERA: FURNITURE AS FASHION	113
CHAPTER 6 OBJECTS WITH ART AND SOUL: THE DESIGNER AS PAINTER	131
CHAPTER 7 LEARNING A NEW UTOPIA: FROM LAS VEGAS TO GRONINGEN	159
CHAPTER 8 THE GOLDEN DESIGN AGE: SWATCH TO BISAZZA AND BEYOND	185
CHAPTER 9 THE ALESSI CORKSCREW AND THE GLOBAL CITY	215
CHAPTER 10 THE END AS AN ETERNAL RETURN: LIGHT, COLOUR AND BACK TO DOMUS	245
EPILOGUE	274
IN THE GARDEN OF EDEN: THE BIGGER PICTURE OF ALESSANDRO MENDINI	276
FOOTNOTES	290
EXTENDED PICTURE CAPTIONS AND CREDITS	292

LETTER TO A FRIEND TRAVELLING THROUGH SPACE AND TIME

The Master has no possessions.
The more he does for others, the happier he is.
The more he gives to others, the wealthier he is.
The Tao nourishes by not forcing.
By not dominating, the master leads.
　　　　Lao Tse, *Tao Te Ching*, sixth century BC

Dear Sandro,

There comes a moment in every author's life and career when they must reckon with their past. If every work is also a form of autobiography, then this book is the perfect opportunity for me – especially because it's about you, the most generous intellectual of Italian design of the twentieth and twenty-first centuries. You were the friend and mentor with whom I've travelled many of the long and winding paths that make a working life worth living, all the while leaving behind words and marks of *quali cose siamo* (who we are), as you yourself titled one of your most chaotic and moving exhibitions.

Writing this book to capture your kaleidoscopic talent meant not only trying to piece together a 'complex and contradictory' body of work – as your friend Bob Venturi liked to call it – but also to recreate the intricate collage (or perhaps puzzle?) of your many lives and intellectual identities, just like the glass mosaics you loved so much and chose as your design tool. Writing about you also meant recalling the grand history of Italian design and its golden age, which is arguably now over. It meant reliving the everyday moments and incidents that (as tends to happen when one has a good memory) seem like just yesterday, especially those occasions when we experienced a flash of inspiration, like a lightning bolt. Such as the time when, while discussing art and design with the brilliant industrialist Aurelio Zanotta, after a moment of reflection he decided to start a new collection of artist-designed furniture, with me as the curator and you as the main – perhaps sole – creator.

It would have been impossible, of course, to include in this book the many other episodes that, over the span of forty years of friendship and collaboration, saw us share significant moments in Italian history and progressive culture. You navigated that critical progressivism with a light touch, clarity and irony – which you always wielded as a weapon against enemies, conventions, or simple intellectual laziness, things not lacking in the world of architects, designers and artists. It was a lesson in professionalism and elegance that I will never forget, and one that only those who knew you well and truly cared for you witnessed in both important and trivial moments, but also absurd, sad, or amusing ones. Because if it's true that life is what happens while you're busy with other projects, then successes and failures, recognition and solitude, admiration and indifference all come and go without any order or logic. This stands in contrast to the modernist myth of consistency and 'market research' which you never believed in – because you were more interested in life outside the project than in the project itself.

So, I left out the story of that summer evening in 1980 when, after the opening of the major international exhibition *Forum Design* in Linz, in a restaurant on the Danube, a lively young woman – during a slightly tipsy conversation – took the hand of the shy new director of *Domus* (you) and smeared it with mayonnaise or mustard. You were astonished but let her do it, and the gesture had all the diners, including Ettore Sottsass, laughing as he announced the defeat of terrorism in Italy. And I only made a brief reference to that evening in 1985 when, as we crossed paths on the stairs of the Zeus space in Milan – you heading down with Anna Gili and me heading up – you greeted me with that ironic smile of yours and said, 'So, it seems we're both changing professions, you and I…' For me, it marked the end of my work as art director at Zanotta, a company you too had worked for with great affection, and you were leaving your beloved role as editor of *Domus*. But not for good – twenty-five years later you would return, and from 2010 to 2011 we directed *Domus* together (alongside other friends who are no longer with us, like the brilliant art director Giuseppe Basile), producing eleven beautiful issues that were destined to become collector's items.

And I could hardly include an even earlier moment from 1979, while you were still the editor of both *Modo* and *Domus*, when you acted as messenger, delivering an envelope to me from someone in that editorial office you clearly loved. You showed me that making magazines is (or was) about falling in love with the very idea of a magazine and with the people who create it. And, just as with love, there's an element of playfulness and fun that comes with the highs and lows of publishing newspapers and magazines. But those were different times – another century, another world and a different Italy. Contrary to the usual narrative of the 'serious' 1970s and the 'frivolous' 1980s, this Italy navigated the shift from revolutionary dreams to the harsh reality of capitalism – no matter how advanced and enlightened – with much less drama.

Many of the utopias and progressive ideas of the 1970s have since evolved into forms that are more compatible with a capitalist culture and society (not yet as fierce as it is today). Your numerous works published in this book reflect this, showing how the anarchic idea of mass creativity found expression through collaborations with countless other creators.

Regarding the impermanence and entropy you often spoke of, in the following texts I won't dwell on perhaps the saddest moment of all: our last farewell in 2003 to the great art critic and mutual friend Pierre Restany. He was the one who introduced you to the court of Gio Ponti and Gianni Mazzocchi, and you collaborated with him on many projects, including the theatrical work *70 Angels on the Facade*, dedicated to Ponti and *Domus*, staged by Bob Wilson at the Piccolo Teatro in Milan.

After writing so much about you for this book, trying to be as objective as possible, my memories have become blurred and altered. But they also inspire hope, or perhaps a kind of utopia, the kind you often talked about: the hope that, as in every good sci-fi story, we might meet again in some future dimension, perhaps on an Einstein-Rosen bridge like the one from the film *Interstellar*, to discuss whether this book manages to capture your talent and imagination. Those qualities brought to life the revolutionary dreams of two generations – yours and mine – that may have failed politically, but not culturally. They left, and continue to leave, subtle signs that another earthly happiness is possible. It wouldn't surprise me if it's true what I've often thought – that you, being so far removed from conventional ideas and concepts of design, were really an extraterrestrial, here to help us Earthlings, confused and uncertain as we are.

My last memory of you as a benevolent Martian is from an evening in 1985. After taking a taxi ride together, knowing I was starting a project called *Società Artisti e Designer* (Society of Artists and Designers), you hesitantly pulled from your pocket a paper titled *Pittura Progettata, Design Pittorico* (Painting as Design, Design as Painting) – a theoretical prelude to your final transition into design as art. You handed it to me shyly and simply said, 'I wrote this, you might find it interesting.'

The hardest part now is to conclude this introduction, which of course comes after finishing the long work of this book. To conclude means to close, to end a dialogue that has lasted so long, even continuing after your earthly departure. The philosopher Massimo Cacciari asserts that something or someone who disappears still exists in some form. So, this book will travel the world, speaking of you, who still and always will exist in the cloud of your writings, sketches and designs – for chairs, vases, bicycles, clocks, coffee makers, armchairs, tables, pools, theatres and museums. But for me, your friend writing to you, without quite knowing exactly where you are in time and space, this is still a farewell, even if just a temporary one.

Certainly, the effort of creating a significant volume like this came with challenges, worries and second thoughts – regrets, as they say in painting. But once the book is completed, closed and printed, there will be no regrets. It is comforting to know that, along with your encyclopedic work, what we experienced – whether near or far, separate or together – now remains for you and for the rest of the world, here and now, in these pages and in the universe of space and time. Forever, I hope.

Ciao, Sandro.

Stefano Casciani

Alessandro Mendini and Stefano Casciani, Milan, 2008

overleaf: Newborn twins Alessandro and Mia Mendini with Savinio's painting *l'Annunciazione*, drawing, 2006

IN SEARCH OF LOST TIME AND SPACE: THE ORIGINS

evident in his thoughtful writings on the great masters of architecture were also on display in his humorous cartoons for the tyre company Pirelli: both are remarkable for the empathy Mendini showed every time he depicted a character entangled in the affairs of life.
In Mendini's work, stories of sentimental experiences, interpersonal relationships, and simple wonder at the unexpected are all told by slender figures against backdrops reminiscent of Lyonel Feininger's engravings, Bruno Munari's negative/positives and even the naïve romanticism of Raymond Peynet. But more interestingly for his artistic biography, many of his drawings and cartoons from the 1950s and 1960s already showed evidence of the abstract, symbolic, and figurative imagination that would go on to play a significant role in Mendini's more famous later projects, from the beginning of his collaboration with Studio Alchimia, through the extensive work with Alessi, all the way to the last day of his working life at the Atelier that bore his name.

MENDINI BEFORE MENDINI

Throughout the 1960s and 1970s Mendini harboured at least two distinct personas. First: that of the intellectual architect in opposition, who was intent on upending the foundations and clichés of a Modern movement that was gradually losing many of its reasons for existence, starting with the very idea of the avant-garde. Second: that of the author (at the time, it was not yet possible to call an architect an artist; many years would have to pass before that would be the case). Through many different means – from writing to drawing and architectural plans to objects – Mendini tirelessly sought and refined the tools to manifest his own expressive dimension. During these years his inclination towards bourgeois subversion became more evident, a quest for measured rebellion against societal conditioning. He embraced a progressive yet complex ideological identity, often expressing it with slogans laden with scepticism and even traces of cynicism, such as:

> *A project never corresponds to the truth*
> *Every piece of architecture conceals a terrorist*
> *Achieve the utmost bad taste possible in a project* [4]

Meanwhile, the more direct, existential and cultural influences, which eventually contributed to shaping his poetic mythology, remained almost dormant. Only by continuing his exploration of new, more individual paths over the years, did Mendini recall the literary and artistic impressions of his youth. These would lend a poetic character and a different dynamic to the later development of his work. Though the direct influence of Marcel Proust and his psychoanalytic novels on Mendini is widely known, thanks to the international fame of the painted armchair that Mendini named after the French writer, there are many other artists – or more precisely, their works – with whom Mendini had the opportunity to interact directly because of the fortuitous circumstances of his birth and childhood.

CASA LA VITA

The house in which Mendini was born, raised and lived much of his adult life was built between 1929 and 1931 by Mendini's grandfather, the contractor Francesco Di Stefano (nicknamed Chichì, he was the father of five children, including Fulvia Mendini Di Stefano, Alessandro's mother), who commissioned Piero Portaluppi for the design. One of the most fashionable architects among the Milanese upper classes at the time, Portaluppi was also remarkable for his reinterpretation of the classic tradition, creating what would become known in architectural circles as the Novecento style.

The building – now known as the Casa Museo Boschi Di Stefano – is set on Via Giorgio Jan,[5] a street that runs parallel to the major thoroughfare of Corso Buenos Aires in an affluent area of Milan. Portaluppi dreamed up a plan for the commissioner and his family that was akin to a small urban palazzo in both structure and dimensions. Great bay windows with impressive ornamentation in Portaluppi's typical style are diagonally set at both corners of the front facade. The interiors are filled with refined artisanal materials and workmanship, including wrought-iron railings and lamps and stained-glass windows.

INSPIRATIONS: FROM GAUDÍ TO PEYNET

In 1926, at the age of 74, an old man perceived as mad by his fellow citizens died in a ward of the poor people's hospital in Barcelona; having emerged, bewildered, from the cave he lived in, he had been struck by a tram. For many years, he had been holed up like a hermit amid the foundations of the barely sketched out cathedral that had been the purpose of his life; a banal accident concluded his exhausting battle against time and people. Thus, the architect Antoni Gaudí, the genius who keenly distilled the most intimate aspects of traditional Spanish culture and who suffered with dramatic sensitivity all of the complexities of contemporary art, passed away in complete obscurity.[1]

When Alessandro Mendini published this text on Antoni Gaudí in 1958, he was 27 years old and had not yet graduated in architecture from the Politecnico di Milano (Polytechnic University of Milan). Nevertheless, he already had his own studio at 14 Via San Maurilio, which he ran with his classmate Mario Brunati. Together, they designed and executed small but significant exhibitions on the work of great masters of the twentieth century, the first of which was a show on Gaudí. The tone of their presentation was both informative and dramatic. Before moving on to a sharp, critical analysis of Gaudí's work, with the few sentences above, Mendini sketched out the character and tragic fate of one of the greatest, and certainly most eccentric, figures in Modern architecture. Here, one can already detect a bitter recognition of the fact that nothing lasts forever, of the impracticality of utopias, and of the challenges of bringing to life and establishing ideas and practices – especially in architecture – that are as innovative as they are unorthodox.

Mendini's calling as an intellectual working with both words and images was already evident by this time, although it was to take unpredictable directions. Naturally shy, but with the confidence of a young man from the affluent Milanese bourgeoisie, Mendini was profoundly drawn to expressionism, and wrote with both admiration and sympathy for the brilliant but eccentric Gaudí, the esoteric Rudolf Steiner and the heroic protagonists of various historical avant-gardes.

For their 1960 exhibition on Erich Mendelsohn, who had died seven years earlier, Brunati and Mendini managed to obtain 25 original drawings from Mendelsohn's widow Luise – most likely through the intervention of Gio Ponti. Ponti had known Mendelsohn ever since the 5th Triennale di Milano in 1933, which Ponti had helped to organize, and where some of Mendelsohn's projects had been displayed as part of a solo exhibition. The invitation for Brunati and Mendini's exhibition included a lovely letter to the two architects, in which Luise recalled the significance of drawing in her husband's work. It also featured a brief text by Ponti praising the two recent graduates for 'the exemplary and spirited cultural initiatives of their young studio'.[2] For them, as for many other Milanese architects, Ponti wasn't just a professor at the Politecnico but also a fundamental part of the Milan design scene, known for the positive eclecticism of his interests as well as his prolific activities as a designer and an extraordinary promoter of architecture and design. Mendini admired Ponti so much that he would go on to refer to him on numerous occasions as the embodiment of inventive imagination, intellectual curiosity, stylistic freedom, and indifference to academic conformity: all qualities that Mendini would himself try to embody.

And yet initially Mendini's ambition wasn't to become an architect. From a very young age, he demonstrated a great skill for drawing – or more precisely, as a cartoonist. Mendini was a humourist, able to tell stories with both minimalist strokes and a graphic richness similar to Saul Steinberg, designed to draw a smile from the reader. And, most of the time, it was a bitter smile, because, after all, there is no comedy without mishaps and drama.

Mendini's sketches conveyed an affinity with the world of contemporary art, rather than being simple satire, especially when compared to other Italian cartoonists who had drawn for satirical magazines, such as the anti-fascist publication *Il Becco Giallo* (1924–31) or the more popular *Marc'Aurelio*[3] (1931–58, for which Federico Fellini drew before becoming a famous director). The storytelling skills that were

evident in his thoughtful writings on the great masters of architecture were also on display in his humorous cartoons for the tyre company Pirelli: both are remarkable for the empathy Mendini showed every time he depicted a character entangled in the affairs of life.
In Mendini's work, stories of sentimental experiences, interpersonal relationships, and simple wonder at the unexpected are all told by slender figures against backdrops reminiscent of Lyonel Feininger's engravings, Bruno Munari's negative/positives and even the naïve romanticism of Raymond Peynet. But more interestingly for his artistic biography, many of his drawings and cartoons from the 1950s and 1960s already showed evidence of the abstract, symbolic, and figurative imagination that would go on to play a significant role in Mendini's more famous later projects, from the beginning of his collaboration with Studio Alchimia, through the extensive work with Alessi, all the way to the last day of his working life at the Atelier that bore his name.

MENDINI BEFORE MENDINI

Throughout the 1960s and 1970s Mendini harboured at least two distinct personas. First: that of the intellectual architect in opposition, who was intent on upending the foundations and clichés of a Modern movement that was gradually losing many of its reasons for existence, starting with the very idea of the avant-garde. Second: that of the author (at the time, it was not yet possible to call an architect an artist; many years would have to pass before that would be the case). Through many different means – from writing to drawing and architectural plans to objects – Mendini tirelessly sought and refined the tools to manifest his own expressive dimension. During these years his inclination towards bourgeois subversion became more evident, a quest for measured rebellion against societal conditioning. He embraced a progressive yet complex ideological identity, often expressing it with slogans laden with scepticism and even traces of cynicism, such as:

> *A project never corresponds to the truth*
> *Every piece of architecture conceals a terrorist*
> *Achieve the utmost bad taste possible in a project* [4]

Meanwhile, the more direct, existential and cultural influences, which eventually contributed to shaping his poetic mythology, remained almost dormant. Only by continuing his exploration of new, more individual paths over the years, did Mendini recall the literary and artistic impressions of his youth. These would lend a poetic character and a different dynamic to the later development of his work. Though the direct influence of Marcel Proust and his psychoanalytic novels on Mendini is widely known, thanks to the international fame of the painted armchair that Mendini named after the French writer, there are many other artists – or more precisely, their works – with whom Mendini had the opportunity to interact directly because of the fortuitous circumstances of his birth and childhood.

CASA LA VITA

The house in which Mendini was born, raised and lived much of his adult life was built between 1929 and 1931 by Mendini's grandfather, the contractor Francesco Di Stefano (nicknamed Chichi, he was the father of five children, including Fulvia Mendini Di Stefano, Alessandro's mother), who commissioned Piero Portaluppi for the design. One of the most fashionable architects among the Milanese upper classes at the time, Portaluppi was also remarkable for his reinterpretation of the classic tradition, creating what would become known in architectural circles as the Novecento style.
The building – now known as the Casa Museo Boschi Di Stefano – is set on Via Giorgio Jan,[5] a street that runs parallel to the major thoroughfare of Corso Buenos Aires in an affluent area of Milan. Portaluppi dreamed up a plan for the commissioner and his family that was akin to a small urban palazzo in both structure and dimensions. Great bay windows with impressive ornamentation in Portaluppi's typical style are diagonally set at both corners of the front facade. The interiors are filled with refined artisanal materials and workmanship, including wrought-iron railings and lamps and stained-glass windows.

Cover of the Gaudí exhibition catalogue in Milan, 1958

Invitation to the Eric Mendelsohn exhibition in Milan, 1960   Cover of the Eric Mendelsohn exhibition catalogue, 1960

IN SEARCH OF LOST TIME AND SPACE: THE ORIGINS

Mendini and twin sister Mia (Maria), 1931

Mendini, Villafranca, Verona, 1935

Art-filled walls of the home on Via Giorgio Jan, Milan, 1982

Mendini's childhood home on Via Giorgio Jan, Milan, 1929

Autoritratto in forma di Gufo, Alberto Savinio, 1936

CHAPTER 1

Intended as a home for Di Stefano's five children – including Marieda Boschi Di Stefano, Alessandro's aunt and the sibling with the strongest artistic vocation – the house was soon also filled with important artworks, collected first by Francesco and later by Antonio Boschi, Marieda's husband. An engineer, an airship pilot during World War I, and later an inventor of industrial patents and an important executive at Pirelli, Boschi was a passionate collector of modern and contemporary art, who often bought works directly from the artists and sometimes even commissioned them. Pieces came from the likes of Umberto Boccioni, Filippo de Pisis, Achille Funi and Mario Sironi – from whom Boschi acquired over forty works, and who also designed furniture for the apartment's dining room. Marieda (nicknamed Aunt Mini by her relatives) was also a great art lover, with a personal calling for ceramics. She served as a reference point for the entire family, not only due to her cheerful and outgoing nature but also her role in Milan's high society.

In contrast with his extroverted aunt and uncle, the young Alessandro was relatively reserved. With a very protective mother and a stern father, the lawyer Vincenzo Mendini, it's perhaps no surprise that he developed a curiosity and fascination for the wonderful worlds represented in the paintings that covered the walls of his childhood home. Born in 1931 (along with his twin sister Maria) on the first floor of the house, Mendini would go on to live in the building for more than fifty years – first with his parents and siblings, then with his own family: Lidia Prandi, an illustrator and journalist who he met at Nizzoli Associati studio and married in 1961 and later their two daughters Fulvia (named after her grandmother, Alessandro's mother) and Elisa, both of whom were born at the end of the 1960s.

From an early age Mendini recalled being particularly impressed by Alberto Savinio's work and appearance:

[...] as a child, I was deeply marked by my acquaintance with Savinio, his books, and also the man himself. Sometimes he came to visit my uncle and I was terribly afraid of him, I thought he was an owl (by the way, do you remember his self-portrait as an owl?)[6]

Brother of the famous painter Giorgio de Chirico, and no less brilliant an artistic talent, Alberto Savinio was uniquely multifaceted and he worked across painting, literature, journalism and musical composition (in this, he was more versatile than his brother). His diverse oeuvre was linked by his humanist and metaphysical approach, which is perhaps best seen in a recurring motif whereby he combined the experiences of people and objects in a single narrative, with modern people and figures from classic tradition meeting and talking, often in a very ordinary drawing room or a slightly cramped attic. Such scenes appeared across his writing and in his books, such as the affectionate tribute to Milan, *Ascolto il tuo cuore, città* (I Listen to Your Heart, City), the stage inhabited by furniture in *Tutta la vita* (A Whole Life) or the more unsettling *Casa la Vita* (Home Life). In some ways, Savinio started a literary trend of 'domestic psychoanalysis' which would later resonate in Mendini's theoretical and narrative reflections on the home.

One piece in particular from the family's collection, *L'Annunciazione* (The Annunciation) – which was painted in 1932 and bought by Antonio Boschi from Savinio's solo show at Galleria Milano in 1933 – featured multiple times in Mendini's writings and drawings. It depicts a curious half-bird, half-human figure sitting in an attic awaiting the visit of a giant messenger (perhaps an angel?) with Greco-Roman features, who evokes the myths of Savinio's youth and stands in contrast with the almost catatonic stillness of the seated figure. The work's irregular slanted corner breaks the classical symmetry of the painting and reinforces its sense of claustrophobia.

According to Mendini, a toy – or rather, the archetypal shape of a toy – pictured in the painting *Objets dans la forêt* (Objects in the Forest), part of a series realized by Savinio in 1927–28, inspired the design of one of his furniture pieces in the 1980s: an entirely mirrored wardrobe made in different versions, including a limited series for Cappellini. Beyond this direct influence, the vibrant colours in Mendini's buildings and objects from the late 1970s onward also bear the mark of Savinio. On a deeper level, Savinio's influence touched the psychological dimension of Mendini's drawings, helping to shape the work that would distinguish him on the international architecture and design scene. Mendini's short stories and works tapped into the same 'animistic' atmosphere that appears in Savinio's dreamlike visions, and both depict an affinity between people, individuals and 'things': daily objects that also live their own intimate, mysterious life.

When, in later years, Mendini set out to compose his own *Recherche du temps perdu* (In Search of Lost Time) – poetic memoirs in the same vein as works by his beloved Marcel Proust – he expressed some of his childhood impressions in writing. Some passages evoke images that seem to have sprung straight from Savinio's mind, recalling those blissful periods of childhood, like Christmas, that are suffused with surprise and wonder:

But if I look even further, before primary school, I remember that on Christmas Eve at my grandparents' house a hum would build with strange whispers and movements in the dark, and at some point us children would be led by hand into the sitting room, where as if by magic, a fir tree shone with ribbons, baubles, chocolate, small chains, candles, cascades of gold, sweets and cotton snow, with a mountain of gifts at its base.[7]

Mendini's early years seem to have been content, lived in the carefree spirit that every child should experience, with stays at his paternal grandparents' home and seaside holidays in Riccione. Benito Mussolini also happened to spend his holidays here, surrounded by armed guards and instilling fear into the other holidaymakers, foreshadowing the darker mood that would arrive with the impending war. In 1940, after Italy joined World War II, the Mendini family fled the bombings in Milan. They initially found refuge in Bedizzole, a small village not far from Lake Garda, and later in Verona. For five years, like many other Italians, they had to endure scarcity of food, lack of heating, and challenges in completing their education. They lived in fear of both the Fascist government and its Nazi allies, who were prevalent in the region and who looted whatever they could.[8] The Mendinis hid their extensive and precious collection of paintings and sculptures by walling it up inside a barn at the house in Bedizzole, together with food supplies. Only Alessandro's youngest brother Francesco – who was born in 1939, and who would later go on to become an architect and Mendini's professional partner for many years – was able to access the contents from a small opening. And yet, even during these dreadful years, Mendini also reminisces about playful moments: times when he started expressing his creativity, trying to comfort Francesco with whatever he could get his hands on:

When the war arrived in 1940 there were no more fir trees to decorate, so my parents made do with some makeshift laurel plants in a pot. It was during those years that I took it upon myself to decorate a wartime tree for my younger brother, using the few things we had. I hung a pencil, an eraser, some Liebig trading cards, a pencil sharpener, a few sugar cubes and some paper cutouts. Those were the festive curiosities of those cold, fearful Christmases, surrounded by the scent of laurel and bombs rather than fir tree, and there were no gifts.[9]

Eventually, the war and its horrors drew to an end, but the Mendinis stayed in the house in Verona, where Alessandro was still attending school. Upon completing his studies, he returned with his family to the house on Via Giorgio Jan in Milan, where in 1950 he enrolled at the Faculty of Engineering at the Politecnico. He later switched to architecture, graduating in 1959. For the young Mendini, architecture school – helmed by Piero Portaluppi, who remained its principal from 1945 to 1963, despite his activism during the Fascist years[10] – served more as an opportunity to immerse himself in Milan's intellectual environment than a place of proper professional training. His classmates included Aldo Rossi and Joe Colombo.

Rather than practicing technical drawing, he preferred to work on the advertising cartoons that his uncle Antonio Boschi helped him create and publish for Pirelli. He also became interested in the work of great, non-conformist architects and soon began dedicating exhibitions to them. He always harboured a particular admiration for Ernesto Rogers's teachings and work. Rogers, the intellectual driving force of the BBPR group (Gianluigi Banfi, Lodovico Barbiano di Belgiojoso, Enrico Peressutti and Rogers), the team behind Milan's enigmatic 1958 Torre Velasca, went from being the editor-in-chief of the relatively light *Domus* magazine to heading up the significantly heavier *Casabella*. Mendini thought of him as a symbol of freedom beyond a faculty still confined by rigid hierarchies and bound by an allegiance to orthodox Modernism.

Mendini was equally captivated by the eclecticism of Gio Ponti – who was not only his professor but also a highly successful professional. Yet even Ponti found himself paradoxically isolated in the environment of the Politecnico, where he was seen more as an inventor of whimsical forms than a high priest of the dominant ideology of Modernism and modernity – which many viewed ideologically and often in a starkly black-and-white way. Mendini and Ponti had a close bond and together they plotted beautiful but impractical projects, such as the Giuseppe Pagano foundation. But Mendini's closeness with Rogers was even stronger, and their student-teacher relationship evolved into Mendini's gradual integration into the editorial team of *Casabella*, where he began work as an archivist. A sign that the Lord works in mysterious ways: Mendini would go on to become perhaps Italy's longest-standing and most famous creator of architectural magazines.

POST-WAR, MODERN ITALY – FROM ARCHITECTURE TO DESIGN

In the February 1946 issue of *Domus*, less than a year after the end of the war, Ernesto Rogers published some horrific data on the consequences of the conflict: 6,702,470 rooms had been destroyed or made uninhabitable, and the 3,460,288 people who had inhabited them had been left homeless. Italy had to be entirely rebuilt from the ground up – from its apartments to its factories. It was a harrowing, unprecedented situation and one that architects, urban planners and designers (though at the time they weren't yet identified by that term) had to deal with: but with what tools? What ideological framework? What should the collaboration with industry – both in terms of manufacturing and construction – look like? Lacking the critical tools to fully grasp the economics of the situation, Rogers and the group of intellectual architects close to him – including Franco Albini, Piero Bottoni, BBPR's Lodovico Barbiano di Belgiojoso and the younger Marco Zanuso – were united in their idea of a utopian ideology: the fight against Fascism and the push for economic and social advancement rooted in socialism and democracy had to be transformed into a creative force, producing a progressive design culture. More concretely, that meant the creation of buildings, objects and projects that served as instruments of progress.

Strategies for this included the planning of new urban interventions – although this would prove almost impossible in a land like Italy, steeped in historical heritage and embedded in a conservative culture that was more interested in preserving than innovating – and architecture with a social (if not socialist) aim. They also included the emergent field of industrial design and, by extension, of design as a whole: a discipline propagandised by Ponti and theorised by writers and critics such as Gillo Dorfles, Paolo Fossati, and Giovanni Klaus Koenig, as well as Bruno Munari, a former Futurist artist turned graphic and product designer.

Did this overlap between the project of post-war reconstruction and the political vision of a 'design for all' inevitably lead to a distortion akin to the compromise that Modernist architects had to strike with Fascism, ultimately succumbing to official academicism? That had been the case for Futurism too: Italy's only original historical avant-garde expression in the artistic sphere, it could have inspired a modern universe of objects, but instead found itself – at least until the war – celebrating the pomp of Mussolini's regime through rhetorical, neo-figurative painting. Fortunately, 1950s Italy was not Soviet Russia, where functional design did exist but lacked a strong aesthetic appeal to its potential users. Italy was a capitalist country with a strong progressive political movement and a rich artistic tradition that was unique in Europe. The exceptional and singular nature of Italian design was born from all of these trends: Futurist inspiration, pre-war Rationalism, the progressive ideology of which Ponti and Rogers were great proponents, and the courage of company executives (from Rina Brion and Cesare Cassina to Adriano Olivetti) who were design pioneers. And it was precisely because of its modernist, utopian character that this work would go on to play a huge role in wider post-war Italian culture.

Mendini and Lidia Prandi, Borghetto, 1962

Mendini and Lidia Prandi, Milan, 1962

Lidia Prandi, Pesaro beach, 1964

Mendini's portrait for enrollment at the Politecnico University, Milan, 1949

Foto eseguita per il diciottenne Alessandro Mendini nell'ottobre dell'anno 1949 per l'ammissione al Politecnico di Milano

One could even go as far as to say that after the war, Italy had few great architects – just great designers. Aside from a few exceptions (such as BBPR's Torre Velasca, Ponti's Pirelli skyscraper, Pier Luigi Nervi's great architectural works and some smaller projects by Franco Albini and Carlo Mollino), Italian architecture in the 1950s struggled to produce anything particularly innovative, but the country's design scene unequivocally embraced modernity and novelty, abandoning all formal and conceptual restraints. The entire range of artistic trends and formal inspirations was reworked into a critical, eclectic language, a continuously transforming nebula that would later be identified as the Italian style of the 1950s: something that the entire international design community would look to with great interest and fascination.

This positively explosive mix of elements attracted – but simultaneously repelled – the young Mendini, who met some of its key players shortly before he graduated. At the time, Milan was still a relatively small city, home to just a handful of design intellectuals. Perhaps that's why Mendini claimed to have felt like a lone wolf in the 1960s:

> *I witnessed the zenith of post-war technical efficiency and its progressive decline into a social and political crisis marked by student revolutions. This was true all around the Western world, but it was prominent in Italy and particularly in Milan, where it also influenced ways of thinking about architecture and design (or rather, Bel Design). From 1960 to 1970, our society underwent this shift in values. In the field of design, this change in perspective led to a progressive criticism of property speculation on one hand and industrial consumerism on the other. Milan was for me – then, as it is now – not just a real place but a psychological one, a world made of emotions and feelings, not projects. My cultural idol was Rogers, and his Casabella. Sometimes I had the pleasure of speaking with him: those were the times when I believed in the Torre Velasca, in neo-liberty, in the Spazio office furniture for Olivetti. I helped Vittoriano Viganò with his drawings when he was planning proposals for the Parco Sempione. But more than the refinement of Magistretti's Carimate club, more than Kartell or Danese or Alberto Rosselli, more than the Castiglioni brothers, I was fascinated by distant cultures; the animist architects: Gaudi, Mendelsohn or Rudolf Steiner.*[11]

Beyond his passion for unorthodox architecture, Mendini harboured a keen interest in the integration of art and design: a theme rarely explored in academic circles but one that he fully embraced. He admired the innovation of Lucio Fontana's *Concetti Spaziali* (Spatial Concepts) with their famous cuts in the canvas. He also appreciated the fabric designs of Fede Cheti, Gianni Dova and Roberto Crippa for the Jsa company in Busto Arsizio, as well as the idea of applied art – quite literally in the case of Piero Fornasetti and his decorated furniture, often made in collaboration with Ponti. As Mendini once said of Joe Colombo, '*I admired in my classmate Joe his ability to be both a designer and a nuclear painter.*'[12] Mendini was friendly with Joe and his brother Gianni and got to know their joint work, which after Joe's premature death in 1971 Gianni would carry on alone.

Another important artistic personality with whom Mendini engaged in a rich intellectual dialogue was the Florentine painter Paolo Scheggi. In the early 1960s Scheggi lived on the same street as Mendini, as a guest at the house/studio of Germana Marucelli – an inventive fashion designer and distant relative of Mendini, for whom Scheggi painted textiles and created jewellery, anticipating the fusion of art and fashion. Nearly a decade younger than Mendini, Scheggi began his artistic exploration in the 1960s, crafting compositions on perforated, overlapping canvasses vaguely reminiscent of Fontana's pieces, that would go on to become his most important and recognizable body of work. Together, Scheggi and Mendini also thought up environmental projects, though none were realised. For a while Scheggi worked at the studio Nizzoli Associati, where Mendini was also employed, as an *ideatore plastico* (form creator).[13]

Mendini with his aunt Marieda Boschi Di Stefano, late 1940s

Architect Mario Brunati, Milan, 1967

Mendini as a student, Verona, 1948

Mendini and architect Mario Morganti, Milan, 1963

Mendini with friends and family members in the studio, Milan, 1963

CHAPTER 1

In January 1965 they conceived and wrote (together with art critic Germano Celant, graphic and industrial designer Angelo Fronzoni, architect Mario Oliveri and sculptor Giancarlo Sangregorio) the manifesto *Ipotesi di lavoro per la progettazione totale* (Hypothesis for Total Design). Here, they outlined a vision of art embedded in ever-broader contexts, one of the cornerstones of Mendini's research. Scheggi pursued these same ideas through various installations, including the 1966 Venice Art Biennale, marking a swift and brilliant career that was tragically cut short due to his untimely death, aged just 30, in 1971. After a period of relative obscurity, Scheggi's work was rediscovered in the 2000s, but just how interesting and visionary it was is still relatively undocumented. Mendini, however, always remembered Scheggi's role in getting him closer to the world of art as a young man.[14]

01.

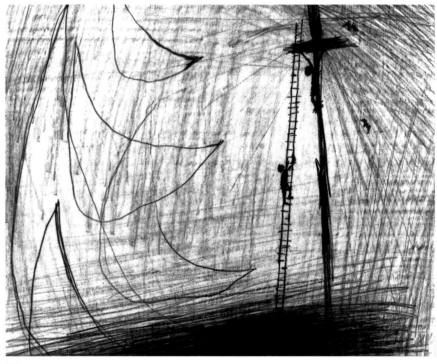

02.

01. *Autoritratto* (Self-portrait), drawing, 1962
02. *Untitled*, drawing, 1960s
03. *Una donna* (A woman), drawing, 1960s

03.

IN SEARCH OF LOST TIME AND SPACE: THE ORIGINS

04.

05.

04. *Donna mappamondo* (World map woman), drawing, 1957
05. *Figura* (Figure), drawing, 1960

06.

07.

08.

09.

06. *Automobile* (Car), drawing, 1960s
07. *Strada che si avvolge* (Winding road), drawing, 1960s
08. *Un anno soffice su sospensioni SAGA* (A smooth year on SAGA suspension), greetings card for SAGA Pirelli, 1954
09. *Pescatore* (Fisherman), drawing, 1960s

IN SEARCH OF LOST TIME AND SPACE: THE ORIGINS

10.

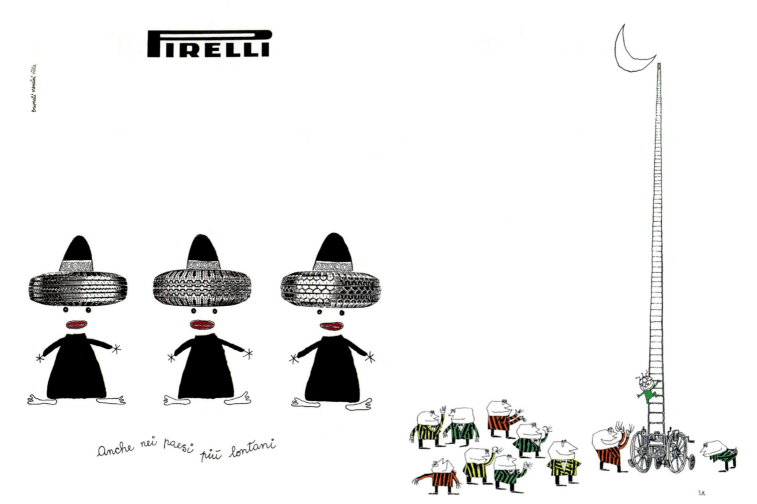

11.

12.

10. Cover of the Pirelli Information and technical magazine,
    Year XI, No.6, December 1958
11. Cover of the Pirelli Information and technical magazine,
    Year XI, No.5, October 1959
12. Drawing for Pirelli, 1959
    overleaf: Global Tools: *primo seminario*
    Vincoli del Corpo (first Body Bonds seminar), drawing, 1975

RADICAL DESIGN: THE GHOST IN THE MACHINE

THE FIRST CASABELLA

Contrary to the myth of *Casabella* as a 'revolutionary' magazine born from the wave of the great counter-cultural movements of the late 1960s – both in culture and politics – the cultural renewal of the magazine under Mendini, and later his group of colleagues and friends from the Radical movement, was a long and sophisticated transformation. Its roots lay in Ernesto Rogers's progressive approach to the title as its editor-in-chief, where he promoted Modernist ideology and social issues in architecture. When Rogers departed the magazine in 1965, publisher Gianni Mazzocchi entrusted the direction of the magazine to the lesser-known and somewhat controversial architect Gian Antonio Bernasconi. Mendini joined *Casabella* initially to oversee its historical archive, organizing documents and materials dating back to previous editors such as Giuseppe Pagano, Edoardo Persico and Franco Albini. Over time, Mendini progressively assumed the role of editor, a position that, during Rogers's tenure, had been carried out by Gae Aulenti and Marco Zanuso.

During those years, Mendini – having left the studio he ran with his former classmate Mario Brunati – also worked as an architect, along with his brother Francesco and Mario Oliveri, in the studio that still carried Marcello Nizzoli's name even though he had long since retired. At the time, Nizzoli Associati was one of the most prominent design groups in Italy, both for its ongoing work in continuing Nizzoli's legacy (he had been a key figure at Olivetti and had designed important buildings for the company as well as for Eni/SNAM), and for its involvement in numerous public buildings, including some international projects. Among the notable projects that the Mendini brothers contributed to were the competition for the headquarters of the Université Libre de Bruxelles (1969); employee housing (1967–69) and management offices (1970) for the Italsider steel plant in Taranto; and the IACP housing estate on Via dei Missaglia in Milan (1966–71). There were strong ties between Nizzoli Associati and *Casabella*, as Oliveri remembers:

To get the [Nizzoli] studio more involved in the cultural field, we proposed a plan to Bernasconi [...] to relaunch the magazine, focused on three key points: Mendini would manage the editorial team, Fronzoni its graphic design; while I would be given a section on building industrialisation (a highly relevant issue at the time). The proposal was accepted.[1]

Like many architects of his generation – and the one before it – Mendini still believed in the utopian idea of architecture as a tool for improving society, or at the very least for creating order in the social contract. Workers were expected to collaborate in enhancing the efficiency of productive structures, but companies and industries were equally expected to provide better living conditions in areas close to the plants, so the workers didn't have to commute. The Mendini brothers found a positive expression for these ideas in modern forms and aesthetics and, in projects like the Italsider headquarters, in a kind of 'pop' version of modernity.

However, Mendini was keenly aware of the contradictions inherent in pursuing progressive, social-democratic ideals – to use a political term – within the largely conservative framework of Italian architecture and construction in the 1960s. This gave many of Mendini's writings of the time a vein of pessimism, evident when he discussed developments such as pre-fabs, which both Mendini and *Casabella* were strongly interested in and generally advocated for. This hinted at a broader rethinking of the still-modernist utopian stance, even as it embraced new technologies in building production.

This sentiment is reflected in a singular, lengthy essay by Mendini in the magazine's February 1969 issue – when Bernasconi was still editor-in-chief – with the peculiar title, '*Metaprogetto sì e no*' (Meta-design: yes and no). The very use of the term *metaprogetto* was meant in a critical sense: after a lengthy and largely positive discussion of theoretical models for domestic and urban living (from traditional Japanese houses to the expansion plan for the city of Bratislava, drawn up by Nizzoli Associati themselves), which Mendini uses as concrete examples of the progressive idea of metadesign, the essay paradoxically concludes with a section titled 'Problematic and self-critical conclusion':

[…] Our belief that it is worth moving from design to metadesign represents the positive side of a coin […] But there is also a negative side: every invention can be used for good or ill, and that's clearly also true in our case. The vortex of political misconduct, bureaucratic inertia, industrial interests, coordination difficulties, authoritarianism and privileges are the negative side of that same coin. It could turn a phenomenon that was conceived to be dynamic into stasis, and deviate the aim of our proposals to such an extent that it might convince us of the need to freeze them temporarily.[2]

To further illustrate these pessimistic predictions, a cartoon strip drawn by Mendini appeared at the bottom of the article. It depicted a stylized geometric figure being progressively disintegrated by an unrelenting flow of words and symbols. In this example, one can sense Mendini's pursuit of a path towards individual (as opposed to collective) liberation. Throughout his entire career, and in particular his leadership of magazines from *Casabella* to *Domus*, he used his exceptional professionalism and ambition to progressively and autonomously define himself, crafting the intellectual self-portrait of an author with many vocations.

As Bernasconi's enthusiasm as editor-in-chief of *Casabella* waned, the group led by Mendini took over at the magazine, involving existing contributors such as the brilliant historian Giovanni Klaus Koenig. Appointed co-editor-in-chief at Mendini's *Casabella*, he would transition from writing serious philological analysis to irreverent alternative stories about architecture under the pseudonym *Lonfo*. The latter is the imaginary protagonist of a metasemantic poem by writer and explorer Fosco Maraini: an animal-like creature that expresses itself in Maraini's untranslatable prose.[3] These curious words bring to mind the hermetic nature of *architecturese* (archispeak), the language reserved purely for the initiated which, for decades, would keep the wider public away from discussions surrounding contemporary architecture – an obstacle to the diffusion of ideas that Mendini consistently sought to remove from his magazines.

RADICAL DESIGN AND ARCHITECTURE

The term 'Radical architecture' was coined by Germano Celant, who had collaborated with *Casabella* when it was led by Bernasconi/Mendini, but the voice of the movement had begun to make itself heard at *Domus* a few years earlier. Ettore Sottsass, who had been linked to Gio Ponti and *Domus* for many years, was the first to introduce the theories of groups and individuals such as Superstudio and Archizoom, who were strongly critical of the Italian design establishment – or at least the faction that aligned with the Modernist Lombard tradition and its branches across Italy, particularly in Rome and Florence.

In the 1960s at the Faculty of Architecture in Florence (particularly in its alternative courses such as Interior Architecture and Industrial Design and Elements of Composition, taught respectively by the 'heretical Modernists' Leonardo Savioli and Leonardo Ricci), a new core of young, critical architects was already forming. Once they graduated and established groups, often with names that spoke of their avant-garde cultural ambitions – such as Superstudio,[4] Archizoom[5] and UFO[6] – they became the central hub of research and experimentation that Mendini published in *Casabella*. The individuals most associated with this movement were Dario Bartolini, Lapo Binazzi, Andrea Branzi, Paolo Deganello, Pietro Derossi, Cristiano Toraldo di Francia, Massimo Morozzi, Adolfo Natalini and Alessandro Poli.

In the second half of the 1960s, the main seats of academic and professional power (which often overlapped) were still occupied by old names from the Fascist era – such as Portaluppi – or the priests of Modernism such as Rogers and Albini. By that time, the revolutionary scope of Modernism had weakened, partly due to the fact that, in the 1950s, Italy had witnessed the beginning of a policy of wild real-estate speculation and the subsequent destruction of both the environment and the historical fabric of entire cities. Curiously, this would rarely be the subject

Casabella issue 367, 1972

Casabella issue 394, 1974

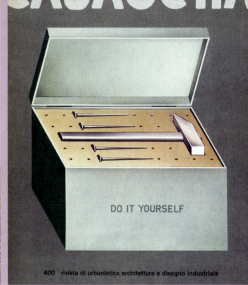
Casabella issue 400, 1975

Mendini's daughter Elisa, 1973

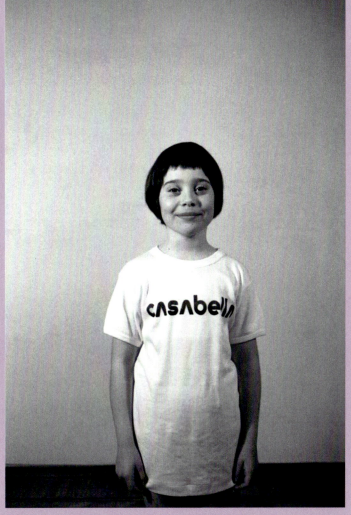
Mendini's daughter Fulvia, 1973

of critical work by the post-avant-garde, of which Radical architecture was certainly a part. Instead, they preferred to focus on experimenting with different expressive languages and new social and cultural conceptions of design problems, often with dystopian undertones.

Mendini started laying the critical foundations for developing this kind of alternative research in his first issue of *Casabella* (issue 349, June 1970). His article *Architettura per l'Uomo Dimenticato* (Architecture for the Forgotten Man) was an exemplary manifesto advocating for people to be given priority over the economy (describing architects as the 'stylists and coach-builders of architecture'). It also emphasized the need to address broader issues that directly involve citizens, such as:

[…] Resource distribution, planning of ecological space, public availability of land, non-speculative industry, giving priority to the development of large-scale social services, limiting the production of superfluous objects, expanding the production of primary and collective objects.[7]

Mendini's claims – which are still relevant today – piqued the interest of a progressive public, but surprised and concerned the establishment because of their radical nature. Immediately after Mendini's article, *Casabella* published an expansive review of *Manifesto*, a magazine founded by a group of dissident intellectuals from the powerful Italian Communist Party, calling it a title 'entirely dedicated to the problem of home and city'. In the same issue, a long article by Germano Celant discussed *Arte come forza-lavoro* (Art as Workforce), openly borrowing Marxist terminology. A historical piece – written, naturally, by Giovanni Klaus Koenig – served as an explanation of the origins of the masthead's new typeface, which was all lower case, with the three letter 'a's replaced with upside-down 'v's, in a reinterpretation of the font designed by Herbert Bayer for the Bauhaus. A perfect paradox: referencing Modernist tradition in a magazine that would become its antithesis and critical consciousness. The cover illustration – Mendini's drawing of an unsettling figure flying over a banal, black-and-white landscape with a large, traditional house – was the most explicit sign that the editor's intentions were to raise doubt rather than create certainties.

Mendini hired the young Franco Raggi as an editor. Having just graduated in architecture, Raggi had started collaborating with Nizzoli Associati (together with Daniela Puppa, also an architect and journalist who would later join the editorial team at *Modo* magazine) before moving to Vittorio Gregotti's studio – which Raggi playfully nicknamed *Gregottificio* (the Gregotti-factory). Gregotti was an Italian starchitect way ahead of his time, both for his cultural authority in Modernist thought and the sheer scale of his work.

The occasion that finally brought Mendini face to face with the young protagonists of Radical architecture was the historic exhibition *Italy: The New Domestic Landscape*, organized in 1972 in New York by the young MoMA design curator Emilio Ambasz. Not only was it the first survey of Italian design ever put on by an art museum outside of Italy but, as Ambasz himself recalled: 'It was impossible for it not to also take into account the problems and critical positions towards the system represented by these perfect objects/products of Italian industry.'[8]

Alongside leading Italian design companies, the curator invited some of the country's most famous architects and designers (including Gae Aulenti, Alberto Rosselli, Ettore Sottsass, and Marco Zanuso) to create futuristic installations. He also asked a number of authors and Radical groups to present their visions in a section called 'Design as Commentary', and it was here that Gaetano Pesce, Ugo La Pietra, Archizoom, Superstudio, Gruppo Strum (who showed some 'photo-novels' with a political theme) and Enzo Mari (who only submitted a text) participated in the exhibition. Mendini – who wrote an important essay for the exhibition catalogue titled 'The Land of Good Design'[9] – travelled to New York for the show, where he was able to get to know all the contributors better. This young cohort, together with the slightly older Ettore Sottsass, would come to represent – despite never having built anything – Italy's architectural avant-garde of the 1970s, and *Casabella* would become their official mouthpiece.

Yet Mendini always kept a certain distance from the most radical practices. While other groups (such as some members of Superstudio) extended their research to projects on material popular culture, Mendini seemed more interested in artistic performance. Even through his participation in Global Tools seminars or the Cavart group with Michele De Lucchi (who would later become one of Sottsass's favoured associates as well as one of Italy's most famous designers), Mendini seemed more focused on testing himself physically, rather than engaging with the broader context: despite many experiences as part of studios, groups and projects, he would always maintain this individualistic touch. Among the many paradoxes of his personality and work, Mendini imagined and designed according to his own, unmistakably individual psychological and artistic features, even while he believed in the power of the group as a collective projection of individual personalities, strengthened by shared contribution. Still, his role as inspirer, supporter and leader always remained distinct.

The Radical *Casabella* stood out for both its graphic design and its contents. It was an innovative proposition, reminiscent of other avant-garde magazines of the time, such as British *AD*, led by Monica Pidgeon. Much as *Casabella* was the result of collective effort, Mendini was still the director in every sense. He was responsible for all aspects of the publication, beginning with ensuring economic success for the publisher, primarily through advertising, which has always been the main source of revenue for industry magazines. Despite *Casabella*'s circulation being much higher than it is today, there wasn't always a healthy economic return, and the magazine started featuring sponsored product profiles which were designed to blend in with the rest of the publication. Though most of them were about construction materials, some were also dedicated to furnishings and objects made by Italian companies including Poltronova and Cassina. This was in keeping with the talent for promoting advertising sales – which could also be called professionalism – that Mendini would bring to all of the magazines that he would go on to lead, from *Modo* to *Domus*.

Compared with other architects and intellectuals of his generation, Mendini was able to maintain a clear view of the realities of the market and of production – as was evident in *Casabella*'s technical pages. Still, he was also able to develop his personal research on the critical themes that were dearest to him, starting with the existential discomfort of the bourgeoisie with which – perhaps reluctantly – he often identified with. These were not yet the times when – first with Studio Alchimia and later with Alessi – he would succumb to the temptation to create actual products, albeit infused with irony and humour, much like his satirical cartoons. Between 1970 and 1975, he imagined and created various pieces, mainly of furniture, some of which were conceived under the title *Oggetti ad uso spirituale* (Objects for spiritual use). Among other pieces this included *Tavolino da salotto* (Drawing room table), a coffin-shaped coffee table made of glass, which was photographed for the marketing material with a naked woman reclining underneath; *Valigia per ultimo viaggio* (Suitcase for the last journey), which was briefly produced as a limited edition for the brand Bracciodiferro;[10] and the *Lassù* (Up there) chair. This last was designed in many variants but made out of wood in only two copies, one of which was burned during a performance, photographed amid the flames and published on the cover of the magazine in July 1974.

In addition to symbolizing the destruction of the chair as an icon of global design – the object that all architects and designers want to work on and of which 'the history of the modern movement is made', as Andrea Branzi put it – this action was an explicit reference to the Buddhist monk who sacrificed himself in the fire he started to protest the Vietnam war (which, at the time, was still raging and which would only end in 1975).

It is important to remember that this was Italy in the 1970s, where most of society was still steeped in conservative culture, not just the bourgeoisie from which Mendini came. Radical gestures were only tolerated within certain aesthetic and ethical criteria: violence, drama, and desperation were not considered appropriate and shouldn't be shown. Mendini's Radical projects (perhaps better understood as works of art, if seen within the context of the era's performance art) were therefore not well-received by conformists, including his architect colleagues who were still siding with the Modernist front. For them, his *Casabella* represented a betrayal of the utopian ideals of the Modernist movement.

Regardless of criticism, Mendini carried on publishing ever-more provocative texts and projects that he commissioned from his large pool of friends and companions, using them as trump cards in the game between conservatism and revolution that he had started. He spent a lot of time wooing Andrea Branzi, the most theoretically loquacious member of the Archizoom group, eventually signing him up for a monthly column titled *Note Radicali* (Radical Notes) that began in issue 370 (October 1972). The Florentine architect used it as a 'forum for discussing the actions of the neo-avant-garde groups' with slogans such as *Distruzione della cultura* (Destruction of culture) and *Distruzione dell'architettura* (Destruction of architecture) for a *strategia dei tempi lunghi* (long-term strategy) and to prepare for *l'attacco finale* (the final attack). His language felt borrowed from far-left political groups and the widespread neo-Marxist revolutionary theories of the time. Mostly, it was useful in perpetuating the myth of the Radical architect (which Branzi identified with) as a subverter of solid values in design culture and the creator of a new era for architecture and design after the identity crisis of the late 1960s.

Casabella also highlighted experimental work in more traditional design disciplines such as clothing and fashion. Despite being considered inferior or lowbrow in the intellectual scene surrounding Mendini, these fields gained importance in the Radical 'cultural revolution' he promoted. This included research by Superstudio (particularly by Cristiano Toraldo di Francia, a group member who was an architect as well as a fashion photographer), and Dressing Design by Lucia Bertolini, a member of Archizoom: a basic form of human environment that she called Nearest Habitat System – accompanied by the slogan *Vestirsi è facile perché l'eleganza è morta* (Dressing is easy, because elegance is dead). In particular the designs of Nanni Strada, a fashion designer and theoretician, stood out: her 1973 *Design Indemodabile* (Unfashionable Design) or *Abito Politubolare* (Polytubular Dress) – a one-piece, assembled with a specially designed two-needle sewing system and created especially for the programme *Il manto e la pelle* (The cloak and the skin) – was shown on the cover of *Casabella* issue 387.

These projects represented an attempt to create an alternative to traditional fashion (as well as a post-Futurist ambition to reconstruct existence itself), but for Mendini they related to a core design principle: the body, around which and for which so much of design and architecture was made. In principle, fashion design was one of Mendini's favourite complementary (not secondary) fields to focus on, both in terms of media – through the issues of *Domus Moda* – but also in terms of design itself, through various installations and collaborations with the industry.

Mendini wasn't shy about highlighting his own work, in the tradition of his idol Gio Ponti, who had freely featured his own projects on the covers of *Domus*. For Mendini, the magazine cover acted as a manifesto for the kind of corrosive and irreverent thought that he wanted to be remembered for – as exemplified by his *Valigia per ultimo viaggio* (Suitcase for the last journey), an immaculate, polished object that could have been made of any material, especially the seemingly indestructible plastics that were so prominent in Italian design of the 1960s and 1970s. The suitcase appeared on the cover of *Casabella* issue 392/393 in the summer of 1974, photographed on bare ground to give the impression of having been abandoned by someone who had literally set off on a journey of no return: a refugee, a migrant or someone who had simply reached the end of their days.

Despite (or perhaps because of) its decidedly avant-garde stance, *Casabella* at that time still had a sizeable circulation and it remained the most respected architectural title in Italy, together with *Domus*. For Mendini and his network, *Casabella* represented a powerful means of disseminating ideas that would otherwise have remained confined to discussions, meetings and workshops.

Pages from the Bracciodiferro sales catalogue, 1973

Cover of Architettura Radicale by Paola Navone and Bruno Orlandoni, 1974

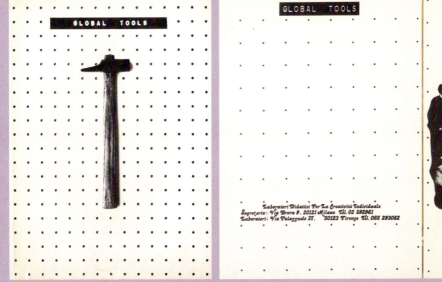

Cover and pages from Global Tools fanzine no. 1, 1974

RADICAL DESIGN: THE GHOST IN THE MACHINE

Mendini sets fire to the Lassù chair, 1974

Almerico De Angelis and Lidia Prandi, Global Tools, 1975

Mendini sitting in the Poltrona di Paglia (Straw Armchair), 1974

Mendini and Davide Mosconi, Global Tools, 1975

However, these events were also influential in their own way, and among them, the most important of the period was arguably the Global Tools[11] 'educational workshops for individual creativity', which would go down in history due to the exceptional line up that joined forces to run them. Alongside Mendini, the group included Ettore Sottsass, Gianni Pettena, Riccardo Dalisi, Ugo La Pietra, Gaetano Pesce, Adolfo Natalini and Superstudio, Andrea Branzi and Archizoom Associati. The young Paola Navone, who would later become the group's coordinator and author – together with Bruno Orlandoni of the canonical book *Architettura Radicale* (Radical Architecture)[12] – also took part. Essentially, Global Tools overlapped with the entirety of Italy's design and architecture 'neo-avant-garde', which was launched and methodically chronicled by *Casabella*. The two fanzines that the group published have in recent years become highly collectable as documents of a period of design history that was as fertile as it was turbulent.

In the 1960s and 1970s, plenty of avant-garde groups formed across different cultural fields. Sometimes they were fronted by extremely talented individuals but often they were a truly collaborative affair. Global Tools was driven by sociocultural motives rather than commercial ones: it aimed to experiment with the fundamental aspects of design, attempting to redefine the concept of design itself through 'global tools' that architects, designers and artists could use to address the complex challenges of designing for a society whose model was yet to be defined. Adolfo Natalini's departure from the group caused a crisis, and the turning point came when the sole sponsor of the group, gallery owner Franco Castelli, decided to withdraw financial support for its research and workshops. The very bourgeois environment that had initially been captivated by the ambitious idea of collective creativity, or even mass creativity, eventually withdrew its economic backing, leading to the ultimate demise of the utopian vision of Global Tools.

ALESSANDRO AND ETTORE

Among the numerous 'militants' of the Radical Design movement, a term fashionable in Italy during the political renewal of those years, the figure that holds the most significance for Mendini is undoubtedly Ettore Sottsass – a creative mind unparalleled in the history of both Italian and international architecture and design. Having trained as an architect, Sottsass had always been interested in the connection between different forms of expression: the visual arts, literature, photography, craftsmanship and of course design on all scales, from objects to landscapes. Over the course of nearly seventy years Sottsass produced an enormous number of projects, balancing research and functionality. Having survived the Fascist government and the disastrous World War II, he developed his critical mindset amid the hardship of the post-war period, aided by exceptional natural talent. Introduced into intellectual circles by his first wife, Fernanda Pivano, he emerged in the 1960s as a reference against the rigidities of Modernism.

Curious about the world, Sottsass embarked on many trips, which took him to India, Japan and notably, the United States. There he met American poets and writers of the new Beat Generation – Allen Ginsberg, Jack Kerouac and Gregory Corso – whose work Pivano would go on to translate and promote with Italian publishers. For Sottsass, these figures became a source of inspiration, both for his writing for *Domus* and also in the use of new cultural and sensory influences to revolutionize industrial design. He enhanced and transformed colours and forms, creating a new kind of functionality. His objects, perhaps mostly famously Olivetti's *Valentine* typewriter, became icons of a new popular design culture. It's not surprising, then, given this exceptional portfolio – a blend of individual expression, devotion to the object as an anthropological phenomenon, and criticism of the commodity system – that Sottsass became a recognised master and a true inspiration for many of the proponents of Radical Design.

Sottsass was an active participant in the Global Tools seminars and his experiments with photography and performance resonated with the group. In *Casabella*, he published *Il Pianeta come festival* (The Planet as a Festival), a fantastic series of visionary projects, and contributed regular columns such as *Per ritardato arrivo dell'aeromobile* (Because of the Late Arrival of the Airplane), where he appeared to write about whatever was going through his head during his long travels, but actually provided keen observations on society and mass culture.

The beautiful 1976 monograph *Sottsass's Scrap-Book*[13] – curated by Federica di Castro, with an introduction by Mendini – was one of two important volumes published by the magazine as part of the *Documenti* (Documents) series. It was also one of the last acts of Radical *Casabella*, which concluded its run with issue 412 in April 1976. Mendini's introduction, both in style and content, bears the unmistakable influence of Sottsass's ideas and it concludes with these disenchanted yet utopian and prophetic words – a kind of guide for both Mendini and Sottsass's pursuit of mass creativity in the 1980s:

If it is true, as the theorists of the neo-avant-garde maintain, that the ultimate goal of heretic architecture today is the technical destruction of culture for a different social use, which consists of society's reclaiming of all individual creative faculties – then Sottsass is the first to work technically on this utopia, to walk the path of hope in this search for identity, so that culture can coincide with man's own nature.[14]

As fate would have it, right after parting ways with *Casabella*, Mendini had the opportunity to settle the score with other, more senior Modernist masters – individuals he had vociferously critiqued in the pages of the magazine – through the exhibition and accompanying book *Il design Italiano degli anni Cinquanta* (Italian Design in the 1950s).[15] It was a playful and dramatic reconstruction of the Italian Modernist golden age presented at CentroKappa, and the curators managed to craft it into something eclectic – in some ways a precursor to postmodernism – and to reshape the discussion on contemporary design.

In the book, Mendini depicted those he saw as forerunners and pioneers of design. His critical preference was for Ignazio Gardella ('the first crack in the tenets of Italian rationalism') and Gio Ponti ('the disowned but de facto father of all the Italian architects that followed him').[16] The former had been a sophisticated innovator of bourgeois architecture with an ahead-of-its-time postmodern approach; the latter an unrestrained experimenter exploring every expressive possibility – even if it meant contradicting himself. Together, they represented the impossible duality that characterised Mendini's work: being an integral part of the system but looking at it from alternative perspectives, attempting to undermine its foundations and always risking marginalization.

FROM CASABELLA TO MODO

In 1976 Mendini left *Casabella*, which had been taken over by Electa, who was not interested in continuing along the same cultural line.[17] The following year he founded *Modo* magazine, reaching out for funding to titans of Italian design including Alessi, Flos, Kartell and Zanotta. For several years *Modo* was hosted by CentroKappa, a think tank physically set inside the Kartell headquarters and led by Giulio Castelli – an architect and the son of Giulio Castelli, the founder of Kartell – and Anna Castelli Ferrieri. In contrast with more traditional, institutionalised magazines, *Modo* adopted an informative, agile approach. While it partially embraced the themes that had been tackled by *Casabella* (which was now under the direction of designer/philosopher Tomás Maldonado, with whom Mendini always shared a dialectic relationship of mutual criticism and intellectual sympathy), it was primarily concerned with a very contemporary redefinition of design, of the market and of business.

On this point, the editor's letters were extremely clear: the companies that had shaped the glory and fortunes of Italian design, as well as those that wanted to find their space in the 'cultured' sphere, had to get up to speed with the new themes of design. Designers, architects, and graphic designers in turn needed to throw themselves into competition with industry, armed with the courage of their new ideas, but also ready to face off with all the players who got to decide what made a product and what its wider meaning was. In his inaugural editor's letter, *Design dove sei?* (Design, where are you?), Mendini stated:

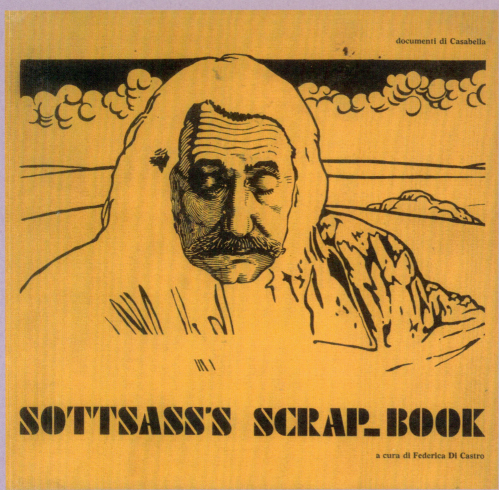

Cover of Sottsass's Scrap-Book with drawing by Tiger Tateishi, 1976

Modo issue 6 with drawing by Milton Glaser, 1978

Mendini with the Modo editorial staff, Milan, 1979

Monumentino da casa, Via Giorgio Jan, 1982

RADICAL DESIGN: THE GHOST IN THE MACHINE

We mean by this term the utopia of a new way [...] of designing, producing, distributing, using, inhabiting, managing – according to evolved production relationships. Modo is looking for all the forces at play in the complex interweaving of the environment's form as its interlocutors [...] politicians, administrators, producers, industrialists, students, designers, workers, artists and technicians, including people who work in marketing, advertising and distribution.[18]

Until a few years prior, even mentioning such interlocutors would have horrified many of those who worked in design, whether of the alternative or the institutional kind. Under the pretext of 'beautiful form', magazines, exhibitions and even some designers and industries would have rather shied away from the uncomfortable issues of consumption, sales and marketing. Mendini, however, had left the 'destructive' phase of his critical work behind him and began a constructive phase of building new scenarios for design. In hindsight, one could say that for him and his associates this new magazine truly marked the transition away from the disenchanted utopias of the 1960s and early 1970s and towards an attempt to directly influence the economic and industrial processes of which product design was an integral part – processes that both shape, and are shaped by, design.

One of the groundbreaking aspects of the discussions presented by *Modo* in its early days was its realism in addressing the problematic aspects of design (and, to a lesser extent, architecture). This realism was, however, always accompanied by a profound appreciation for quality, novelty and the unprecedented. As for the editorial team, Mendini surrounded himself with younger collaborators who came from different cultural backgrounds but who all shared an interest for a new kind of information on design: more concrete but not cynical, pragmatic but still utopian, inspired by progressive ideas but also understanding that the 'pedagogical' supremacy of experts over operators, particularly those in the design industry, no longer had much foundation.

Valerio Castelli was the magazine's art director, journalist Claudia Donà dealt with industry issues and Nives Ciardi – a psychologist and writer – interviewed unusual personalities (such as astrologist Lisa Morpurgo). The managing editor was Franco Raggi, who Mendini had already worked with at *Casabella* and who had taken part in the Global Tools seminars. For *Modo* he penned incisive articles and significant interviews. After leading both *Modo* and *Domus* simultaneously from 1979 to 1980, Mendini decided to dedicate himself exclusively to *Domus*, so Raggi went on to become the editor-in-chief of *Modo*, maintaining an openness to the concrete themes raised by *Modo* since its beginnings.

Among the magazine's contributors were art critic Lea Vergine, credited with 'discovering' Body Art; Barbara Radice, the editor-in-chief of *DATA* magazine and later Ettore Sottsass's second wife; and Cristina Dosio Morozzi, a journalist, the wife of Massimo Morozzi, and from 1987 to 1995 the third editor-in-chief of the magazine. Giovanni Klaus Koenig, as he had previously done for *Casabella*, told curious stories about design with a comedic streak. Often, these dealt with his favourite topic, public transport – like the Milanese Jumbo Tram, which he himself designed with Roberto Segoni. Lidia Prandi, Mendini's wife, was also on staff. She had already collaborated with some of Mendini's performances in the early 1970s, with the knitted wool costume for harp player Ines Klok[19] and as part of the Global Tools seminars, in an overlapping of art and life which happened in the most natural and sentimental of ways. Lidia wrote – and continued to write even after Mendini left to start at *Domus* – on the most current themes in design, with a particular focus on the methods and processes of production, but also on new designers, about which she published a book for *Modo* in 1994.[20]

From the first few issues, the magazine also featured some satirical cartoon strips by Francesco Tullio Altan, who was just starting his career. Known as Altan, he would go on to become one of Italy's most famous cartoonists, with an international reach thanks to characters such as the dog *La Pimpa*. For *Modo*, he drew a curious metaphysical character who grappled with existential contradictions, and later (under Franco Raggi's editorship) he also made sarcastic visual comments on the condition of architects and designers, through characters such as the disenchanted factory worker *Cipputi*, one of the most famous subjects he used to describe Italy's permanent cultural crisis.

The presence of cartoon strips in the magazine was no coincidence – partly a nod to Mendini's early vocation as a cartoonist and partly because, from the 1960s through the 1970s and much of the 1980s, Milan was the most vibrant hub of Italian publishing, especially for image-based magazines. *Linus* was the country's most popular 'cultured' cartoon monthly, hosting strips such as Charles Schulz's *Peanuts*. Conceived by Marcello Gandini, it featured writers such as Umberto Eco and Altan. Other 'alternative' titles were also important: *Pianeta Fresco*, edited by Sottsass and Fernanda Pivano with Allen Ginsberg; *In* by Ugo La Pietra, another friend of Mendini's and an experimental artist and architect; Andrea Valcarenghi's *Re Nudo*, the most politicized title in an alternative and counter-cultural sense. While *Modo* was described as a 'design information monthly', its varied contributions made it interesting to an educated, curious public, not just insiders. The magazine opened its pages to all the major themes, from the contemporary furniture market to design education, as well as to contributions from younger voices.

For example, in 1978, before I had even graduated in industrial design, Mendini asked me to conduct some interviews for *Modo* on designer training. At the time, Milan's design community was much smaller, almost familial, particularly within the Radical (or ex-Radical) circles, so for this interview Mendini organised a dinner in a restaurant in Brera – the city's creative district – which Ettore Sottsass, Ugo La Pietra and Franco Raggi attended. We started a conversation on the very topical subject of design schools, starting with the new ISIAs (Istituti Superiori per le Industrie Artistiche) such as the one in Rome, the first public design faculty in Italy, where I completed my studies. Mendini was a friend of the writer and professor Renato Pedio, himself the true soul of the ISIA together with its director Aldo Calò; he went on to write an editor's letter defending ministerial bureaucratic complications.[21]

Those were some of the best years for progressive Milan, during which it solidified its identity as the true 'capital of design'. This definition would, over the years, pay off handsomely as a product of city marketing. But even at the time, the city of Gae Aulenti, Cini Boeri, Rodolfo Bonetto, the Castiglioni brothers, Vico Magistretti and Marco Zanuso, as well as Sottsass and Mendini themselves, was already effectively the world's design capital, thanks to the strong synergy between designers and industries. Milan had an irresistible appeal to an international public as the place to get up to speed on design, particularly on the annual occasion of the Salone Internazionale del Mobile. A certain Lombard rigour and understatement led these leading designers not to just fly the flag, but to approach every situation – be it cultural, commercial or even existential – with commitment and intensity.

In this context, Mendini – with his reserved demeanor and measured expansiveness – embodied the concept of the critical-operational intellectual (to borrow a term from Bruno Zevi) who acknowledged the complexity of his role and that of his profession within the society he sought to engage. This approach also helped him prepare for the most significant media venture of his career – perhaps of his entire life's work – the post-modern reinvention of *Domus*, with which he would attempt to overturn the existing balance within the culture of design and functionalist architecture.

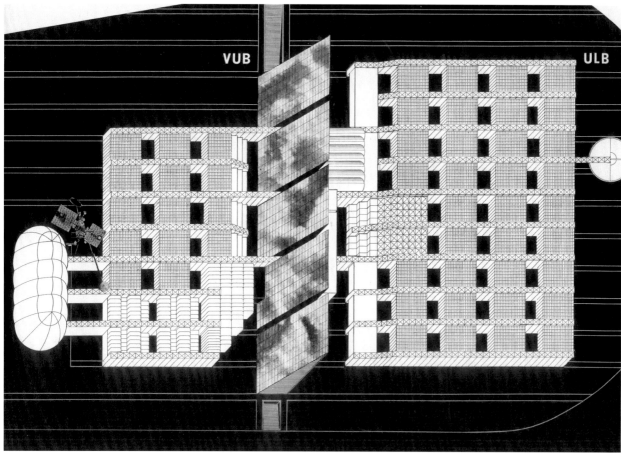

13.

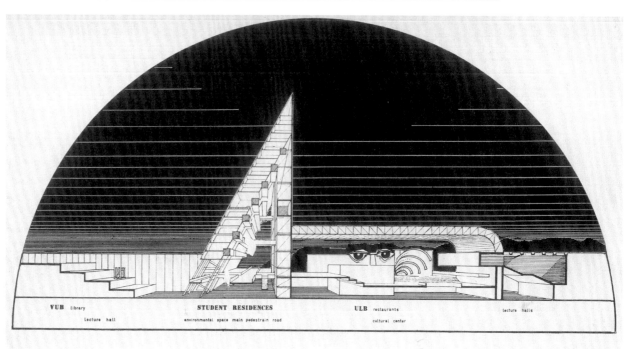

14.

13. Project for the Université Libre de Bruxelles (by Nizzoli Associati), drawing, 1960
14. Project for the Université Libre de Bruxelles (by Nizzoli Associati), drawing, 1960
15. Diedron Disco Complex (by Alessandro and Francesco Mendini and collaborators), Cappella Cantone, Cremona, 1972
16. Plan for Diedron Disco Complex (by Alessandro and Francesco Mendini and collaborators), Cappella Cantone, Cremona, 1972

15.

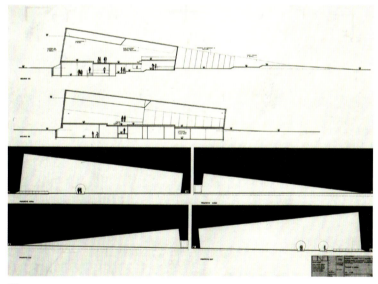

16.

RADICAL DESIGN: THE GHOST IN THE MACHINE

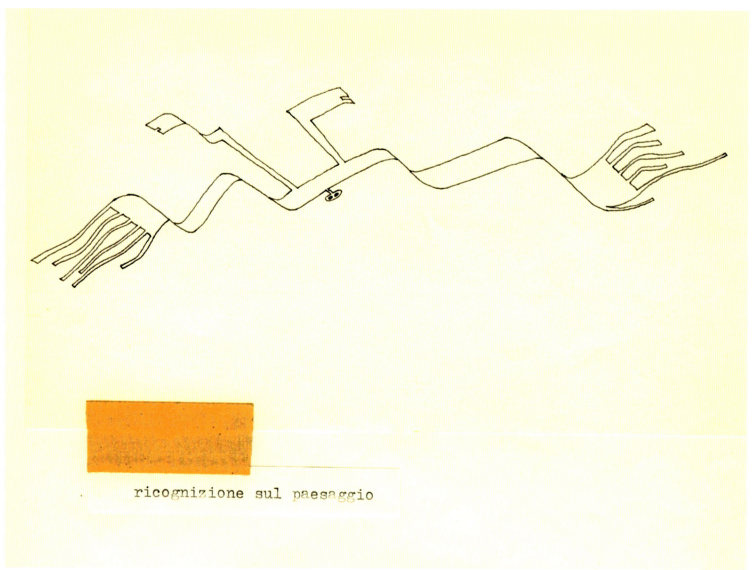

17.

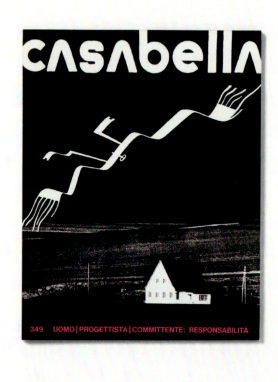

18.

17. *Urbolante: Ricognizione sul paesaggio* (Urbolante: Landscape reconnaissance), drawing, 1970
18. Casabella issue 349, 1970
19. *Oggetti ad uso spirituale* (Objects for spiritual use), drawing, 1970

poltrona caverna

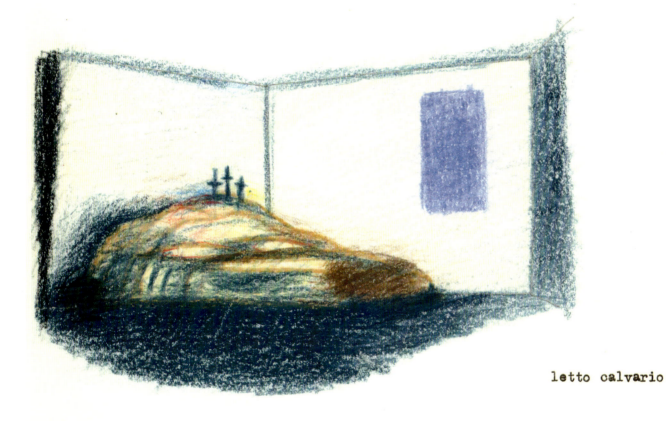

letto calvario

tavolo dolmen

19.

RADICAL DESIGN: THE GHOST IN THE MACHINE

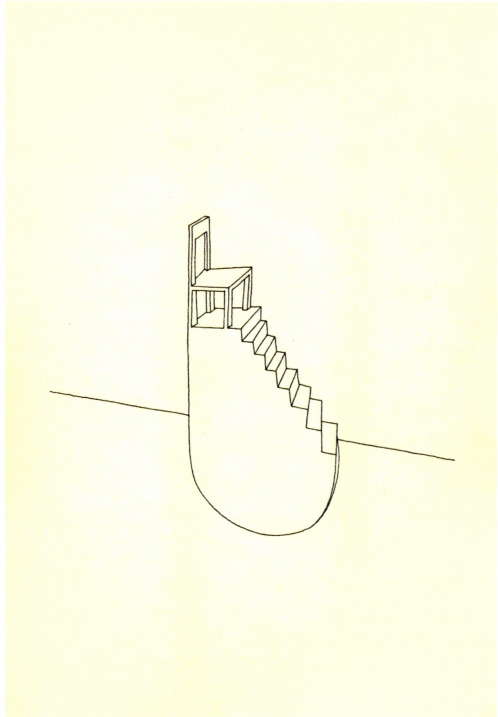

20.
21.

20. *Monumentino da casa* (Small monument for the house), drawing, 1970
21. *Oggetti ad uso spirituale* (Objects for spiritual use): *Sedia 'Elevazione' oppure 'Erezione'* ('Elevation' or 'Erection' chair), drawing, 1970
22. *Monumentino da casa*, 1974

22.

RADICAL DESIGN: THE GHOST IN THE MACHINE

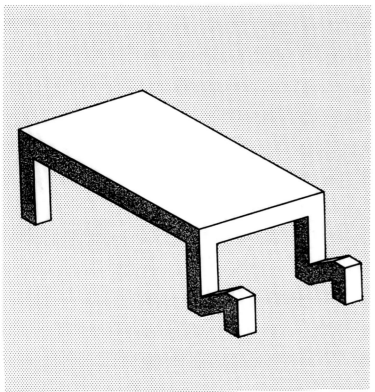

23.

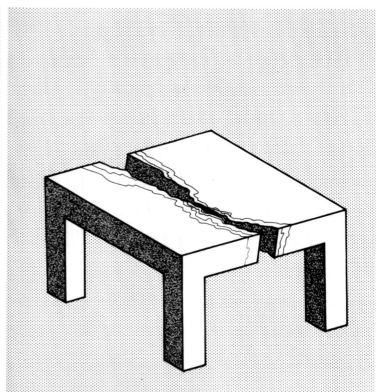

24.

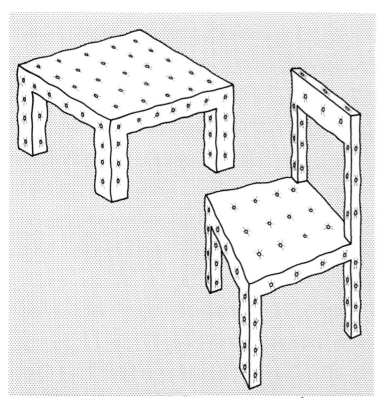

25.

23. *Objects for spiritual use: Tavolo preghiera (Prayer table), drawing, 1972*
24. *Objects for spiritual use: Tavolo voragine (Chasm table), drawing, 1972*
25. *Objects for spiritual use: Tavolo e sedia capitonné (Upholstered table and chair), drawing, 1972*
26. *Mobili da meditazione, mobili da guerriglia (Meditation furniture, guerrilla furniture), drawing, 1960s*

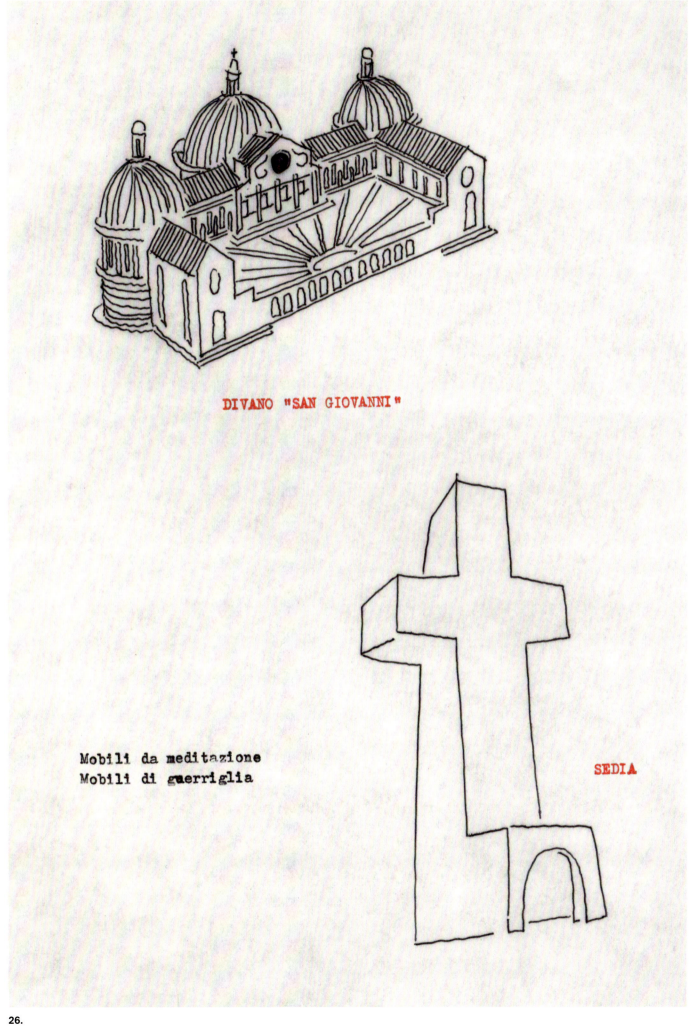

DIVANO "SAN GIOVANNI"

Mobili da meditazione
Mobili di guerriglia

SEDIA

27.

TAVOLO DOLMEN
DOLMEN TABLE

28.

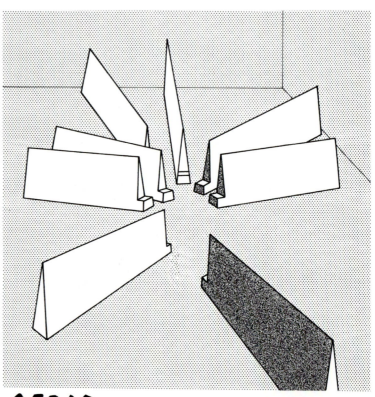

SEDIA

29.

CHAPTER 2

56

30.

31.

27. *Objects for spiritual use: Poltrona, tomba da soggiorno* (Armchair, living room tomb) for Gufram, 1974
28. *Objects for spiritual use: Tavolo dolmen* (Dolmen table), drawing, 1972
29. *Objects for spiritual use: Sedia* (Chair), drawing, 1970
30. *Lampada letargo* (Letargo lamp) for Bracciodiferro, 1973
31. *Lampada senza luce* (Lamp without light) for Bracciodiferro, 1973

32.

33.

32. *Lassù* (Up there) chair, partially burnt version, 1974
33. *Sedia terra* (Earth chair), 1974
34. *Monumentino da casa* performance, Piedmont hills, 1974

CHAPTER 2 58

34.

35.

36.

37.

35. *Sedia grano* (Grain chair), 1974
36. *Valigia per ultimo viaggio* (Suitcase for the last journey) for Bracciodiferro/Cassina, 1974
37. *Tavolino da salotto* (Drawing room table), 1975
    overleaf: *Untitled*, drawing, 1979

RADICAL DESIGN: THE GHOST IN THE MACHINE

PROUST: A KITSCH REVOLUTION FOR THE COMMON MAN

TOWARDS A NEW ITALIAN DESIGN

In 1976 siblings Alessandro and Adriana Guerriero founded Studio Alchymia, with the slogan *Progettazioni di immagini per il XX secolo* (Designing images for the twentieth century). Initially based on Milan's Via dell'Orso, in the creative district of Brera, they later moved to a basement studio in the centre of the city at the address 55 Foro Bonaparte. It was here that they began their ascent to international fame as a leading force in post-Radical design during the late 1970s and early 1980s.

Alessandro Guerriero had studied architecture at the Politecnico and, like Mendini, he held progressive beliefs. However, for political reasons, he ultimately decided not to graduate.[1] Having gained experience in graphic design and media, he also began to make *mobili e oggetti 'illusionistici'* ('illusionistic' furniture and objects) with ironic titles and descriptions such as the (fake) fireplace *Fuoco di Sant' Antonio* (The Fire of Sant' Antonio), the foldable table *Ultima Cena* (Last Supper) and the *Credenza* wardrobe, which had a door designed like a fanciful baroque portal. In the early years, the Guerrieros were joined by Bruno and Giorgio Gregori, designers and refined illustrators who remained a constant presence in the studio until it closed its doors in 1992.[2]

The name Studio Alchymia (which would later change its spelling to Studio Alchimia – which is how it will henceforth be referred to in this book) was drawn from Alessandro Guerriero's interest in numerology and esotericism. The accompanying slogan clearly emphasized design as an imaginative process rather than a purely technical discipline. His strong intellectual curiosity led him to connect with various figures from the Radical design scene, and from 1977 Studio Alchimia began producing experimental objects by Franco Raggi (*La Classica* lamp), Lapo Binazzi/UFO (*Paramount* lamp), Liisi Beckmann (*Congiunto* and *Consorte* table and chair) and Bruno Gregori (*Cor'Engrate* clock) – though most of these were pieces that had already been designed and were simply reissued by Studio Alchimia in limited series.[3]

The first collaboration between Guerriero's studio and Mendini arose in 1978, with the exhibition *Incontri ravvicinati d'architettura* (Close Architectural Encounters) at the Palazzo dei Diamanti in Ferrara, which also included work by Branzi and Sottsass. Mendini's contribution to the exhibition was sarcastically titled *La Stanza del Secolo* (The Room of the Century),[4] which featured old furniture he'd salvaged from junkyards, either left as it was, or re-painted with motifs borrowed directly from avant-garde abstract patterns. This was the first time he put forward the idea of the banal house, crammed with kitsch elements, as a reference model for an equally banal way of planning and designing.

The exhibition was one of the many shows that, throughout the 1970s and 1980s, contributed to redefining the Italian cultural approach to architecture and design in the wake of the Radical era, but it was particularly important because it represented a new phase for Mendini's work. Two pieces from *La Stanza del Secolo* would end up in Studio Alchimia's production, even if only temporarily: the *Kandissi* sofa and the *Proust* armchair, which was destined to become the most famous and representative piece of Mendini's oeuvre.

The armchair's first physical iteration was created through the collaboration with Studio Alchimia,[5] but Mendini had been ruminating on the idea of 'Proust furniture' for a few years. Back in the early 1970s when he was working with Bracciodiferro, Mendini had travelled through France with Cassina's art director Francesco Binfaré, visiting the places where Proust had lived. Originally, the intention was to create textiles for Cassina inspired by the imaginary memory of Proust's novel *In Search of Lost Time*, but the project ended up taking a different direction.

Mendini had previously experimented with modifying iconic pieces of design. In his series *Redesign del Movimento Moderno* (Redesign of the Modern Movement) he took classic chairs, including Thonet's *No.14* and Gio Ponti's *Superleggera*, made by Cassina, and adapted them, either decorating them or transforming them. His irreverent intent was evident in his transformation of Gerrit Rietveld's *Zig Zag* Chair, rendered with a back shaped like a large cross, which recalled Mendini's Radical, religious – or rather, sacrilegious – themed designs. But the direct application of a Proust-era painting style onto a stylised armchair represented a new design methodology and the piece marked a decisive turning point in his work as an artist and designer. Mendini himself recounted the origin, evolution and meaning of the *Proust* armchair as follows:

> *As for Proust, I was referring on one hand to his descriptions of place and time, to his infinite play on memory; and on the other hand to the painting styles of Impressionism, Divisionism and Pointillism. I found a perfect ready-made in an eighteenth-century-style armchair and chose some details from Signac's paintings, particularly those depicting meadows. I combined them as a texture that invades the entire armchair, both the fabric and the wooden parts, dissolving its form into a kind of nebula. Beyond the idea of creating a design piece starting from something entirely unrelated to the usual design process, I also wanted to achieve this result: to make a culturally valid object starting from a falsehood, because the redesign in question was done on a kitsch armchair, still mass-produced in a 'faux antique' style.*[6]

The *Proust* armchair ultimately created ripples across the design world: despite having been dismissed by critics for being too intellectual or in 'bad taste', such a deliberately kitsch object caught the eye of the more general public, who in some respect could identify with a piece of furniture that could have been plucked from one of Italy's bourgeois salons of the past. The piece also encapsulated many other characteristic traits of Mendini's new phase: an interest in pure, simple surfaces and an attraction for colour, or rather 'multicolour', which from then on would become the calling card of all of his work, across design as well as architecture – from armchairs to corkscrews and lamps to sideboards, culminating in the multicoloured monumentality of the Groninger Museum.

However, in 1978 the *Proust* armchair was created as a one-off piece for the Ferrara exhibition. It was not designed with mass production in mind – or even limited production – but rather as a demonstration of Mendini's critical intentions. The same applies to the other pieces from *La Stanza del Secolo*, such as the *Kandissi* sofa – an ironic homage to Kandinsky, the father of abstractionism – and the *Spaziale* table and its chairs (which, until then, had only existed as drawings).

A meeting between the two Alessandros – Mendini and Guerriero – provided the opportunity to rethink the *Proust* armchair as an item that could be produced in a small series. That's when the pair came up with the concept of a true collection of furniture and objects under the title *Bau-Haus I*, which Studio Alchimia would go on to produce, asking a selection of designers from the post-Radical scene to submit ideas for new products. After some initial hesitation about the name – a clear reference to the Bauhaus school of Johannes Itten, Walter Gropius and Mies van der Rohe that spawned much of the modern design that the Radicals sought to challenge – Mendini grasped Guerriero's intentions. He wanted to put forward an ironic refoundation of design through the poetics of single post-Radical authors, continuing his expressive experience and following the utopian hypothesis that even 'anti-design' objects had a chance to exist on the furniture market.

While Mendini brought his existing *Stanza del Secolo* pieces to the collection, Ettore Sottsass, Paola Navone, Andrea Branzi, Michele De Lucchi and Swiss architects Trix and Robert Haussmann designed new pieces of furniture and objects. Launched with a poster designed by Giorgio Gregori, the exhibition of the *Bau-Haus I* collection opened in 1979 inside the Studio Alchimia space on Foro Bonaparte. Other than the *Proust* armchair, Mendini also presented his *Kandissi* sofa, the *Kandissone* tapestry and the *Ondoso* coffee table, which was inspired by the aesthetics of the 1950s in the organic shape of its top, its celluloid coating and its conical metal legs. Also on display were a series of neomodernist armchairs and furnishings by Andrea Branzi and storage pieces by Paola Navone with linoleum panels. Ettore Sottsass contributed his *Svincolo* floor lamp (featuring two neon tube diffusers and a rectangular structure coated in Abet plastic laminate); a bookcase with steel shelves and a structure also coated in Abet laminate; the small table *Le Strutture Tremano* (The Structures Tremble), with a glass top supported by a frame of multicoloured tubes, as well as other lamps and objects.[7]

Alchimia Group, Triennale di Milano, 1986

Ettore Sottsass and the Proust armchair, Studio Alchimia, 1979

Mendini and Franco Migliaccio painting the Proust armchair, 1988

PROUST: A KITSCH REVOLUTION FOR THE COMMON MAN

Poster for Studio Alchimia Bau-Haus Side One collection, 1979

Studio Alchimia production, spread from Architectural Review, ITALY special issue, 1982

CHAPTER 3

Even for those familiar with and fond of the 'pop', ironic look of Sottsass's industrial product designs – such as the iconic *Valentine* typewriter for Olivetti – seeing pieces so different from his previous production, or rather, that took his ironic language to the extreme, was a startling surprise. The exhibition's overall aim felt explicitly provoking and bewildering, and reactions were mixed: much of the design establishment and specialist press preferred to ignore it, but there were also those who didn't spare Sottsass and Mendini from harsh criticism for participating in this unprecedented and unexpected provocation.

> The latter in particular was affected by these malicious critiques, convinced that his position was not conservative or, even worse, reactionary. On the contrary, he saw himself as open to understanding and expressing a culture of images and design that acknowledged the concrete and psychological transformations being experienced by the average Italian: the petit-bourgeois individual in the ebb of the revolutionary aspirations of the 1960s and 70s. It was exactly these changes that led Mendini and his peers to come up with the theory of Banal Design in this period.

In contrast, the show's reception from non-specialist media was very different. Within an Italian culture still linked to the idea of 'Bel Design', Alchimia's approach was too unusual and provocative to go unnoticed. The studio's inability to fit in with the establishment went on to explicitly characterise its identity, as did the way in which it moved closer to the worlds of fashion, art and even collecting, rather than traditional design and industry. This was a true, healthy shake-up of the system, which generated new authors and new means of expression.

> Some designers only grasped the most superficial aspects of Alchimia's provocations, such as the use of multicolour and materials like plastic laminate. Many participants in image culture (advertising, graphic design and experimental theatre such as that of director Mario Martone)[8] adopted Mendini's stylistic traits, his formalist and sarcastic method, before other designers did. Sometimes, though, these followers misunderstood the group's intentions. While Alchimia saw their work as a serious rejection of the role of the avant-garde and the negation of design as the last resort for idealist illusions about planning, some followers saw it as a mere trend or, even worse, a style.

Mendini and Guerriero – at least from the *Bau-Haus I* collection onwards – were the studio's leaders. In accordance with Mendini's theory-praxis, the studio worked towards a concrete materialism, considering design a field of expression like any other. Similarly, design could combine well with other expressive forms – fashion, art, music, or theatre – and like them, it could gather inspiration from everyday life: from objects and things, beautiful or trivial, which were part of ordinary existence. That's why Sottsass made use of plastic laminates inspired by old *latterie* (dairy shops), metal sheeting used in the construction of bus steps, or souvenir ceramics. For Mendini, it meant referencing Kandinsky and Italian Futurism, and for Branzi, it was Soviet Constructivism and Rationalism, in a rapid stylistic chase.

> Mendini's aim was not to consider colour and geometric shapes as symbols of modernity, but to give them the opportunity to exist autonomously, transforming them from symbols into signs: potentially infinitely multipliable in both variety and quantity, especially on the surface of products and on materials rethought as decoration, from fabrics to celluloid to plastic laminate. The Alchimia group's abandonment of the functionalist criteria that defined the Modernist understanding of design would become the most important expression of 1980s Italian design, in the context of a postmodern condition that had come of age in all aspects: philosophically, from the point of view of design, and in relation to the existential struggle that Mendini was always fascinated by.

38.

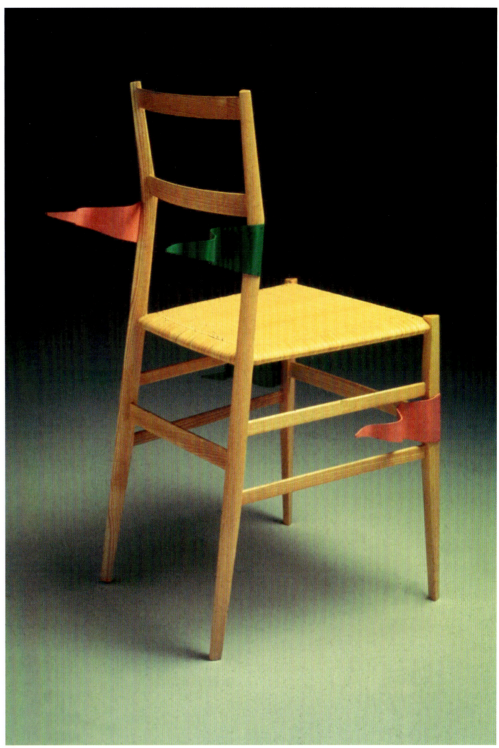

39.

38. *Diagramma teorico* (Theoretical diagram), drawing, 2013
39. *Redesign di sedie del movimento moderno* (Redesign of chairs from the modern movement): *Superleggera* by Gio Ponti, 1978

PROUST: A KITSCH REVOLUTION FOR THE COMMON MAN

40. Redesign of chairs from the modern movement: *Sedia Universale* by Joe Colombo, 1978
41. Redesign of chairs from the modern movement: *Zig-Zag chair* by Gerrit Rietveld, 1975
42. Redesign of chairs from the modern movement: *Thonet no. 14*, 1978

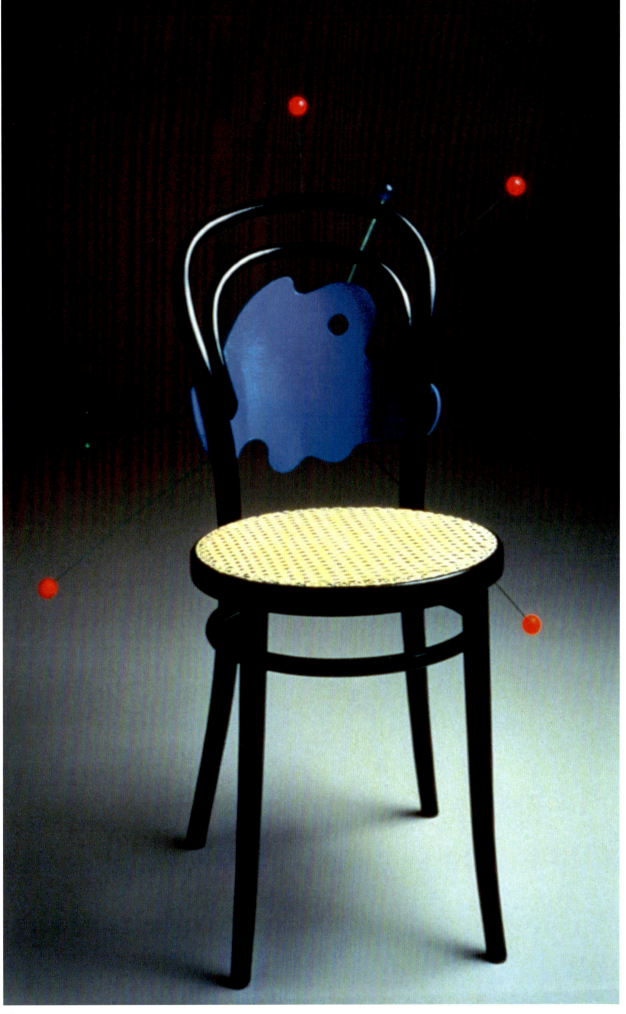

42.

PROUST: A KITSCH REVOLUTION FOR THE COMMON MAN

43.

44.

43. *Ondoso* coffee table, Alchimia Bau-Haus Side One collection, 1979
44. *Kandissi sofa*, 1978
45. Redesign of chairs from the modern movement: *Wassily* by Marcel Breuer, drawing, 1978

45.

46.

46. *Kandissone* tapestry, 1978
47. *Poltrona di Proust* (Proust armchair), 1978
48. Left: study for variant of the *Proust* pattern
    Right: *Proust* laminate for Abet Laminati, 1990

47.

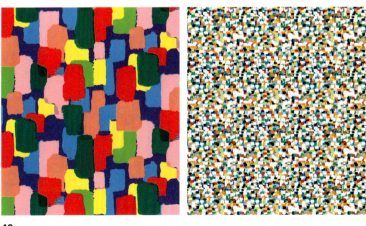

48.

PROUST: A KITSCH REVOLUTION FOR THE COMMON MAN

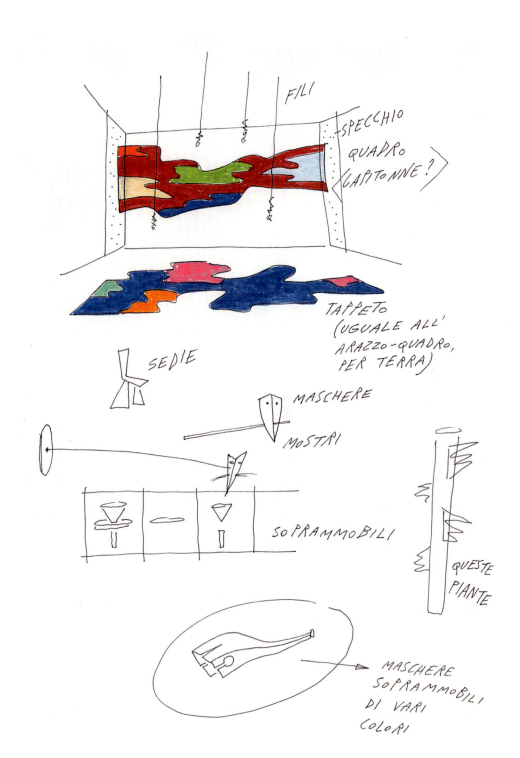

49.

49. *Casa di Ambrogio Milan*, drawing, 1983
50. *Kandissone* tapestry, drawing, 1978
    overleaf: *Move every thing a little*,
    Tea & Coffee Piazza, Alessi, drawing, 1983

50.

PROUST: A KITSCH REVOLUTION FOR THE COMMON MAN

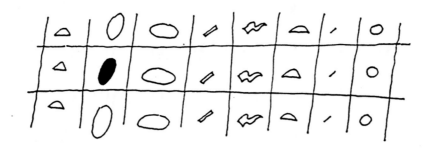

MOVE EVERY THING A LITTLE

FROM POSTMODERN TO NEOMODERN: THE ALESSI AND DOMUS YEARS

THE PROJECT OF POSTMODERNITY

In the late 1970s, several essays were published in Europe using a key term that framed the discussion around the end of modernity. In 1979, French philosopher Jean-François Lyotard released *La Condition postmoderne: Rapport sur le savoir* (The Postmodern Condition: A Report on Knowledge), outlining what he saw as the momentous shift from nineteenth-century idealism to twentieth-century techno-scientism – and with it, the crisis of progressivism. Two years earlier, however, Charles Jencks had already adopted this term from philosophical discussion and used it in the title of his pamphlet, which made waves in the sleepy field of architectural criticism. *The Language of Post-Modern Architecture*, published in 1977 both as a monographic issue of the British magazine *AD* and as a standalone volume by Rizzoli, analyzed the system of modern design and architecture, which by that point had become fully integrated with the system of production and capitalist society.

> With this publication, the London-based American critic managed to obtain global success, to the extent that his definition ended up becoming a historical juncture in design culture. The basic thesis put forward by Jencks may appear straightforward: postmodernism meant everything that came after Modernism – or more specifically, after its failure. Cities didn't improve thanks to Modernist utopias, nor did living conditions improve thanks to the objects that were inspired or produced by Modernism. Having come to terms with this fact, he concluded, why not devote oneself to stylistic variation, to formalism, to referencing the ancient or perhaps even the Modern itself? Indeed, Jencks declared the end of Modern architecture, or at least of the Modern movement in architecture. But it's hard to pinpoint when this actually happened. Was it before or after World War II? With the advent of Nazism and Albert Speer's sombre, monumental settings? The closing of the Bauhaus and the diaspora of its masters? Or was it actually in the mid-1950s with Le Corbusier's Notre-Dame-du-Haut in Ronchamp, where the architect repudiated geometric abstraction in favour of an organic expressionism of his own?

While much of the discourse on postmodernism was tediously esoteric, Jencks's provocation clearly struck a chord with Mendini, who had been aware of these themes for a while – the entire suite of *Casabella* issues that he directed, as well as the performances, the anti-design objects, the *Proust* armchair and the other objects for Studio Alchimia, are all proof of this. It convinced him to survey the international state of design to understand how and through which authors this postmodern movement was taking place, whether it was really that relevant, and how long it might last. *Modo* magazine didn't seem fit for this purpose because of the extreme diversity of its content and its close focus on product design issues, and perhaps also its reliance on a group of stable sponsors whose concerns it was necessary to focus on. It was imperative to find a more powerful means of communication and research, and this came to Mendini in the form of *Domus*.

DOMUS: SUCCEEDING GIO PONTI

When Gianni Mazzocchi, the publisher of *Domus*, faced the challenge of finding a successor to Gio Ponti – who, after 50 years almost uninterrupted at the helm was no longer able to lead the magazine due to his advanced age – Mendini emerged as a favoured candidate. Of course, Mendini's impressive background which already included editing (and, in the case of *Modo*, founding) two important magazines certainly played a part. However, the key factor seemed to be the shared connection between *Domus*'s authoritative and charismatic critic Pierre Restany and the architect and artist Marcello Pietrantoni. Mendini held Pietrantoni in great esteem, and wrote about him in the art magazine *Data* in December 1976;[1] Pietrantoni mentioned Mendini to Restany, who, 'having never met him', examined his work and suggested him to Mazzocchi as the new editor-in-chief of *Domus*.

> Mazzocchi and his daughter Giovanna (who had started helping him direct the publishing house) welcomed Restany's suggestion. After intense conversations on the new editorial project, and with Gio Ponti's blessing, the first issue of the magazine led by Mendini hit newsstands in July 1979. Mendini recalls: 'The handover with Ponti was particularly

warm; it took place just between the two of us in his living room, with a bottle of champagne.'² Despite having the same graphic design as the previous issues, its content already signalled a different cultural direction, with long articles on pre-fabricated buildings, a few pages on design and a large section on art (edited as usual by Restany and Lisa Licitra Ponti, Gio Ponti's eldest daughter, who had long been collaborating with him). In the preface to the issue, Mazzocchi announced its new course under the editorial direction of Mendini, who, he said:

*[…] truly understands the cultural and prestigious value that Domus holds throughout the world [and] will know how to enrich it further, injecting his sensibility and intelligence into it.*³

Restarting *Domus*'s great engine was a challenge that required both courage and commitment from Mendini. Succeeding Ponti meant taking on his important inheritance – a relatively easy task for Mendini, given his knowledge and admiration for the master – while at the same time continuing to develop a true editorial enterprise, which was already famous across the world. This fact had been celebrated in 1973, on occasion of the magazine's 45th anniversary, with an exceptional retrospective at the Musée des Arts Décoratifs of the Louvre in Paris. The exhibition *1928/73 Domus: 45 ans d'architecture, design, art* had been a triumph. The most important historians and art and architecture critics, as well as some of the best artists and architects of the time, contributed to the unique, two-volume catalogue. Influential intellectuals Giulio Carlo Argan and Marshall McLuhan, Konstantin Melnikov (one of the last remaining figures of the Russian avant-garde), Archigram prophet Peter Cook and the revolutionary Swiss critic and curator Harald Szeemann were all involved. The entire international intelligentsia of arts and design agreed: *Domus* continued to play a leading role in identifying and exploring the figures and trends central to the development of a cosmopolitan visual and material culture.

This official endorsement by the Louvre and other outreach activities helped extend *Domus*'s fame – and what today would be called its brand – on the international scene. Its authority in all areas of expression and of design was reinforced, and *Domus* was established as the most important means of communication for architects, designers, producers and their patrons, both current and potential. On the one hand, Mendini's vision and project for *Domus* was to continue Gio Ponti's dream: to make *Domus* the global 'bible' for enthusiasts and professionals in the arts, architecture and design, the indispensable source of information on new designs, objects and products. At the same time, it was necessary to make a clear break from the magazine's past: however glorious, it was still laden with Pontian optimism, fundamentally biased towards those who benefited from current systems, and often ignorant of great social problems, issues and new mass behaviours.

Once again, Mendini found himself at a crossroads. His time at *Casabella* had ended abruptly because of the new publisher's aversion to his editorial line, an experience he didn't want to repeat. But he also didn't want to renounce his Radical, personal political positions, which he had expressed clearly in a text from 1975 for the first Global Tools seminar on the Body:

*We are left-wing intellectuals. Many of us are bourgeois, few are proletarians. We move within strange situations, in more or less official ways we produce a great magma, which could be defined as left-wing culture. A precise destiny looms inexorably on this transient culture […] The bourgeois intellectual, by introducing a proletarian stylistics into his elite culture, vents his innate sense of guilt, playing a necessary role towards the death of a late culture which needs to end as soon as possible.*⁴

Mendini would carry on this vision of work through his artistic and research practice, but as an intellectual who was also part of the industrial system, he was aware of the transformations taking place in Italian society. He would have to take this into account when producing an international magazine as important as *Domus*, particularly in a new edition adapted to a difficult time that was nonetheless full of unexpected opportunities for industrial design.

Perhaps the event that carried the most severe consequences was the 1973 oil energy crisis, which profoundly affected the Italian economy and its development through the mid 1970s. From 1976, the two historical political parties *Democrazia Cristiana* (Christian Democracy) and *Partito Comunista Italiano* (PCI, the Italian Communist Party) tried to implement an alliance, with the dual aims of relaunching the country's economy and bringing democratic and workers' forces into the planning and control of fundamental economic and political choices, following the model of German social democracy. The result was, first, a dramatic worsening of political tensions and then the PCI's sharp decline at the 1979 general election.

A period of relative 'social peace' followed, and with the progressive elimination of workers' disputes, Italian capitalism essentially regained control of both economy and society, instigating a postmodern and neo-industrial restructuring. The rapid introduction of robots for automated production played a large role in this process. Fiat Auto was world-leading in the research, production and use of these machines, so that from 1985 onwards the Termoli[5] factory alone could produce 2,100 engines for the FIRE 100 (Fully Integrated Robotised Engine) car every day – more than one a minute. This new engine, designed by Rodolfo Bonetto, allowed Fiat to meet the demands of its globalized market.

Fiat's example was followed by thousands of other companies, which aspired to gain new segments of the international market by investing in technology and updating their manufacturing systems, but also by making use of small businesses, so-called 'subcontractors'. These artisanal businesses became the foundation of sectors such as furniture design and fashion: their production could adapt quickly to the fluctuations of the market as well as to changing tastes.

Mendini was well aware of this new infrastructure for Italian industry and he tried to become its interpreter, as designer and promoter as well as design communication guru in his role at *Domus*. His experience designing seemingly improbable furniture with Studio Alchimia served as a workshop for what, over the following decades, would become some of his most important design production projects – through which he was always mindful of continuing a great Italian craft tradition.

Mendini turned to his friend Ettore Sottsass for help with the new graphic identity and layouts of *Domus*. Sottsass simply added some characteristic graphic signs to the pages, and a red-and-white striped band to the top of the cover, arguing: 'magazines on newsstands are often shown vertically, one in front of the other, so even if it'll be half-hidden, you'll always be able to recognise *Domus*.'

In truth, the magazine's main graphic innovation was its cover concept. Mendini decided to do something that had not been done before on an architecture or design magazine – at least not as part of a regular series. He featured portraits of artists, architects and designers on the cover, introducing creatives who embodied new directions in their field, just as a cultural or entertainment figure might represent their work or even a cultural trend.

He commissioned photographers Occhiomagico (composed by Giancarlo Maiocchi and Ambrogio Beretta first, and later Maiocchi on his own) and Maria Mulas, with airbrush retouching by illustrator Emilie Van Hees, who highlighted the features of each person's face, emphasizing both their physical and intellectual traits. The series included portraits of the 'up-and-comers' of the early 1980s, such as Frank Gehry, Peter Eisenman and Richard Meier; more established authors such as Tomás Maldonado, Enzo Mari, Meret Oppenheim, Philip Johnson and entrepreneur Rina Brion (head of Brionvega); and historical, verging on mythological figures such as Andrea Palladio. For the first number in this new series, Mendini chose Aldo Rossi who was, rightly or wrongly, considered the main Italian exponent of postmodernism.

Mendini's interventions on the editorial team were less radical. Marianne Lorenz kept her role as editor. Originally Austrian, Lorenz had been living in Milan since graduating in architecture, and she was in touch with the most important international architects of the time. The art section remained in the hands of Lisa Licitra Ponti, who looked after

Portrait of Mendini by Tiger Tateishi for Domus, 1979

Mendini with Gio Ponti, Milan, 1979

 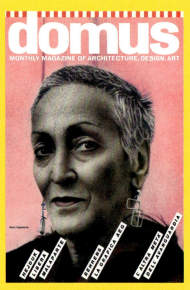  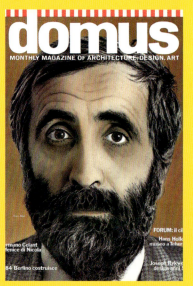

Domus (l-r): Aldo Rossi (issue 602), Meret Oppenheim (issue 605), Morris Lapidus (issue 610), Enzo Mari (issue 607), all 1980

her father's memory and archive after his death, and who knew and followed closely the authors of a variety of contemporary art trends. Pierre Restany acted as editor-at-large, travelling frequently and participating in the most important international exhibitions.

Mendini also added me to the team, while I was still a student at Rome's ISIA and curated the exhibition *Design Formazione* (Design Formation) at Rome's Palazzo delle Esposizioni. He entrusted me with the task of overseeing design, alongside Maria Grazia Mazzocchi, the daughter of the publisher and journalist. Other collaborators included Rosa Maria Rinaldi, and notably, for the special issues on fashion, some of the authors from *Modo*: Nives Ciardi, Claudia Donà, Daniela Puppa, Barbara Radice and Franco Raggi (though, notably, none of *Casabella*'s historical contributors). This large ad hoc group represented a new cultural and economic project: an operational nucleus, fortified by *Domus*'s substantial resources, embodying Mendini's cultural visions. On several occasions, Mendini himself spoke of how indispensable it was to share projects and objectives in increasingly large groups; this would remain a constant feature of his work over the course of his decades-long career.

> *My way of working and thinking is methodical, everything proceeds slowly and in an organized fashion, things are studied and debated. To achieve this, I need two souls. The introverted one, looking inward, deep and isolated: sketching, writing, creating organisational charts, reading and studying. Then the organized, discursive one, linked to discussion and realization of projects. Therefore my time is divided between these two modes [...] Just as with magazines, creating groups is also a passion of mine which gives me a lot in return.*[6]

Studio Alchimia was also involved in the magazine's art direction, with Alessandro Guerriero and graphic designer Mauro Panzeri – who looked after layouts – and Occhiomagico studio creating images and portraits for the next series of covers. In this series, the cover model was presented in the context of a virtual environment, thanks to the first photo-editing techniques that allowed the merging of photography and illustration.

Directing the new *Domus* – an operation that was both intellectual and commercial – was a complex task but one that Mendini approached in a similar way to *Casabella* and *Modo*. He afforded a lot of freedom to his trusted and trustworthy editorial team, even if it was made up of young, relatively inexperienced creatives. He encouraged contributions on themes that evoked his lively curiosity, but also on topics that the editors were passionate about. Editorial meetings to make strategic decisions could be brief. One-on-one dialogue could also happen between the director and the editors. The relationships were always friendly and on equal footing, although with a useful vein of detachment and irony. As a director who considered himself *primus inter pares* (first among equals), Mendini also took upon himself the responsibility to talk with the publisher. Increasingly in this capacity he dealt with Giovanna Mazzocchi, rather than her father, who by then was the deus ex-machina of the whole company of Editoriale Domus.

Giovanna agreed to an openness towards new initiatives that enriched the editorial activity even further. The magazine promoted design competitions, published important books – such as *Il Design Italiano degli Anni Cinquanta* (Italian Design in the 1950s) for the eponymous exhibition at CentroKappa – and planned international editions, including one for the US market, for which Emilio Ambasz was consulted.[7] The activities of Centrodomus also resumed: relocating to the Rozzano offices of the Editoriale, it became a research centre, focusing on themes such as decoration with the Research on Decor, while the historical premises on Via Manzoni in Milan became home to a space to put on exhibitions and presentations in collaboration with the companies closest to the magazine and the publishing house.

In this 'factory of cultural information', communication happened in a rapid and efficient manner both internally and externally, despite the fact that this was before the advent of the internet, email and smartphones. The world beyond the team was reflected in editorial decisions that attracted an increasingly large and international public. Other than a calendar of engagements managed by his assistant Monique Mizrahil, Mendini's unique 'diary' consisted of many yellow Post-It notes on his otherwise almost empty desk, bearing the names of the most important people in industrial and design culture, written in Mendini's unmistakable handwriting with his trusty Tratto pen.

1980: THE FIRST YEAR OF A GOLDEN DECADE

In 1980, when he hadn't yet turned 50 – often considered the age of maturity for an architect – Mendini experienced an exceptional coincidence of facts, situations and collaborations that indelibly marked his work and destiny. The start of his editorship of *Domus* coincided with a frenetic period of exhibitions (first on his own; later with Studio Alchimia) which were completely new for the Italian public: the project/subject of the exhibitions were the research, narration and provocation of ideas surrounding the culture of living.

Until then, design exhibitions – including the great, important show on the 1950s at CentroKappa – had been limited to documenting history, authors and issues around design as a business. Meanwhile, pure and creative research was confined to contemporary art exhibitions, mostly at galleries and not inside museums, which at the time were still extremely conservative (design museums didn't exist at the time in Italy, not even in Milan).

Two major exhibitions – and a smaller, less famous one – signalled the maturity and importance of Mendini's new design visions, all in 1980. These were the international exhibition *Forum Design* in Linz, Austria, in June; *L'oggetto banale* (The Banal Object) at Venice's Architecture Biennale, in July; and *La Superficie Modificante* (The Modifying Surface) at Milan's Centrodomus, in September.

The *Forum Design* exhibition in Linz, organised by the local Österreichisches Institut für Visuelle Gestaltung (Austrian Institute for Visual Design), aimed to give the widest overview of the positions coexisting at the beginning of the 1980s on the international design scene. A pavilion built on the Danube and designed for the purpose by the Austrian avant-garde group Haus-Rucker-Co (who Mendini had already featured in *Casabella* when he was the magazine's editor-in-chief) displayed different design approaches, organized across three sectors.

Alessi and Zanotta were chosen to represent Italy in the *Concezione industriale del design* (Industrial Design Concept) sector, curated by Mendini, with a set-up designed by Achille Castiglioni, to display their attitude towards innovation and research in product design. Other countries were represented by companies including Citroën, Siemens, Honda, Nikon, Seiko and previously unknown figures such as the industrial/fashion designer Kenzo. The *Strategie individuali* (Individual Strategies) section presented a series of authors, architects, designers and artists, all of whom were extremely refined interpreters of the contemporary condition. Among others this included Rebecca Horn, Mario Merz, Ettore Sottsass[8] – who brought a series of furniture pieces designed by Alchimia – Òscar Tusquets and Lluís Clotet. Finally, the *Aspetti tematici* (Thematic Aspects) section, which was also curated by Mendini with exhibition design by Studio Alchimia, gathered a few original interventions on topics including space equipment (*Space Design*, curated by Barbara Radice and based on NASA archives), fashion (*Fashion Design*, put on by the Fiorucci D-Xing research centre) and *Banal Design*.

The *Banal Design* section displayed a series of conventional objects that had undergone a process of redesign through the use of colour and decoration. Alongside these objects, there was a small architectural model, with four different facades that had been designed by Mendini, Alessandro Guerriero, Andrea Branzi, and Bruno and Giorgio Gregori, based on a project published in a manual for surveyors. There was also a series of paintings representing details from suburban architecture, focused on the use of decoration. That was the first public appearance for the idea of the 'banal', which was becoming the main focus of the theory and practice of Mendini and Studio Alchimia. Mendini was increasingly emerging as the group's main source of inspiration: despite being able to maintain complete authority on his designs, he continuously exchanged ideas and collaborated with the rest of the team.

Domus, Michele De Lucchi
(issue 617), 1981

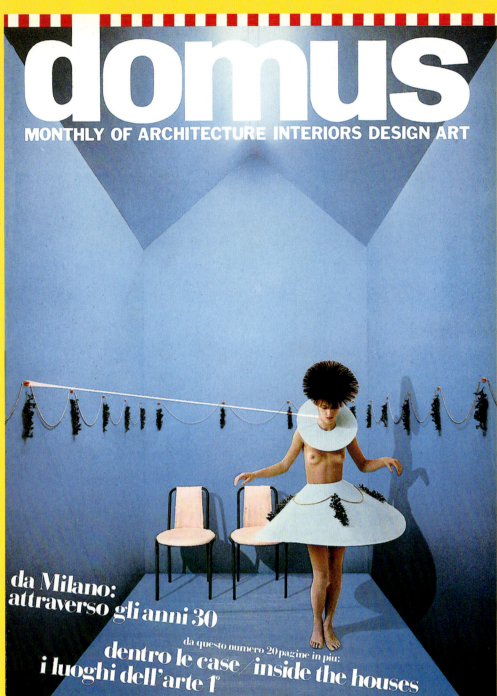

Domus, reconstruction of the Arredare come esistere installation (issue 624), 1982

(l-r): Domus, Emilio Ambasz (issue 639), 1983; Domus, Piero Busnelli (issue 642), 1983; Centrodomus publications, 1981

FROM POSTMODERN TO NEOMODERN: THE ALESSI AND DOMUS YEARS

Mendini in the Stanza Banale (Banal Room), Architecture Biennale, Venice, 1980

Mendini and Richard Meier working on Tea & Coffee Piazza project, 1983

Mendini, Milan, 1980s

Together with *Italy: The New Domestic Landscape*, the show organized by Emilio Ambasz in 1972 at MoMA in New York, *Forum Design* was probably the most important major design exhibition of the second half of the twentieth century, due to its large scale, the refined contributions of so many artists, architects and designers of the time, and the expansive catalogue *Design Ist Unsichtbar* (Design Is Invisible) – unfortunately only ever published in German.[9] But its success also had to do with the atmosphere of enthusiasm and human affinity between then-emerging personalities, which I was also a part of – having been invited by Zanotta, for whom I was curating the art direction at Mendini's recommendation. Participants including Ettore Sottsass, Achille Castiglioni, Barbara Radice, Alberto Alessi, Laurids Ortner (an architect from the Haus-Rucker-Co group), artist Rebecca Horn, industrialist Aurelio Zanotta and Alessandro Guerriero all met inside and outside of the exhibition's great pavilion, for theoretical discussions but also for convivial moments.

> Linz's great event had international critical resonance, particularly in the field of industrial design. The Swiss-German theorist and curator François Burkhardt – at the time the director of Berlin's Internationales Design Zentrum (IDZ) and later, for many years, the director of the Centre Georges Pompidou's Centre de Création Industrielle (CCI) – who was also intellectually close with Sottsass first, and Mendini later, was still writing very positively about it in 1983:

The event had a significant influence [...] In particular the exhibition and section on Banal Design, with Sottsass's new programme manufactured by the Italian Alchimia group, contributed to bringing great vitality to the critical debate [...] Suddenly, people realised that if innovation in architecture was coming out of the USA, design innovation still came from Italy.[10]

THE BANAL OBJECT

The most famous occasion for a presentation of Mendini's theories on the banal and on redesign was Venice's Architecture Biennale, which opened in July 1980, a month after the Linz exhibitions. This edition went down in history as the postmodern Biennale, because of the *Strada Novissima* (New Road), curated by the Biennale's director Paolo Portoghesi, and the *Teatro del Mondo* (Theatre of the World) by Aldo Rossi. The *L'Oggetto Banale* (The Banal Object) show, curated by Mendini, was commissioned by Portoghesi and designed by Franco Raggi, Paola Navone and Daniela Puppa with the collaboration of Studio Alchimia. It was presented in the same space that was playing host to the *Strada Novissima*: the ancient, spectacular Corderie of the Arsenale, which for decades had remained the unused property of the military, and which Portoghesi gave back to the Italian and international public – an act of self-described 'urban cultural guerrilla'.

> Like the show in Linz, the exhibition consisted of a series of anonymously-designed objects of daily use – a vaporizer, an espresso coffee maker, a bottle of liquid soap – on which the authors intervened with small decorative elements (spikes, circles and other abstract motifs). Codified like a system of signs, with only slight formal variation, these motifs were similar to the stylistic elements that Mendini had used in the chairs that comprised his *Redesign of the Modern Movement* series. Next to these objects, which had been transformed from trivial to 'interesting', there was an architecture model 'for surveyors', like the one in Linz and, hanging from the ceiling, Arduino Cantafora's painting *La Città Banale* (The Banal City) – all displayed in a space representing the waiting room of a train station.

The whole set-up was an allegory of 'banality' as the starting point for a rebuilding of meaning in design. The spirit of the exhibition was half-comical (the decorated objects) and half-unsettling (the painting and the architecture model). The ideas it represented were also theorised and documented in the book *Elogio del Banale* (Ode to the Banal), inspired by Mendini, curated by Barbara Radice and published on the occasion by Alchimia.[11] Mendini's article is the most caustic and significant of all the pieces in the volume and, as was his habit, Mendini posed questions in terms that left no room for illusions:

> *The exhibition on the banal object [...] is based on the following considerations. Series in large quantities contain and imply the concept of the banal. The multiplication of a masterpiece is an intellectual utopia [...] One can hypothesize a banal design methodology, a neo-banal design and architecture that is aware of itself [...] Why not exploit the natural, intimate and mythical relationship that exists between man and an object considered 'ugly' in every mass society? For a banal man, banal objects and things: a paradoxical celebration of conventions, the triumph of genuinely missed opportunities, an availability towards an aesthetic fiction that corresponds to the fiction of everyday life [...] The banal is applied art, adapted to everyday life [...] but it's also the non-violent 'unhappy conscience' that's typical of the mass man who knows he can no longer pursue the proletarian mirage [...] We urgently need a disconcerting, disorienting, desecrating provocation, aimed at focussing attention on objects with no quality, to reflect on today's design malaise.[12]*

Although apparently cynical, the text's stark language simply represented what had already become his work's overall perspective: unhappy design. Franco Raggi's contribution to the volume provided a more constructive vision, which still, however, reiterated and reinforced Mendini's pessimism:

> *As designers, stating the necessity to analyze the banal universe is perhaps a paradox. This is born as a provocative act towards a stale architecture and design culture, that is moralistic, presumptuous, isolated, populist and aristocratic [...] Compared to the dead-end of the avant-gardes and the rhetoric of non-design, the proposal of a Banal Design is a polemic act that re-connects the design of instrumental goods to their conditions of real use.[13]*

This unique but sincere reading of the idea of Banal Design, which at the beginning Raggi supported wholeheartedly, is still interesting many years later. It sounds like an invective but also, at the same time, an earnest suggestion – directed at both Italian designers and the industrial establishment. The criticism certainly annoyed the conservative ranks 'who are not able to overcome the fall of their rational myths', and who reacted to the provocation by entrenching themselves behind the defence of Italy's 'Bel Design', of the industry's exports and the market more generally.

The importance of Mendini's theories on Banal Design and the exhibitions that attempted to represent them didn't go unnoticed by the most cultured and discerning critics, like Andrea Branzi, who'd long since left the Archizoom group and had become a singular designer-cum-theoretician figure. In his book on new Italian Design, *La Casa Calda* (The Warm Home), he dedicated an entire chapter of critical exploration to the banal, with many references to postmodernism:

Through re-design, design presents itself as an act that enhances but doesn't modify reality. Curiously [...] banal design reaches an emancipation which matches [...] postmodernism's position about the end of the development for modern architectural culture.[14]

> Branzi's long, complex theoretical reflection was perhaps best expressed through some observations, which referred to the *Redesign of the Modern Movement*, Studio Alchimia's products and the different 'rooms' that Mendini dedicated to the theme of the banal:

The operations of re-design consisted of interventions of decoration on found objects or famous design products. The idea was to illustrate the impossibility of designing something new compared to what had already been designed... The 'Banal rooms' were places where everyday life was reconstituted in an exemplary manner, in an undramatised, agnostic way that was, however, full of presences of what Modern culture had been: a serene domestic universe that was also devoid of development.[15]

Michele De Lucchi, Martine Bedin, Casciani, Mendini, Achille Castiglioni, Ettore Sottsass, Linz, 1980

Mendini with Casciani at Forum Design, Linz, 1980

Cover of the Forum Design exhibition guide, Linz, 1980

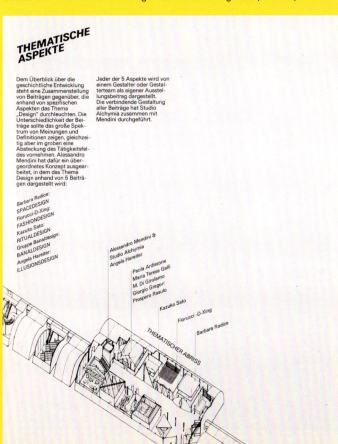

Pages from the Forum Design exhibition guide, 1980

FROM POSTMODERN TO NEOMODERN: THE ALESSI AND DOMUS YEARS

Branzi developed a critical view of Mendini and Alchimia's work, but this didn't prevent him from collaborating with both of them on a number of occasions, to the point of creating an entire furniture collection with Guerriero called *Animali Domestici* (Pets), produced by Zanotta. He didn't fully consider though, that in the development of Mendini's research, the use of decoration – whether that was simple patterns or concrete, stylistic forms – didn't aspire to achieve beauty, but aimed instead to bring design and the form of products (and, possibly, also of architecture) closer to mass sentiment.

THE CENTRODOMUS: THE MODIFYING SURFACE

This was the direction of the *Ricerca sul Decoro* (Research on Decor), which Mendini and I conducted together with a group of collaborators: Carla Ceccariglia, Guido Jannon, Giannino Malossi and Paola Navona. Among the results were a publication and a show, titled *La Superficie Modificante* (The Modifying Surface), which took place at Centrodomus in 1980, with exhibition design by Studio Alchimia. In addition to this, the group developed targeted research for the companies and industries that supported it: Abet Laminati, Alessi, Fiat and Zanotta. With different approaches, these companies would go on to use this information to develop design strategies or – as was the case for Abet Laminati – actual products. The research, as journalist Rosa Maria Rinaldi summarised in the publication, was:

> *Organised into four sectors – architecture, furniture and objects, automobiles and fashion. In each of which, decoration is systematically examined through an inquiry that examines its details, isolates it from its context, and treats it as a totally independent project, both long-lasting and ephemeral, but above all, contemporary.*[16]

In the design guidelines resulting from the research, Mendini solidified his idea for decor, or decoration, as a design element with a life of its own: it became an abstract sign that could be used for patterns applied to surfaces (on textiles, laminates or other industrial surfaces) but potentially also become the shape of the design itself. An eloquent example of this idea is his design for teapots and other objects realised for Alessi as part of the 1983 *Tea & Coffee Piazza* collection: in one of his drawings, Mendini sketched individual decorative signs – an oval, a semi-circle, some small flags and parts of a line – which, when combined, created the shape of the objects themselves.

While the collaborators of *Ricerca sul Decoro* would go on to develop their work in various, interesting and personal directions, Mendini would never leave this 'dangerous' decorative deviation from the line of positivist Modern design. Instead, he would make it a starting point to tread his own, one-way path towards an integration between design, psychology and art, which would eventually lead him back to his initial vocation as an illustrator. First, though, he had to (and was able to) demonstrate his abilities as a tireless cultural organiser, someone who was able to lead the most important design magazine in the world while simultaneously managing his own expressive and cultural research, creating and setting up exhibitions, and also taking on the art direction of a company like Alessi. There, he found his alter ego in Alberto Alessi, the great Italian industrialist and intellectual, who was able to simultaneously think up and create a new vision for design, for products and for the factory itself. Thanks to the leadership of Alessi and Mendini, whose approach was as pragmatic as it was visionary, the factory would soon begin to fulfil its potential as a place for humanistic culture.

OBJECTS AS ARCHITECTURE

A young graduate when he joined his family's storied business in 1970, Alberto Alessi already had an innovative vision for entrepreneurship. Alberto was the elder son of Carlo Alessi Anghini, the head of the company at the time, and the grandson of founder Giovanni Alessi Anghini (and, on his mother's side, of Alfonso Bialetti, the brilliant inventor of the coffee maker Moka Express). As a young man,

Alberto felt that design, and particularly collaboration with high-level designers, had the potential to relaunch a sector like that of steel household goods. Previously, these items had been relegated to continuing a century-old tradition of pre-established shapes and functions – which was reassuring in terms of guaranteeing revenue, but not well-suited to changing tastes.

Alberto's first direct approach to production was very experimental – he restructured the process, dividing production into *Programmas* (Programmes) each of which corresponded to a different period, or typology. In 1970, aged 24, he suggested creating a series of multiples in stainless steel, under the label *Alessi d'Aprés*, commissioning important artists to design them. The project only became a reality two years later, and went on to include works by Giò Pomodoro, Piero Consagra, Andrea Cascella and even a drawing by Salvador Dalí, which wasn't made into an object at the time but was picked up again in 2023. Meanwhile, architects Franco Sargiani and Eija Helander were tasked with redesigning the company's corporate identity and planning the new *Programma 8* – which consisted of containers and trays in different materials. With their rigorous geometry, these items already represented a clear rupture with the brand's historical production and its other bestsellers.

Sargiani also introduced Alberto to Ettore Sottsass, who would soon become one of Alessi's most important designers,[17] first with the items for *Programma 6* – products for hotels, restaurants, cafés and communities – and then with inventions such as his iconic oil-and-vinegar set in crystal and steel. After a long gestation (1971–74), the latter would go on to become one of the company's bestsellers, an evergreen still in production today.

Alessi honed his skills as a design manager (this is the label that his role would be given many years later, though it usually denoted a more limited and less strategic position) with professionals such as Sargiani and Sottsass. It was with Mendini, however, that he began to rethink the entirety of the production and to compose a strategic vision for product development.

The opportunity for Mendini to create his most important collaboration with industry came via *Modo* magazine, of which Alessi was one of the sponsors. Ready to tread new ground and new design strategies, Alberto Alessi saw Mendini as a unique theoretician and designer, who was able to combine intellectual reflections on the industry's complex workings together with an approach to design that was simultaneously high-brow and accessible. For his part, Mendini felt he had found the opportunity to put his critical/operative working method into practice through this company. It would allow him to operate between theory, historical systematization and design strategy, an objective that he described in the preface to his book *Paesaggio Casalingo* (Homely Landscape),[18] which outlined the shape of the long research he started for Alessi in 1977:

For a long time, I had been looking for the opportunity to focus my attention on one specific type of object, in order to classify and evaluate it comprehensively. Amongst the many types of object, I've always been intrigued by certain systems of things found in the home, beyond the more overt phenomenon of furniture. I believe that a comparative and complex study of the historical evolution of a specific, unified system of objects is one of the most up-to-date and comprehensive ways to define its potential future in design.

[…] That's why I chose a remit that is not too broad but instead fairly well defined – what I call the 'homely landscape'. By this, I mean the collection of accessories that, in a home, community or café, are linked to food and drink: objects that are as interesting as they are socially simple and widespread. It's for these reasons that I turned to Alberto Alessi, having identified in his stainless steel kitchenware company the organic group of products that I wanted to investigate to develop my thesis. I found in him someone who had already, through his experiences and of his own accord, developed intellectual needs that were similar to my own. What followed were many conversations that were as pleasant as they were challenging, often held with a third person – Ettore Sottsass.[19]

At Alessi, the storied friendship between Sottsass and Mendini developed into a loyal 'competition' between the former's sensitive professionalism and the latter's cultural interests. Both, however, paid close attention to the emotional relationship that people have with everyday objects – a shared interest that led them to develop a more sophisticated understanding of product design, as Sottsass had explained back in 1970, when he wrote for *Domus*:

I was beginning to think that if there was any point in making objects, it was that they should help people live in some way. I mean, they should help people recognize themselves and liberate themselves […] In short, if there could be a reason to design objects, it could only be to perform a kind of therapeutic action […] to imbue objects with the function of awakening the perception that everyone has or can have of their own adventure.[20]

Translated into the world of industry, this philosophical attitude toward 'designing objects' meant being able to effectively reach a very large public, (literally) putting in their hands tools that would help them consciously engage with humble everyday actions. These include those related to the nourishment of the body – after all, the greatest and most powerful spiritual machine we possess – where household items and cooking utensils play a crucial and indispensable role.

In picking a title for this operation of the historical and analytical resystemization of Alessi's production, Mendini chose a name which was influenced by the innovative spirit of the not-so-distant exhibition curated by his friend Emilio Ambasz at MoMA. The difference was that the revolutionary idea of a 'New Domestic Landscape' was replaced with the more soothing notion of the 'homely' landscape, a term that, at the time, also evoked family traditions (or even home-style recipes) which were still very much present in 1980s Italian society.

It's interesting, then, to see Mendini's and his collaborators'[21] efforts to make Alessi's many products – created over many years with seemingly random intent – fit a coherent logic, expressed through a limited number of 'programmes', numbered from 1 to 9, each with specific genealogies, characteristics and market objectives. The numbering of these programmes referred approximately to the order in which they were produced, starting from 1 – which included products from 1921, the year the business was founded through to the 1930s – up to 9, still in progress at the time the book *Paesaggio Casalingo* was released in 1979.

In fact, *Programma 9* was made up of one model alone, the first Alessi espresso coffee machine, which was designed by Richard Sapper and which marked the beginning of a long history of espresso coffee makers that would become a hallmark of the company. Through it, Alessi was able to gain a competitive foothold in a portion of the market that had previously been left relatively untouched by competitors. This new kind of product would also lend itself to creative ventures blending art and design, with pieces such as Riccardo Dalisi's reinterpretation of a series of characters (such as Italian actor Totò, among others) as coffee makers. Another friend from the *Casabella* years, Dalisi – thanks to Mendini's invitation and Alessi's support – went on to become a moderately successful designer.

The career of Austrian-born architect Hans Hollein received a similar boost from Mendini and Alessi, who commissioned him to design the *Paesaggio Casalingo* exhibition, which was hosted by Milan's Triennale between December 1980 and March 1981. An eccentric architect and the heretical heir of Viennese Modernism, Hollein should be rightfully considered part of the Radical movement, yet he was also a refined exhibition designer, starting with the important show *MAN transFORMS: Aspects of Design* at New York's Cooper-Hewitt Museum in 1976.[22]

There, together with co-curator Lisa Taylor, Hollein had investigated the less obvious aspects of product design, and presented items including multiple shapes of bread (laid out on a large table in a room that was reminiscent of da Vinci's *Last Supper*) as well as work tools, Ettore Sottsass's conceptual photographic musings and medieval sculptures. All this was in keeping with a position that was best summarized by his slogan *Alles ist Architektur* (Everything is Architecture).

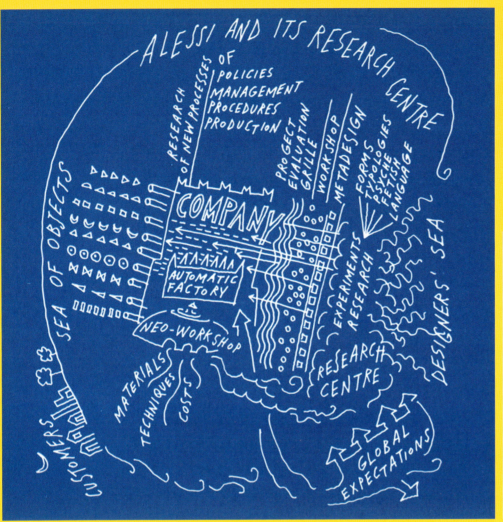

Theoretical drawing for Centro Studi Alessi, 1991

Paesaggio Casalingo for Alessi, 1980

Hans Hollein and Alberto Alessi in Alessi's Paesaggio Casalingo catalogue, 1980

Tea & Coffee Piazza for Alessi, 1983

FROM POSTMODERN TO NEOMODERN: THE ALESSI AND DOMUS YEARS

For the *Paesaggio Casalingo* exhibition at Milan's Triennale,[23] the first of a long series in which Alessi would present its projects, Hollein designed a long, tall, white arched structure, which referenced classical times and Roman aqueducts. At the base of each arch an armoured display cabinet contained historical Alessi products, arranged in order of their 'programme'. Above the cabinets, new products were brightly lit by neon tubes which seemed to transform them into artworks worthy of the museum-like setting. Meanwhile, the first arch, through which visitors would enter the exhibition and which was visible from both sides, was dramatically broken in two.

Even though it might be simplistic to define Hollein as a postmodern architect, given how multifaceted and imaginative his work was, the exhibition design of *Paesaggio Casalingo* can be considered a forerunner of that tendency, which would come to prominence in the architecture world at the Venice Biennale the following year. And yet Hollein's exhibition design maintained its relevance for a long time; it was used again by Alessi in numerous other exhibitions – including one 30 years later for *Oggetti e Progetti* (Objects and Projects), a great historical exhibition at Munich's Die Neue Sammlung museum, which Mendini curated.[24]

FROM HISTORICAL SYSTEMIZATION TO POST-MODERN EXPERIMENTATION

In 1979, during the re-ordering of Alessi's production into programmes, Mendini began the first and most important of his design collaborations with Alberto Alessi, which would go on to impact many other future projects in decades to come: *Tea & Coffee Piazza*. Under this banner, the leading figures in postmodern architecture (or what was then taking shape as such) were invited to design a tea and coffee set: Americans Michael Graves, Charles Jencks, Richard Meier, Stanley Tigerman and Robert Venturi; Austrian Hans Hollein, Spaniard Òscar Tusquets, Kazumasa Yamashita from Japan, and among the Italians, Paolo Portoghesi, Aldo Rossi and Mendini himself.

It's not surprising that, even here, one can recognize elements of the design strategy that Mendini had favoured ever since his Radical period: the creation of a group with which to have both theoretical and practical discussions (in this case, on the subject of food and its ritual objects), with an internationally diverse membership, where everyone retained their own vision despite being devoted to a common goal.

In the Modernist design climate of the time, some orthodox Modernist critics and designers saw *Tea & Coffee Piazza* as a reckless provocation. But the project had two strategic aims: one was immediate, the other would become paramount to Alessi's production. In a very timely manner, Mendini had grasped the importance of the postmodern phenomenon, which would become crucial in the development of international design culture. Through this project, he revealed to the public the movement's main protagonists, who also became fundamental in relaunching Alessi's image with architects, designers and a specialist audience.

The project's English-language title, which evoked Charles Moore's Piazza d'Italia in New Orleans (1978), reflected the project's awareness of the American scene, as did the fact that it included several American architects. These were the same figures that Mendini relied on at *Domus* to rebuild the magazine's international reputation and to answer a not-so-secret question: if the beating heart of global capitalism was still the United States, why not draw from that developing design scene – which knew everything about the mechanics of the market, of production and commercial success, and was still able to glean both culture and profit out of it?

The case of Michael Graves is exemplary here. Initially a heretic Modernist architect, Graves later took postmodernism to the level of Disney fantasy with projects like his office building for the company, which deployed Snow White's seven dwarves as column supports. Thanks to Alberto Alessi's intuition and guidance, he also became a designer of many best-selling household items (perhaps most famously a kettle with a bird-shaped whistle) which were forerunners of the 'cartoonish' design that, in the 90s, opened new mid-to-low-end markets for Alessi.

This supergroup gathered by Mendini was as cultured and detached in its expressive coolness as *Casabella* and the Global Tools project had been wild and passionate in their utopias. But the collaboration was successful, like a true research and development laboratory, in identifying among the authors of *Tea & Coffee Piazza*, the new designers who were best suited to reimagine a different 'homely landscape' for Alessi. Or, rather, a landscape of household items, conceived not just as everyday tools essential for preparing and consuming food, but also as elements of important domestic and public rituals.

In some ways, paradoxically, the project retraced the steps of the 'material culture' ideas developed by the Global Tools project, but this more commercial project was expressed in a more refined manner. The Japanese artist Kōichi 'Tiger' Tateishi, a friend and collaborator of Sottsass, produced stunning 'historical' sketches, hand-drawn and coloured for Alessi. And precious full-scale models of the *Tea & Coffee Piazza* sets were produced, an example of the way in which, in the 1980s, Italy's production of home furnishings exemplified a new industrial culture that successfully married tradition with innovation.

Always keen to highlight his individual approach, Mendini made his contribution to *Tea & Coffee Piazza* a personal manifesto of his poetics. Both the teapot and coffee pot were not only shaped like his favourite decorative motifs, but in one of the limited-edition serigraphs produced for the occasion by Alessi, they appeared adorned with the *Galla Placidia* pattern, developed by Studio Alchimia. This pattern would go on to appear in various different colourways and dimensions in future Mendini projects, from Swatch watches to Alessi corkscrews.

The collaboration with Alessi marked the beginning of a new era for Mendini's work, after he made peace – or at least a truce – with industry. After this point, he was able to put into practice his transition from anti-design to design, from design to architecture, and from decoration to painting.

51.

51. Entrance to the Space Design section in the exhibition Design Phenomene, Forum Design, Linz, Austria, 1980
52. Entrance to the Fashion Design section in the exhibition Design Phenomene, Forum Design, Linz, Austria, 1980

CHAPTER 4

52.

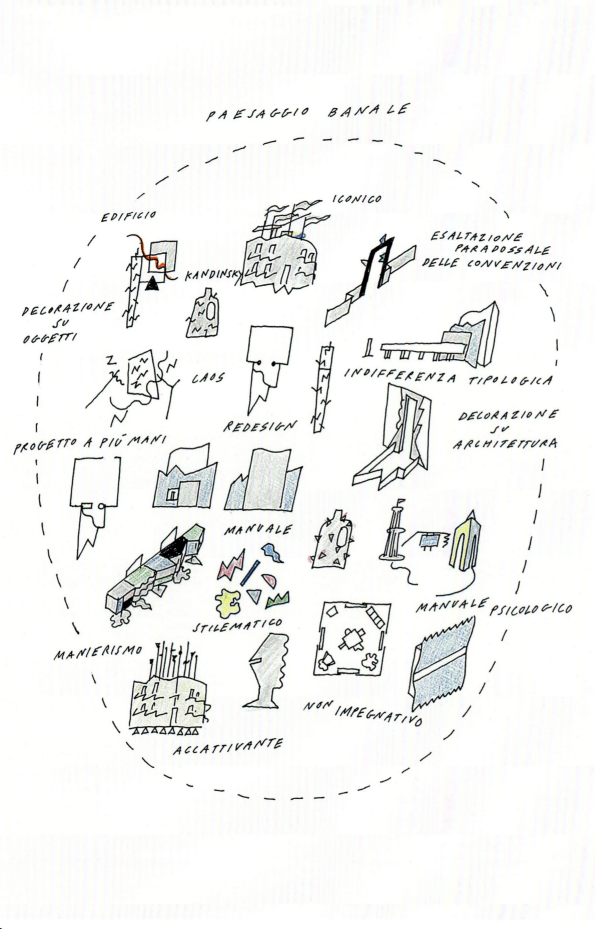

53.

53. *Paesaggio banale* (Banal landscape),
    drawing by Giorgio Gregori, Alchimia, 1980
54. *Untitled* (Psychological study for Casa di Giulietta
    exhibition in Verona), drawing, 1982

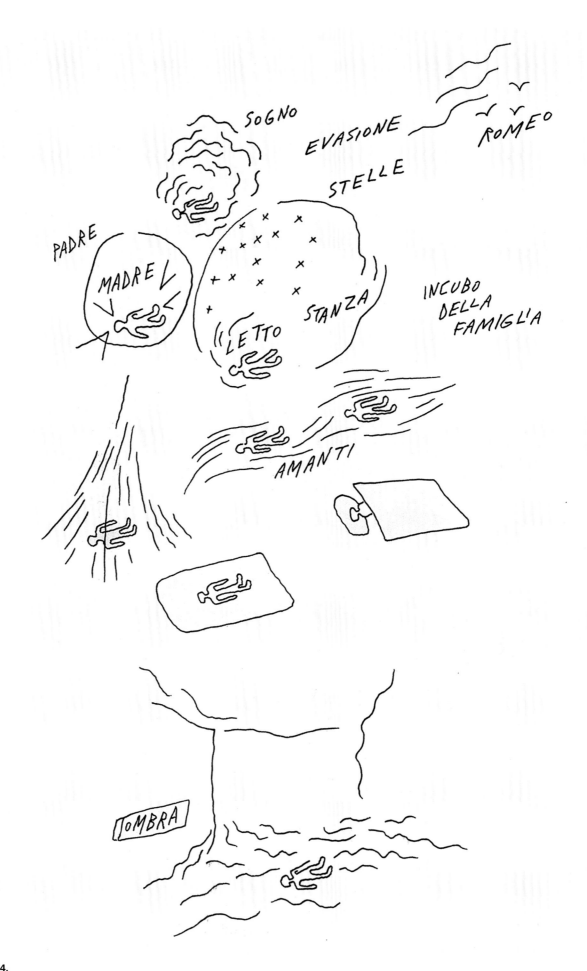

54.

55.

55. *Untitled* (first drawing for Mobile Infinito), drawing, 1980-1981
56. Redesign of objects: Lamp, for the *L'Oggetto Banale* (Banal object) exhibition, First Biennale of Architecture, Venice, 1980
57. Redesign of objects: Vaporizer, for the *L'Oggetto Banale* (Banal object) exhibition, First Biennale of Architecture, Venice 1980

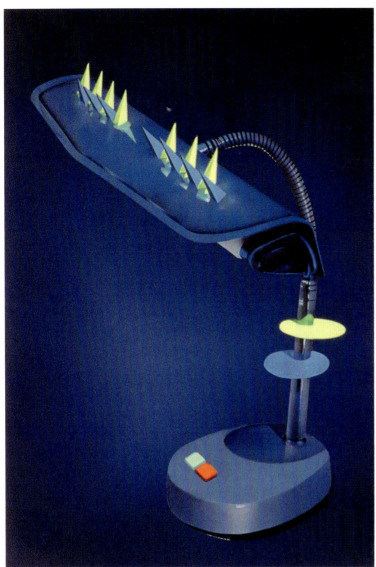
56.
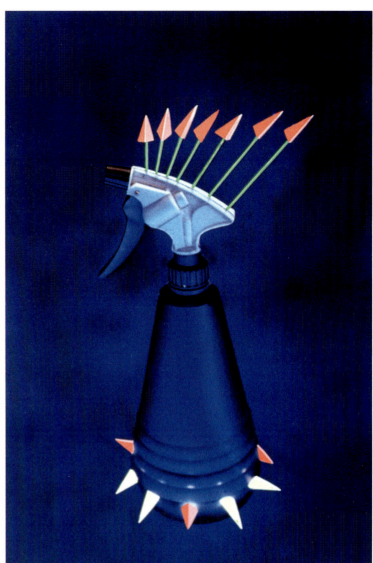
57.

FROM POSTMODERN TO NEOMODERN: THE ALESSI AND DOMUS YEARS

58.

59.

58. *Tea & Coffee Piazza*, tea and coffee set for Alessi, drawing by Maria Christina Hamel, screen print, 1983
59. *Alessi Programma 6: Tea & Coffee Piazza*, tea and coffee silver set for Alessi, 1983
60. Redesign of objects: coffee maker in painted aluminium, for the *L'Oggetto Banale* (Banal object) exhibition, First Biennale of Architecture, Venice, 1980 (limited edition 1994)

60.

FROM POSTMODERN TO NEOMODERN: THE ALESSI AND DOMUS YEARS

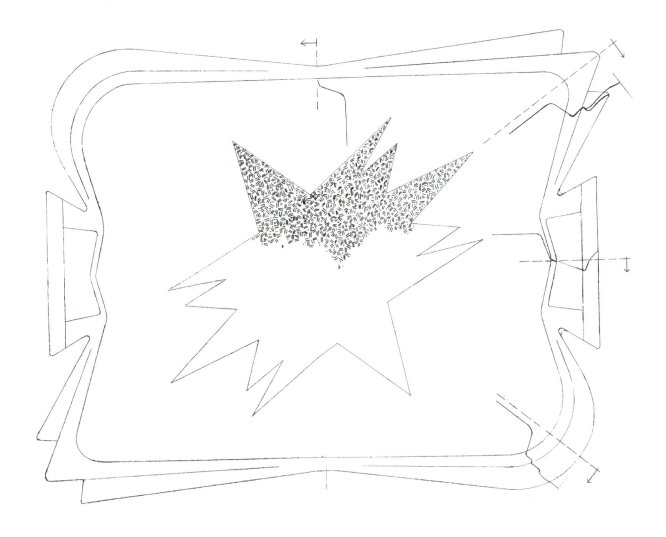

61.

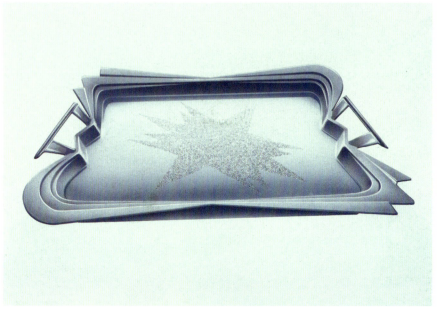

62.

61. *Alessi Programma 3,* steel tray, technical drawing, 1978
62. *Alessi Programma 3,* steel tray, illustration by Tiger Tateishi for *Paesaggio Casalingo* book, 1978
63. *Alessofono*, redesign of the Saxophone made by Alessi, black chromed brass with gilded decorations, coral and gold, project with Maria Christina Hamel, 1994
    overleaf: *Arredi Vestitivi* (Wearable Furniture), drawing, 1982

63.

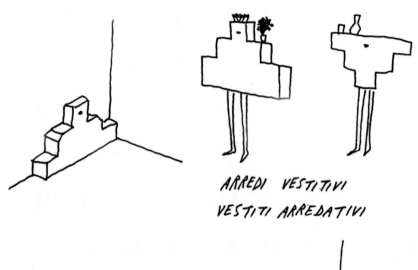

ARREDI VESTITIVI
VESTITI ARREDATIVI

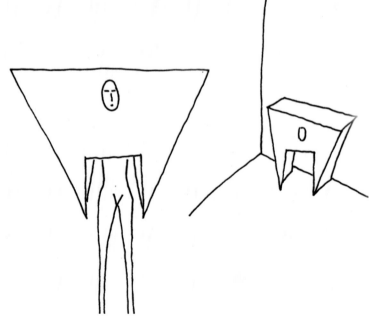

ENDLESS EPHEMERA: FURNITURE AS FASHION

THE EPHEMERAL IS ETERNAL: FASHION AS DESIGN, DESIGN AS FASHION

Fashion prescribes the ritual according to which the commodity fetish demands to be worshipped.[1]
Walter Benjamin, *Paris, Capital of the Nineteenth Century*, 1939

Fashion and design? They are an endless flux, a flowing magma that merges body, clothes, objects, surfaces, buildings.[2]
Alessandro Mendini, 1998

The 1980s were characterized by rich and novel artistic expression across creative fields from pop music to design, an improved economic climate fuelled by the increased consumption of the middle classes, and relative stability in terms of world peace. In fact, it is sometimes referred to as the second 'roaring' decade of the twentieth century – with the happy distinction that, unlike the 1920s, it wasn't followed by a global conflict. For Mendini, the 1960s and 1970s were marked by a personal and ideological crisis, as he took on Radical positions that contrasted with his initial progressive approach to design. The 1980s brought a sudden rise to success and international fame, but also an increasing awareness of the inescapable mechanisms of capitalist economics. Even within this framework, however, the critical designer found a way to carve out his own space for free and irreverent exploration.

During this time of profound, almost psychoanalytic introspection, Mendini maintained the scepticism and irony that had enlivened his drawing since his early cartoons. For example, in the initial sketches for his *Tea & Coffee Piazza* set for Alessi, Mendini's tea and coffee pots look like amusing characters scurrying across a table – in one sketch, a coffee maker even becomes an alien character from another planet. His images and installations had always had an ironic, almost comedic, component. The geometric features (small flags, lightning bolts, half-moons and triangles) and anthropomorphic features (eyes, noses, mouths and hands) that characterized his work from the early 1980s onwards appeared even more naive and almost cartoonish when used as decorative patterns and textures for textiles and clothing.

An intellectual interest in fashion was of course not new, nor Mendini's invention. Perhaps the most important forerunner to Mendini's interest in the subject was the German philosopher Georg Simmel (1858–1918), author of works such as *Lectures on Kant, The Problems of the Philosophy of History* and the 1904 essay 'Die Mode' (Fashion).[3] This brilliant analysis of clothing, which starts from psycho-sociological considerations (the need to imitate; the search for other people's approval), goes on not only to define the mechanisms of a system that remains essentially unchanged to this day, but to highlight its logical application to other fields of production. If it is clear that, as Simmel stated, 'as soon as anything that was originally done only by a few has really come to be practiced by all – as is the case with some items of clothing and certain forms of social conduct – such conduct can no longer be termed fashion', it follows that such an attitude can apply to longer-lasting products like furniture.

One of the key tenets of the Modern movement in both architecture and design was that of the 'ideal home', in which the inhabitants' fundamental needs would be solved once and for all. Unfortunately, this rather utopian notion (which Mendini had already challenged with his idea of 'anti-design') didn't take into consideration the inescapable human need for fashion. As Simmel wrote:

> *Every single fashion has the admirable ability to present itself as if it wants to live forever. Whoever buys furniture that ought to last a quarter of a century buys it according to the latest fashion, and doesn't pay the slightest notice of whatever was in fashion two years before. However, it's evident that within a couple of years, the power of fashion's attraction will abandon the current furniture, just like it abandoned its predecessors, and the acceptance or refusal of their form will be decided by objective criteria of another kind.*[4]

Mendini was particularly interested in these other 'objective criteria'. Even if consumers didn't know how to express their desires and expectations, an architect or a designer needed to be able to intuit, understand and anticipate them. This visionary ability was the lesson of great fashion designers and the secret of their global success, which Mendini adopted in his own way, adding sophisticated intellectual reflection to his powerful creative intuition. Even the idea of the first Bau-Haus collections with Studio Alchimia, and those that followed for Zanotta, Design Gallery, Zero Disegno and other clients, were steps towards his personal *rifondazione dell'universo* (refounding of the universe). In order to build this universe, Mendini grabbed any opportunity to send unsettling, disconcerting messages to culture, to the industry and to the buyers of the infinite commodities produced in a post-capitalist (or neocapitalist) society.

Mendini's almost scientific interest in fashion initially emerged through exhibitions – several of which were organised with Studio Alchimia – which centred around the body and its decoration. Most notable among these was *Arredo Vestitivo* (Wearable Furniture), a combination of furniture and clothes worn by otherwise naked models. This was presented as part of a performance, in connection with a special *Domus* publication on furniture, that took place in the shop of popular fashion designer Elio Fiorucci in Milan. That evening in February 1982, just off Corso Vittorio Emanuele II (the street on which to see and be seen), drew hundreds of passersby to witness the eccentricity of postmodern design.

Mendini kept fuelling his challenges to the Modernists, who adhered to the strict principles of functional architecture and saw such projects and his editorial direction as continuous provocations. He even recalled how during those years, some architects he knew stopped greeting him, or were uncomfortable bumping into him, due to his radical shift in cultural direction.

Yet Mendini had no intention of backing down from the positions he held at *Domus*. In this pre-digital era, the magazine had become an efficient and profitable (for the publisher at least) platform, where Mendini moved pawns, rooks and kings across several chessboards like a Grandmaster. He published, republished and commissioned both famous and unknown authors to write about the industry and the market in its broadest sense, with international authority. Emboldened by the magazine's leadership position in design communication, Mendini even dared to produce two special issues of *Domus: Moda 1* and *Moda 2* (*Fashion 1* and *Fashion 2*), which were entirely dedicated to style, fashion design and trends in clothing and dressing.

The evidence of his momentous transformation from Radical intellectual to appreciator of the ephemeral, which would go on to have powerful consequences on his work and that of his associates, was his first editor's letter for *Domus Moda 1* titled *Cosmesi Universale* (Universal Cosmetics). Cloaked in a faux-naive language, which Mendini had sharpened in his writing over his long time as a critic, journalist and editor, his ruminations on design's past, present and future had a disenchanted tone, but were at the same time romantic, pointing to new and different perspectives on work. This would have been unthinkable in the orthodoxy of rationalist, Modernist design. Over 40 years later, that editor's letter feels like a manifesto of Mendini's whole oeuvre, with visionary significance, presenting the revelation of a molten, incoherent future for design that has now become our present as designers, authors or simple individuals:

> *I'd like to share a little of what's going through my architect's mind these past months, when I set about doing my job – that is, designing things that people use, not just buildings, but also coffee-makers, furniture, hats or t-shirts [...] It still happens today, though it was more a rule of the past, that those who design think they're making something true, certain and exemplary that will last for eternity, something whose meaning is never going to change. For me, it's quite the opposite: in these times of uncertainty, a few minutes after drawing something [...] it no longer appeals to me, it's already outdated and obsolete, often I don't even enjoy seeing it made into the corresponding object. I'm more interested in the mutability than the stability of things, indeterminacy rather than certainty, the baroque sense rather than the rational one.*

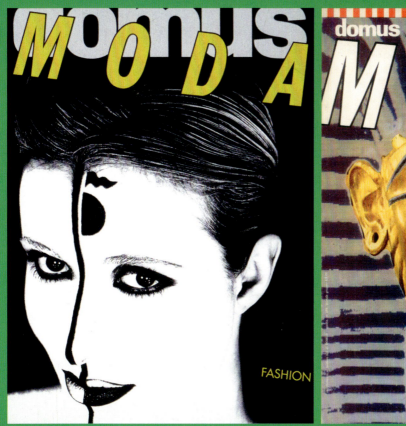
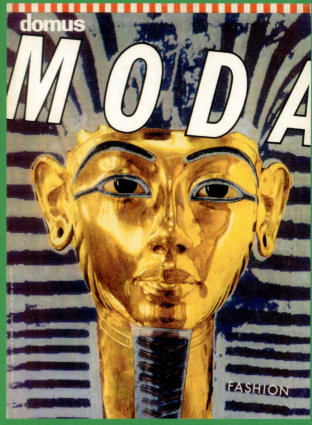

Covers of the special issues Domus Moda 1 and Domus Moda 2, a project by Alchimia and Occhiomagico, 1981

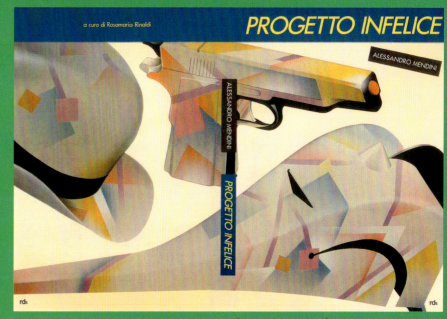

Cover of Mendini's Progetto Infelice (Unhappy Design) book, 1983

Alchimia invitation for Arredo Vestitivo performance at Fiorucci shop, Milan, 1982

ENDLESS EPHEMERA: FURNITURE AS FASHION

> *[...] Perhaps I want to give precedence to the fleeting breaths of life over the finality of death, to a design driven by love rather than function. That's why I try to think of architecture the way a fashion designer thinks about a garment, and why I consider a garment like the smallest architecture, the smallest and most virtuoso space built around a person, intimately fitted to the body: a free and infinitely changing habitat, according to the anarchic game of 'decoration'.*
>
> *[...] And I tell myself: if only architecture had its own catwalk shows, that it had a seasonal character, and it changed like the decoration on a skirt!*
>
> *Then I tell myself, decoration is a mass exhibition, because everyone knows how to decorate, and if design truly coincides with decoration, then the logical consequence is that everyone knows how to design. In fact, that's my ultimate fixation when I design: I think that everything I can create already exists, that every new design is only ever a 're-design', that all the forms of the cosmos belong to an endless flux of 'universal cosmetics', shimmering dust, particles, illusions on bodies, clothes, objects, buildings, the world.*[5]

The whole special issue followed this manifesto of irregular thought. There were classic features on transient fashion trends, some reportage on eccentric characters such as the Milanese Anna Piaggi, a fashion icon and influencer ahead of her time who dressed differently almost every day, and an interview by Barbara Radice with Issey Miyake, the fashion designer closest to design's methods and the inventor of new dressmaking techniques.

Domus Moda 1 included a peculiar reportage on a stripper's outfits, accompanied by photography by Gabriele Basilico, who wasn't yet famous for his dramatic urban landscapes. *Domus Moda 2* featured a long, curious article on bras written and illustrated by Dario Bartolini, a former Archizoom architect, who had specialized in lingerie design.[6] And then there was the most didactic piece of all: *Dal corpo alla città* (From the body to the city), a title that playfully riffed on the famous Modernist slogan, *Dal cucchiaio alla città* (From the spoon to the city), attributed to Ernesto Rogers. Rosa Maria Rinaldi wrote about the latter, a project by Mendini[7] which consisted of applying his characteristic decorative features to a naked body, a garment, an Alessi coffee maker prototype, Alchimia furniture, and a tower for Milan's Carnival, following the idea of cosmetic improvement through signs as universal decoration.

And by the end of reading – or simply browsing through the kaleidoscope of images that Mendini and his collaborators generated for *Domus Moda*, one couldn't help but wonder how much of it was irony, a mockery of the Modernist establishment still reigning in Milan, once the 'moral capital' of Italy. Or perhaps Mendini had already sensed that his city – or in fact, the entire country – was rapidly on the way to becoming the model ground for extreme consumerism, thanks to a flourishing economy, particularly in the fields of design, furniture and fashion. This was perfectly aligned with the new social and political order, in which an all-encompassing, all-determining lifestyle – from the sofa in one's living room to one's clothing and car – was understood as a series of status symbols to be displayed both publicly and privately.

UNHAPPY DESIGN, HAPPY LIFE?

In the first half of the 1980s Mendini published two books that are very helpful in understanding his work. Their titles alone are telling: *Architettura addio* (Farewell to Architecture), published by Shakespeare & Company in 1981 and, in particular, 1983's *Progetto Infelice* (Unhappy Design). The first was just text, bound by an imageless cover. The book aimed to justify his decision – which turned out to be only temporary – to abandon architecture as a profession and a means of expression. The second – issued by RDE, also the publisher of *Modo* magazine – revealed the provocative intent behind his storytelling, through text and images, as well as the improbability of his claimed renunciation of design.

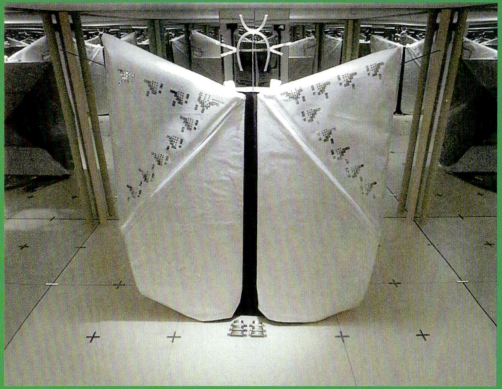

Anna Gili's Abito Monumentale for Black Out installation, Triennale di Milano, 1985

Detail of wall design by Mendini and Anna Gili for Anna Gili's Nulla, Idea per un ambiente performance with Abito Sonoro, 1984

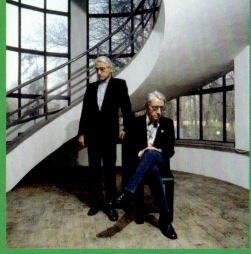

Mendini and his double, sculpture for Black Out installation, Triennale di Milano, 1985

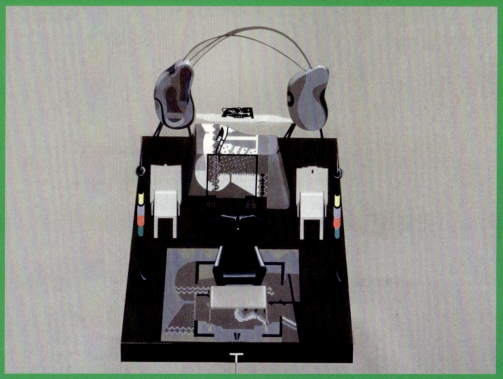

Black Out installation drawing for the Affinità Elettive exhibition, 1985

ENDLESS EPHEMERA: FURNITURE AS FASHION 117

The cover of the first edition of *Progetto Infelice* featured an illustration of a model from *Tender Architecture*, an installation made for an exhibition sponsored by Alcantara in 1983 at Milan's Padiglione d'Arte Contemporanea (PAC). The second edition featured an illustration of a pair of shoes, hat and gun, covered with Mendini-like motifs, drawn with an airbrush by Bruno Gregori for Alchimia. The text was essentially an anthology of his critical/political writing from *Casabella* onwards. But the book also contained a collection of diverse visual materials, which described his intellectual journey from Radical crisis to the rediscovery of decoration as an exit strategy from the impossible task of following Modernist principles. In other words, within the contradictory nature of existence, design couldn't help but reveal a condition of unhappiness, or at least the awareness that even design itself could never be a definitive solution. Nor could it represent the achievement of a condition of expressive satisfaction: in whatever moment, the ideal conditions that created it could reveal themselves to be wrong, false or outdated. A new objective emerged: cyclical, infinite design. Even just by acknowledging its own transience, this attempt could become a useful experience for the continuation of intellectual work.

The *Mobile Infinito* (Endless Furniture) project, which consisted not just of furniture but also a performance, was a prime example of this new approach. It was created by Mendini along with Studio Alchimia and a small army of other designers and artists in September 1981, just two days before the seismic opening of the first Memphis exhibition (which halted the traffic in the centre of Milan, as curator Rainer Krause recalls).[8] *Mobile Infinito* was staged by the theatre troupe Magazzini Criminali – provocatively right in front of the austere Politecnico di Milano building – with set design by Franco Raggi and costumes by Daniela Puppa. Among the operation's many meanings, for Alessandro Guerriero there was surely the intention of going beyond the idea of 'collections', started by Studio Alchimia and picked up by Ettore Sottsass's Memphis. But for Mendini, it meant something more.

> Rather than creating individual objects, he wanted to design one large, composite piece of furniture that could potentially extend infinitely, as it was made from isolated elements that were as disconnected from each other as possible. Though 'furniture systems' were still very popular on the market, Mendini disguised the individual elements through a variety of decorative interventions, creating an 'exquisite corpse' in the finest Surrealist tradition.

The exhibition invitation and catalogue featured black-and-white drawings and Mendini's symbolic sentences. Designed by Mauro Panzeri and published by Alchimia Editore, the catalogue credits included entries such as: 'Coordination: Paola Navone'; 'Interior decoration of furnishings: Bruno Munari, Gio Ponti & Luigi Veronesi'; 'Ornaments–caryatids: Andrea Branzi'; 'Furniture legs: Denis Santachiara'; 'Handles: Ugo La Pietra'; 'Flag: Kazuko Sato'; 'Cage: Michele De Lucchi'; 'Lamp: Piero Castiglioni', and so on, up to Achille Castiglioni's 'ready-made'; 'magnetic decorations' by Sandro Chia, Francesco Clemente, Enzo Cucchi, Nicola de Maria and Mimmo Paladino (basically, the whole Transavanguardia movement created by the critic Achille Bonito Oliva); and Ettore Sottsass's 'Lampade Ombra' (Shadow Lamps), which never made it past the design stage. It also included Mendini's dazzling aphorisms on the home, such as:

> *The house has a floor as sticky as honey*
> *Feet stick to it*
> *And you can't get out anymore*[9]

He also wrote a sceptical but poetic introduction:

> *While the design method with which 'real furniture' is constructed says: organize, differentiate, assemble, produce, doubt, check, act; the non-method of endless furniture says: Think, accept, get closer, remember, tell, believe, rest, don't live in the house, but live in its endless essence. While 'real furniture' is reasonable and complete, infinite furniture has a risky, unfinished destiny.*[10]

HAPPY LIFE?

So if the fate of a new possible design was 'risky and unfinished', always at the risk of unhappiness, wasn't it better, then, to live a happy life? By a unique turn of events, in just a few months Mendini would reach a significant moment in his life, once again tied to his work on surfaces, the body and clothing. He curated an exhibition/census of young Italian designers, titled *L'Oggetto Naturale* (The Natural Object), which took place in Prato in 1982, under the broader title *Unforeseen consequences: Art, Fashion and Design*.[11] Students from Florence's Istituto Superiore per le Industrie Artistiche (ISIA), who worked with Paolo Bettini, were among those invited to participate. Bettini was a dynamic, authoritative teacher whom Mendini greatly admired – to the point of making him the cover star for the issue of *Domus*[12] which featured the exhibition.

Among the students included in the exhibition was Anna Gili, who was about to graduate from ISIA. Mendini and Gili developed an intellectual empathy and a personal friendship, which was to last for a long time, and which spawned a number of collaborations and performances focused on clothing – or rather Gili's interpretations of clothing.

The first performance consisted of the *Abito Sonoro* (Sonorous Garment), a monumental white-and-gold dress, made of metal and fabric, brought to life by a dancer that emitted disquieting primal noises while performing an erratic choreography. The *Abito Sonoro* was first shown in 1984 at the Speciale gallery in Bari, which was founded by Mendini's friend Tarshito (the name given to architect Nicola Strippoli by his guru, Bhagwan Shree Rajneesh).

A show titled *Nulla* (Nothing) at the Alchimia Memorie e Luoghi del XX Secolo gallery in Firenze followed, and, also in 1984, one at Milan's PAC, where the performance was interpreted by dancer Maria Fernandes Iglesias. The *Abito Sonoro* also appeared in Mendini's installation *Black Out*, a collaboration with Alchimia, for the exhibition *Affinità Elettive* (Elective Affinities)[13] at Milan's Triennale in 1985, and later, in 1986, at Düsseldorf's Kunstmuseum.

In the following years, collaborations between the two designers would continue, with Anna Gili becoming a constant and supportive presence for Mendini. She also served as a source of inspiration for some of his design projects, particularly for Alessi.

64.

65.

64. *Rampichino*, Cinelli bike screen-printed for Alchimia Fast Design, 1985
65. *Vasi di Manici* (Vases with handles) for Alchimia Fast Design, 1985
66. Cover of the *Mobile Infinito* (Endless Furniture) catalogue, drawing by Mimmo Paladino, Alchimia, 1981

IL MOBILE INFINITO

66.

ENDLESS EPHEMERA: FURNITURE AS FASHION

67.

68.

69.

67. *Mobile Infinito* (Endless furniture): *comodino* (bedside table), project with Alchimia, 1981
68. *Mobile Infinito* (Endless furniture) Japan: *comodino* (bedside table), project with Alchimia and Sinya Okayama, 1985
69. *Mobile Infinito* (Endless furniture): *tavolo* (table), project with Alchimia, 1981
70. *Mobile Infinito* (Endless furniture): bookcase, back laminate panel by Gio Ponti, project with Alchimia at Milan Polytechnic, 1981

70.

ENDLESS EPHEMERA: FURNITURE AS FASHION

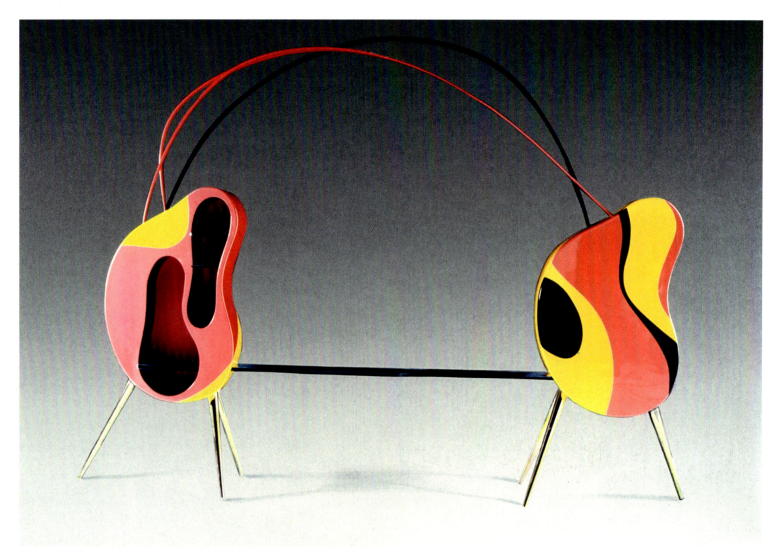

71.

71. *Black Out*, bar cabinet for the installation *Black Out*, Triennale di Milano, 1985
72. *Tender Architecture*, drawing for the Alcantara installation, Materiali Idea exhibition, PAC, Milan, 1982

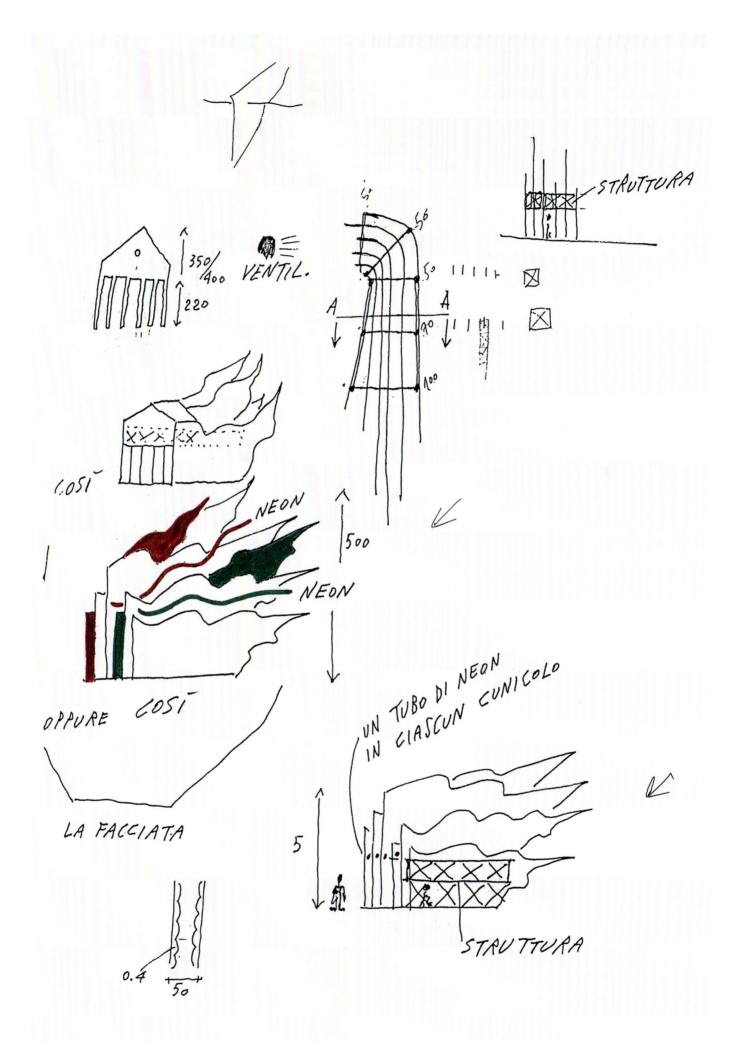

73.

73. *Nulla, Idea per un ambiente* (Nulla, Idea for an environment) performance with *Abito Sonoro* (Sonorous Garment) by Anna Gili, installation on the wall by Mendini with Gili, Florence, 1984
74. *Abito Sonoro* (Sonorous Garment) performance by Anna Gili, PAC Milano, 1984
75. *Arredo Vestivito* (Wearable Furniture) performance for Fiorucci (with Alchimia), Milan, 1982
76. *Ambienti di Transito* (Transit Environments) performance, Alchimia with Stefano Casciani and Carla Ceccariglia, Naples, 1983
   overleaf: *Zabro* chair/table, Nuova Alchimia collection for Zabro (Zanotta), drawing, 1984

74.

CHAPTER 5

126

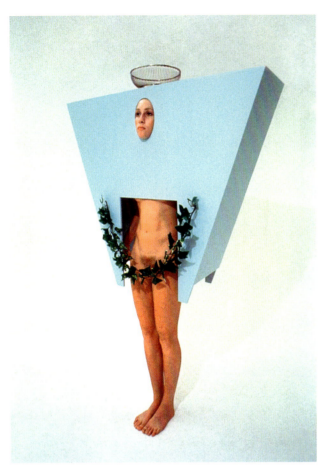

75.

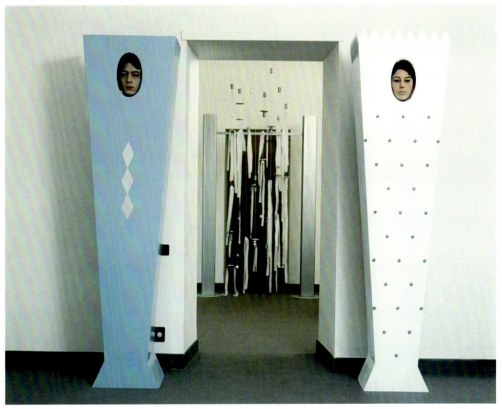

76.

ENDLESS EPHEMERA: FURNITURE AS FASHION 127

 6 COLORI + BIANCO FONDO

SMUSSO
LIMITE SERIGRAFIA

18 GIU. 1984

OBJECTS WITH ART AND SOUL: THE DESIGNER AS PAINTER

ANIMATED OBJECTS FOR POST-MODERN PEOPLE

The Parker Pen:
A pen he bought in New York drove him to write extremely salacious stories until they sent him to the asylum, where they made him responsible for the library.
   Ennio Flaiano, *Diario degli Errori. Racconti di New York*, 1965[1]

When some of Mendini's objects that had escaped destruction were put on trial, the rightful accusation against them was that they were Physical Advocates of Self-Denial [...] Though seemingly social, they were impossibly solitary; though seemingly present, they actually preached absence. Encased in everyday forms and familiar colours, they were paradoxically filled with evocative meaning, yet at the same time concealed their true intentions, masquerading as caricatures of cultural disguises.
   Emilio Ambasz, *Favole del Design: Una Raccolta di Favole per Bambini Scettici*, 1994[2]

Do objects have a soul? Despite the extensive volume of literature on design, this is a question not often posed – and even less frequently answered. It's a delicate topic, not often broached when we discuss the things we surround ourselves with – the things we somehow can't let go of, for reasons we don't fully understand. Ennio Flaiano, one of the great Italian writers of the twentieth century, who co-wrote several of Fellini's memorable films, posited that indeed objects might have a soul, albeit a rather magical and not particularly benevolent one.

Emilio Ambasz, who had remained a close friend of Mendini's ever since the exhibition *Italy: The New Domestic Landscape* at New York's MoMA, and who on numerous occasions acted as an interpreter of his work, offered a different perspective. He argued that objects, whether animated or not, are of secondary importance. What matters more is how the creator – in this case Mendini – uses those objects as a means of self-discovery, even if it involves disguising themselves or 'masquerading as caricaturse of cultural disguises,' as Ambasz wrote in the preface to the book on Atelier Mendini[3], published for the opening of the Groninger Museum in the Netherlands.

Despite his doubts about the actual usefulness of design, in the first half of the 1980s Mendini worked for a robust group of companies that were trailblazers in the design and furniture scenes. Chief among them was Alessi, where he continually strengthened his relationship of respect and intellectual exchange with Alberto Alessi. There was also Driade, which, under the leadership of Enrico Astori and Adelaide Acerbi, recruited designers with strong personalities who helped the company make its mark on the international stage. Mendini created the *Sabrina* armchair for them in 1982. A redesign of a *bergére* reminiscent of 1950s motifs, his version was upholstered in a fabric inspired by a 1927 tapestry by Bauhaus artist Gunta Stölzl and became a kind of homage to the famous Modernist design school started by Walter Gropius.

Of course, Mendini was still in touch with Cassina, with whom he had made part of his *Redesign del Movimento Moderno* series. At the Meda-based company, art director Francesco Binfaré continued to play a significant role, particularly in guiding the more avant-garde experiments often led by Gaetano Pesce. Mendini also had a relationship of mutual respect with Aurelio Zanotta, founder of the eponymous company Zanotta, which had been a regular advertiser in *Modo*. Curious, brilliant and visionary, Aurelio Zanotta was essentially also the company's art director. He was commercially savvy, but also had a strong experimental streak, and collaborated with many of the Milanese masters, from Achille Castiglioni and Marco Zanuso to Gae Aulenti and Enzo Mari, as well as other Italian talents, such as the Turinese trio of Piero Gatti, Cesare Paolini and Franco Teodoro.[4]

The consultancy work that I carried out for Zanotta between 1980 and 1985 was more focused on communication projects and exhibitions rather than the development of products. However, Aurelio Zanotta and his expert technicians worked on both prototypes and production models for some genuine inventions in 'pop' furniture, including the inflatable armchair *Blow*, and *Sacco*, a beanbag chair designed by Gatti, Paolini and Teodoro, which was dryly described in the Zanotta

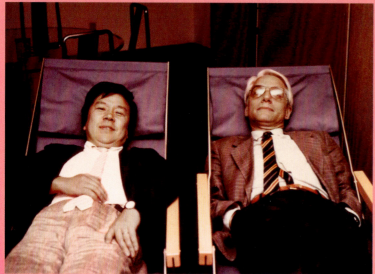
Mendini and Toshiyuki Kita, Los Angeles, 1985

Aurelio Zanotta and the Zabro chair/table, 1984

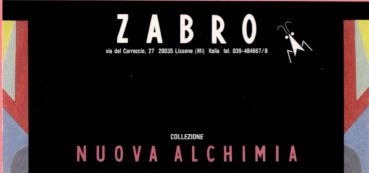
Zabro Nuova Alchimia collection catalogue, 1984

At the Temporary Contemporary conference, Los Angeles, 1985

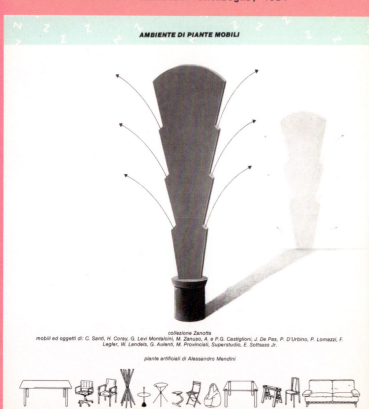
Invitation to the Ambiente di Piante Mobili exhibition, Milan, 1981

CHAPTER 6

catalogue as an 'anatomical armchair with foam polystyrene sphere padding'. *Sacco* enjoyed huge success in Italy, in part thanks to its appearance in the surreal TV sketches of comedian Paolo Villaggio.

Some of Zanotta's projects with Mendini were born in the spirit of collaboration with Studio Alchimia, including the 'Research on Environment' developed in the summer of 1981.[5] The project began with the creation of an 'environment archive' that gathered images of the work of the artistic avant-garde, and then extended into the creation of images for the company's advertising campaigns. The latter combined scenarios from the avant-garde with products such as the reissue of rationalist furniture by Giuseppe Terragni or Gabriele Mucchi. The advertising campaigns for these products were mostly published in *Domus*, in the prime back-cover position, and the research project was complemented by exhibitions of objects and furniture produced by Zanotta, which dealt with the same themes.

The first of these exhibitions, in 1981, was *Ambiente di Piante Mobili* (Furniture Plant Landscape) for which Mendini designed a series of artificial wooden plants. These were meant to recreate a natural landscape indoors, creating an unexpected juxtaposition between nature and its imitation. The 'Furniture Plants' were reminiscent of Giacomo Balla's wooden 'Futurist Flower' sculptures from the early 1920s, but they were (at least potentially) functional – one piece that looked like a large cactus, titled *Atomaria*, would become a floor lamp, produced as part of Zanotta's *Zabro* collection.

In January 1982, to coincide with the exhibition *Anni Trenta Arte e Cultura in Italia* (1930s Art and Culture in Italy) at Milan's Palazzo Reale, Zanotta presented rationalist pieces of furniture by Giuseppe Terragni, Giuseppe Pagano, Gino Levi-Montalcini and Gabriele Mucchi at Centrodomus, in a setting that ironically reinterpreted one of the metaphysical spaces from Luigi Moretti's architecture: the *Palestra del Duce al Foro Italico* (Mussolini's Gym at the Foro Italico). Mendini dedicated a *Domus* cover (designed by Occhiomagico with Alchimia) to the Zanotta exhibition. The design featured a female nude 'swimming' through an imaginary, life-size reconstruction of what an American magazine sarcastically branded 'Mussolini's bathroom'[6] – in response, we adopted the name as the title of our own exhibition.

This representation may seem innocuous today, but the relationship between rationalist architecture and Fascism – explored by Andrea Branzi's sarcastic sculptures, including the exhibition's *Mickey Dux*, a cross between Mussolini and Mickey Mouse – was a delicate subject, and the unprecedented presence of a nude on the cover of a 'serious' magazine like *Domus* still felt like a scandal at the time. At the very least, the exhibition and campaign created surprise, curiosity and interest in the rationalist furniture that Zanotta had successfully reissued.

NEW CRAFT AND MULTIPLIED ART

With the characteristic spontaneity that distinguished him from other furniture producers, Aurelio Zanotta made a proposal to Mendini: to design – or rather redesign – one of Zanotta's upholstered pieces for the high-end market. Mendini responded with a leather-upholstered version of the *Zona* sofa. With its generous proportions, the *Zona* had a simplified – almost banal – structure, but it was of the highest technical and manufacturing standards. Using a special leather in the colour range that Zanotta had commissioned by Andrea Branzi, Mendini planned a 'redesign after Léger': he picked a 1924 picture by abstract painter Fernand Léger called *Abstraction*, and used it as decoration for the material, studying the application of the pattern to the sofa's different areas and modifying its colours in accordance with the new colour range. To achieve the complex decoration for the sofa's seat and backrest, Zanotta developed a new assembly technique for joining different shapes, a process similar to quilt-making – a patchwork with invisible stitching.[7]

Interestingly there is an analogy between Mendini's redesign/ready-made operation and Léger's own 'copy and paste' method, of which *Abstraction* is an example. In his 1971 essay *Léger and L'Esprit Nouveau*, the critic Christopher Green described this method: 'The following years [of Léger's work] were dominated by the process of variation on a standardized idea.

> *Eléménts Mécaniques* (1924) was an almost exact enlargement of a 1922 painting. In order to make *Abstraction* (1926), Léger took a third painting, making some minor changes. Within the limits imposed by manual skill, this is truly painting as industrial production.'

Thus, through Mendini's interpretation, the *Zona* sofa became a non-sofa: a three-dimensional tapestry. Through a canonical process of banal redesign, it acquired symbolic value, embodying the decorative 'weak thought' highlighted by Mendini in his 1983 text *Nuovo Design* (New Design):

> *A design is a temporary event, provisional and artificial, barely linked to the static coldness of reality and of authenticity, it is linked to the vibration of what appears and what is unknown, where the fleeting breaths of life prevail over the finality of death, and loving design prevails over functional design [...] Hence the fixation [...] that today not only furniture but also decoration can prevail over design and architecture – or even technically oppose them. Decoration disappears into thin air as quickly as it appears, and in that fleeting moment when it exists, we are morbidly drawn to it, it makes even the driest structures energetic, tense and violent.*[8]

As the 1990s approached, in part thanks to his conversations with Mendini, Zanotta was the first furniture producer to sense that a new and more radical shift was taking place in the very concept of the industrial object. This shift allowed for objects to be envisioned not just as the unlimited repetition of a single form, but also as having limitless possibilities for variations in form and materials – a concept reminiscent of the diversified series approach, which would eventually expand to other sectors and brands – including Swatch, for whom Mendini would later design and coordinate a similar project.

> This perspective is reflected in the increasingly frequent experiments undertaken by Zanotta in the production of 'hybrid' typologies, such as the *Zabro* chair/table and other innovative pieces created in collaboration with Mendini. Some of these pieces even made it into production, such as the large multi-coloured table *Macaone*. In fact, the *Zabro* 'Nuova Alchimia'[9] collection, developed from 1983 to 1984 under the supervision of Alessandro Guerriero with Mendini as the sole designer (with contributions from Bruno Gregori), represented this trend perfectly. Catering to the select few, products were being transformed from functional tools into collector's items.

At first this was partly motivated by a desire to revitalise artisanal techniques – the much-discussed trend for 'new craftsmanship' – and Italy was fortunate to still have a vibrant and active production network. Enzo Mari's 1981 exhibition *Dov'è l'artigiano?* (Where is the artisan?)[10] was pivotal in understanding the unique context of Italian design and industry at the time.

> However, it became increasingly clear that the intricate surface treatment of the colourful and highly decorative *Zabro* furniture – tables, armchairs, coffee tables and consoles named after curious insects (like Andrea Branzi's *Animali Domestici*), which had a primitive, sculptural appearance crafted from untreated tree trunks – was primarily aimed at enhancing the expressive quality of the furniture. With this collection, Mendini and Aurelio Zanotta once again anticipated a growing trend that was emerging more broadly in the field of pure expression, and captured it within the furniture industry.

MANY SUCCESSES AND ONE DEFEAT: LEAVING DOMUS

By the time he was in his early 50s, Mendini was considered the guru of New Design. While Ettore Sottsass, by then almost 70, was still the undisputed leader of innovative large-scale product design, it was clear that Mendini possessed an original, forward-thinking vision that caught the interest of many brands. This perspective was often lacking in other designers – some of whom, though they were considered masters in their fields, were so focused on their commercial work that they struggled to design outside the strict confines of production and market demands – and was highly valuable to businesses. Mendini spearheaded many new collaborations: he designed furniture for Baleri Italia and Elam UNO, lamps for Eleusi, objects for the silversmith Cleto, watches and jewellery for the Swiss brand Türler, handles for German company FSB and even decorations for the bodywork of Renault cars. Mendini also got many of these companies to advertise in *Domus* – an important part of the magazine's success.

At the same time, Mendini continued his research and experimentation across different media, including making a collaborative record with the pop band Matia Bazar, titled *Architetture Sussurranti* (Whispering Architecture).[11] The project followed a design collaboration between Alchimia and the fashion designer Cinzia Ruggeri, a close friend of Alessandro Guerriero and one of the early buyers of an original *Proust* armchair. Ruggeri designed clothes for Antonella Ruggiero, the lead singer of Matia Bazar, who had an extraordinary voice and who would go on to have a long solo career.

In the spring of 1985, at the peak of this era of professional success, Mendini and a group of other designers were presented with the opportunity to go on a 'tour' of the United States, sponsored by a number of important American retailers and two Italian manufacturers, Zanotta and Oluce – the lighting company known for bestsellers by Joe Colombo and Vico Magistretti. The tour involved a series of talks in Dallas and Houston and concluded with a public conference in Los Angeles, in a building designed by Frank Gehry (who at the time was not particularly famous, but to whom Mendini had already dedicated a cover of *Domus*). The conference, which brought together the visiting Italian designers with American architects, was titled *Colonizing the American Marketplace: Contemporary Italian Industrial Design*, and it became a forum for its participants to discuss the similarities and differences between America's and Italy's design cultures.

Among others, attendees included designers Bruce Burdick, Perry King (who worked for Olivetti with Santiago Miranda) and Doug Tompkins (founder of the Esprit group); visual designer for public space Deborah Sussman; editor of *Arts+Architecture* Barbara Goldstein, Japanese designer Toshiyuki Kita; Alessandro Guerriero for Alchimia, and myself, as Zanotta's consultant and co-curator of the event.

At the conference, Mendini gave a talk titled *Ogni oggetto è diverso da ogni altro* (Every object is different from another).[12] Largely inspired by one of his articles for *Domus*, it focused on the emotional approach to design in post-industrial culture, and the relationship between design, the body and fashion. He also talked about new forms of consumption, diversified series, and everything that a designer could be, or become. This was summarised in the two sentences of the article from which the title of his talk was taken:

> *I believe that an appropriate slogan for the object of the future could be this: 'Every object is different from another', which means adapting objects to the diversity of humans. Indeed, 'every human is different from another'.*[13]

The tour was well-attended, especially in Los Angeles, in large part due to the participation of Mendini and Achille Castiglioni: design virtuosos as well as personable and charismatic speakers who had never before given talks in the US. The media coverage was very valuable in communicating the importance of design, of Italian companies, and of the magazine that, by then, Mendini personified, just as Gio Ponti had done from its founding until his death.

It's therefore hard to understand why, in 1985, shortly after returning to Italy, a troublesome period began for Mendini at *Domus*. Misunderstandings, differences in opinion on editorial lines and perhaps pressure from the advertising team led to the end of what had been the magazine's most successful period of international revival, an accomplishment unmatched by subsequent editors (though this was arguably also due to changing cultural and economic conditions).

Mendini's departure was melancholic for many reasons. It signalled the end of an era of integration between communication and design, the interruption of many plans he still wanted to carry out and the end of a relationship with an editorial team that was very close to him – not least his faithful friend Pierre Restany. Even more painful was the fact that he was not allowed to say goodbye to the readers of *Domus*, as is the established journalistic tradition whenever there is a change in editorship, where Mendini would have likely employed his usual fair play.

However, for his dedicated and loyal readers – and there were many of them at the time – it was perhaps even better to read the honest words that he was able to express in *L'architettura. Cronache e Storia* magazine. Thanks to the generosity of its editor Bruno Zevi, who agreed to host his ideological 'enemy', Mendini was paradoxically given the chance to say farewell to his readers in the pages of his magazine's biggest competitor.

Dear reader of Domus,

You may have noticed that the September 1985 issue does not include the piece in which I, for the past five years, have addressed you with a short 'communication' on the opening page of the magazine.

In fact, as of that issue I am no longer the editor of Domus. A disagreement with the publisher, stemming from political reasons and editorial policies, led me to resign suddenly, and the separation was so abrupt that I was denied the opportunity to publish a 'Farewell to readers' in Domus. Therefore, I am writing my farewell and my thanks to you and the editorial team from the pages of L'architettura magazine, led by Bruno Zevi, who with his great generosity has already taken a stance on this dispute and now is hosting this 'Farewell' despite the ideological distance between us. But I don't want to bore you with these matters; instead I wish to express the deeper reasons that led me to step away from the magazine.

[…] I left Domus at its 'maximum possible' revenue. Beyond this point, the Domus formula can no longer guarantee independent information for the reader. This is the problem: if the premise for an architecture and design magazine is to express a 'cultural project', one must define in advance a cap for the business and remain within it. In the delicate balance between editorial project and cultural project, one must not succumb to the idea of transforming the magazine into a major business. Only this limitation can ensure autonomy, because otherwise one becomes uncritical and acquiescent to industry (especially the furniture industry) and directly links editorial content with advertising revenue. In other words: bid farewell to the development of a questioning line, an approach based on research and our true responsibilities, and instead give free rein to the demands of a debased consumerism, which since the 1960s has been marking a negative point in the not-always heroic history of Milanese design.

[…] This is one reason for my crisis: seeing many of the ideas that I have so 'thoughtfully' put forward over these years triumph under the guise of 'mere' mannerism […] As for myself, as a 'human being', I'm not interested in design: I use design not because I want to design, but because I want to communicate, because my issue is 'communicating'. My life in itself has no planned intentions, it doesn't want to realize objectives or projects: it is an accumulation of experiences, more or less normal or exceptional or alienated or secret events, all attempts at communicating, which is my personal vocation.

[…] Therefore, in analyzing myself, I find myself indifferent to techniques: I don't have the fortune of having one technique prevail over another. Thus, drawing, words, objects, a magazine (Casabella), another (Modo), yet another magazine (Domus), exhibitions, lectures, poetry, installations, are all possible and provisional materials through which I can develop this obsessive idea of 'expressing myself'. But what to communicate?

[…] At the height of energy and social power, it is legitimate to feel the need to go through a crisis. […] So: what are we, what should we be instead, where does our (my) 'search for the self' hide? It is necessary to find a 'truer and more precise' reality, to transform and radically transfer our point of observation, to withdraw from our usual environment, to regress and embark on a complex integration into a different atmosphere, to risk the unknown of no longer knowing how to produce, to leave our dear things behind, what we have already built and capitalized on: loved ones, places, methods, work, moral structures, our (my) image itself. We need to show up armed only with what can be held in the space of the mind and in the dimension of the body: among many other things, it's also good to leave Domus![14]

Domus issue 627 featuring Mussolini's Bathroom exhibition by Andrea Branzi and Alchimia, 1982

Andrea Branzi, invitation card for Mussolini's Bathroom exhibition at Centrodomus, Milan, 1982

Mussolini's Bathroom exhibition at Centrodomus, Milan, 1982

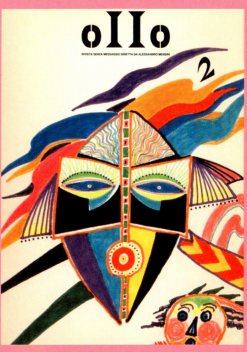

Ollo magazine issue 2, 1990

OBJECTS WITH ART AND SOUL: THE DESIGNER AS PAINTER

Twenty-five years would pass before the publisher, at a critical time for *Domus*,[15] called Mendini back to produce eleven 'collectable' issues (as the editorial promotion described them). This new *Domus* project was something that he and I would embracd with enthusiasm, but also with an awareness of the profound changes that had taken place in culture and society over the course of a quarter of a century.

DESIGNED PAINTING AND PAINTERLY DESIGN

In the 1980s, the trend for materializing the expressive content of artistic research into objects, environments and installations came back to the fore. From Arte Povera, which after a period of crisis had experienced a significant re-evaluation of its key figures' work, to certain strands of neo-expressionism, artists rediscovered the value of space as a place for experimenting with new perceptions. Even the renewed appreciation of sculpture, a form of expression that for many years had been confined to a narrow circle of enthusiasts, was significant in terms of a revived interest in the tangible presence of art in the environment. In the 1980s, the work of artists such as Piero Gilardi, Jannis Kounellis and Merz was considered at its highest level; even members of the Transavanguardia movement such as Enzo Cucchi and Mimmo Paladino, having established their own expressive dimensions, translated a certain spatial quality that was already present in their paintings into sculptures and environments.

> There was a peculiar but predictable symmetry between art that was moving closer to design, or rather to the concrete form of objects, and the strong interest of the design avant-garde in artistic expression. This was evident from the fact that Cucchi, Paladino and Sandro Chia – all artists who had already contributed to the great 'collage' of *Mobile Infinito* – would, by the end of the 1980s contribute projects to the *Mobili d'Artista* (Artist Furniture) collection that Zanotta asked me to curate in 1989.

Even the paintings that Mendini started painting in 1985 (or rather, had executed according to his designs) reflect aspects of a broader phenomenon: the renewed convergence between art and design. Some of the formal motifs in these paintings had already appeared in the decoration of his early furniture for Zanotta. This convergence highlights the alignment of two traditionally distinct fields: one focused on the production of unique works of art, and the other, at the opposite extreme, on mass production. Yet both share a common vocation: to express 'metaphors of the present' when cultural and productive conditions allow.

> Mendini began to theorize about this intersection between art and design in the months leading up to his resignation from *Domus*. In a chance encounter in September 1985, after he had left the magazine and I had left Zanotta, he made an ironic comment about the fact that we were both changing careers. Beyond speaking about the specifics of our professional circumstances, his remark could also be taken to refer to the greater freedom of expression that we were both looking for. He was finding this through his work in painting, which he combined with his work in consultancy, design and soon also architecture, something he returned to in partnership with his brother Francesco.

Just one year later, his first solo show, *Dipinti* (Paintings), was held at the Zeus space. These works, created using various techniques including tempera on paper, enamel on canvas or wood and oil on canvas, were all titled *Senza Titolo* (Untitled), perhaps as a form of modesty – the shyness of an artist who was just starting out – or maybe to give the viewers a chance to interpret the abstract forms and compositions. The paintings incorporated decorative elements previously used in his furniture and objects, while introducing new ones – some geometric, others inspired by nature, like large multi-coloured leaves.

> Mendini had mentioned these ideas to me before presenting them, explaining that he was developing the concept of designed painting, or painterly design. Curiously, this coincided with the period around 1985 when I was beginning to work along similar lines with the Società Artisti e Designer (SAD) in Zurich. We found ourselves on common ground, with shared interests that led to Mendini writing a presentation text for SAD's major exhibition at Zurich's Galleria Margine in 1987.[16] And when publisher Giancarlo Politi was preparing the first monograph dedicated

entirely to him, *Alessandro Mendini*, published in 1989, he asked me to write a piece that connected the different forms of expression in his work; it was titled *Canzoni per la fine del secolo: Alessandro Mendini dal design alla pittura* (Songs for the end of the century: Alessandro Mendini from design to painting).[17]

On the book's cover, there was an image of his 1987 solo show at Kaess-Weiss gallery in Stuttgart: two paintings, one of which featured the motifs of the *Kandissone* tapestry from 1979, hung on the walls of the display space, which were also painted in the same colours as the artworks. This created the effect of a unified environment where the three-dimensional space and the two-dimensional paintings became indistinguishable. The foundational text for this almost natural leap from simple decoration to painting is Mendini's 1986 essay *Pittura Progettata, Design pittorico* (Designed Painting, Painterly Design). In it, Mendini asserts the freedom he finds in the act of painting, which is not bound by functional necessities or programmatic goals.

Yet his was a calculated form of painting, executed with a precision that imparts a certain coldness, precisely because the artist does not seek to evoke particular emotions but simply to express his state of mind. Conversely, it is *design pittorico* that can fulfil this emotional function, as furniture and objects remain, in some way, extensions of the person, the individual, their memories, and cultural imprint—imbued with a warmth that painting has lost over the centuries, having become a medium so ancient and consecrated by conventions and traditions. Mendini's approach to painting was cerebral and philosophical:

Just like I'm looking for a PITTURA PROGETTATA [designed painting], I can also find a DESIGN PITTORICO [painterly design]; the former is cold, rarefied and cerebral (as it is anti-painting), the latter is warm (as it is anti-design). My painting is cold, my design is warm: they correspond to a poetic vision of the world that is detached and 'half-fantastic', suited to the NUOVO UOMO DECORATIVO [new decorative man] – that man who today, at the end of ideologies, has 'conquered', reached a 'superficiality' of an 'aesthetic', 'neo-abstract' kind.

[…] My inter-disciplinary painterly game is constrained by the rigour of its rules. The dispute is only 'pictorial'. Linguistic games intertwine, combine and repeat infinitely in the abstraction of lines and drawn surfaces, in a system that's valid only within itself. The indefinite wanderings of the mind give rise to the development of a representative mechanism (treatise-like), in man's eternal attitude (which I make mine) to incessantly 're-design' the world's image matrix.

My painting is like a circle: everything that happens within it has perhaps already happened, in different forms, in other cultures and places. Given the inadequacy of 'real' design to confront the world, it is replaced by my 'personal vision': a continuous work, without end and without justification, an endless formalistic network of stylistic devices and visual references – the only type of 'quality' I know how to offer.[18]

In 1987, Vittorio Fagone, an art critic and co-curator of the important international exhibition *Documenta 8* in Kassel, invited Mendini to show some of his recent work. He chose to present both some paintings and the model of a 'Universal Museum' he designed with Alchimia. Based on a panopticon structure, it was decorated on its surface with decorative architectural motifs – arches and columns – inspired by the *Ollo* series[19] (a magazine and furniture collection), which could also be found in the paintings he showed.

This marked the beginning of a new phase in Mendini's work, where architecture, design and painting merged into a seamless continuum, reflecting a newly 'liberated' vision of the project. This approach ultimately led him to create his masterpiece, the Groninger Museum in the Netherlands.

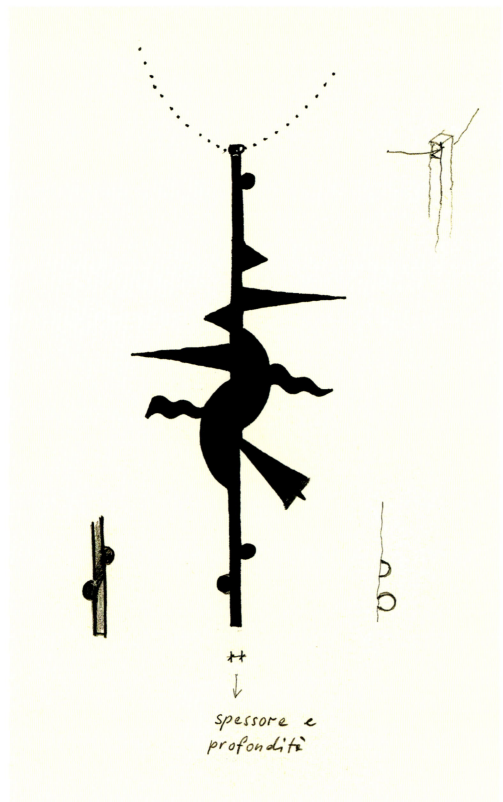

77.

77. *Gioiello d'oro* (Gold jewel) pendant for Cleto Munari, drawing, 1983
78. *Gioiello* (Jewel) pendant for Cleto Munari, 1983
79. *Untitled*, nitro painting on wood, 1986

78.

CHAPTER 6

79.

80.

80. *Untitled*, nitro painting on wood, 1986
81. *Untitled*, nitro painting on wood, 1986
82. *Untitled*, nitro painting on canvas, 1986

81.

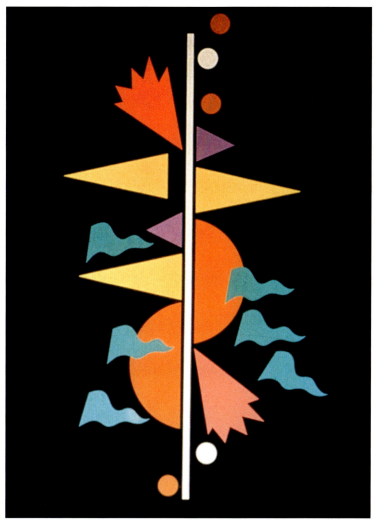
82.

OBJECTS WITH ART AND SOUL: THE DESIGNER AS PAINTER 143

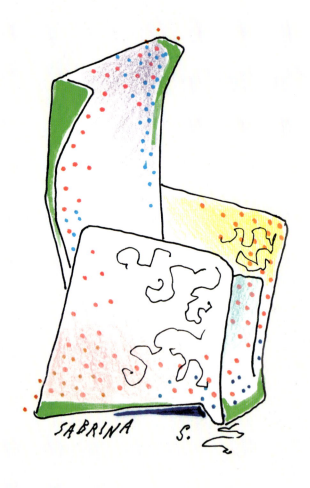

83.

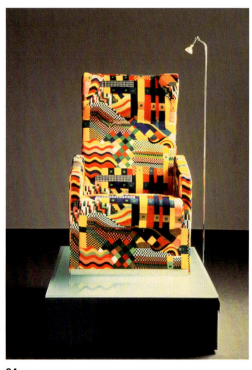

83. *Sabrina* armchair for Driade, drawing, 1982
84. *Sabrina* armchair covered in Bauhaus fabric for Driade, 1983
85. *Omaggio a Gropius* (Homage to Gropius) steel handles for FSB Brakel, 1986

84.

CHAPTER 6   144

85.

OBJECTS WITH ART AND SOUL: THE DESIGNER AS PAINTER

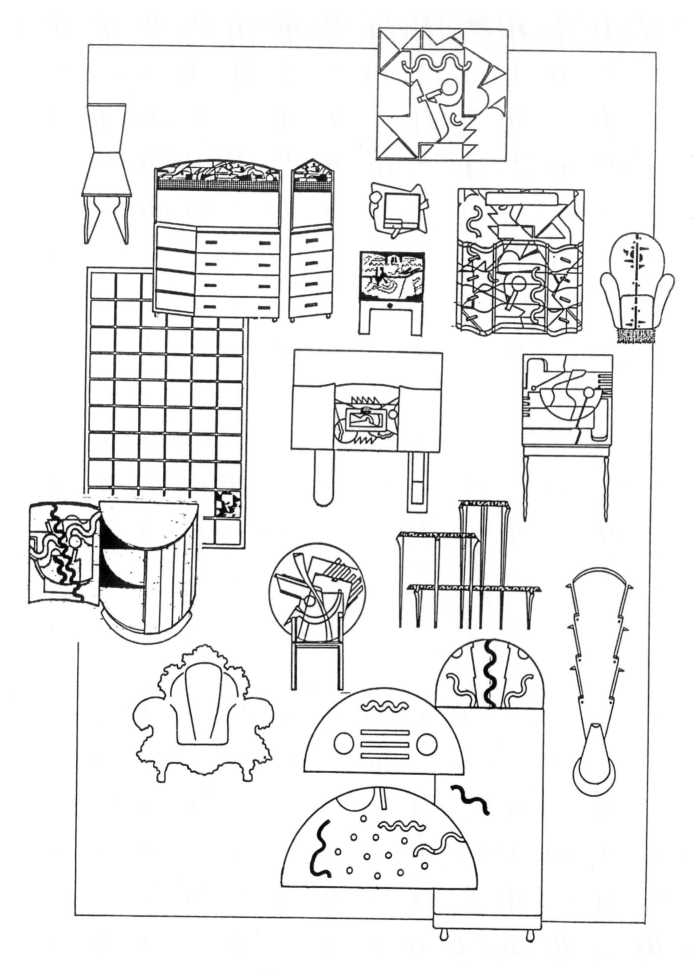

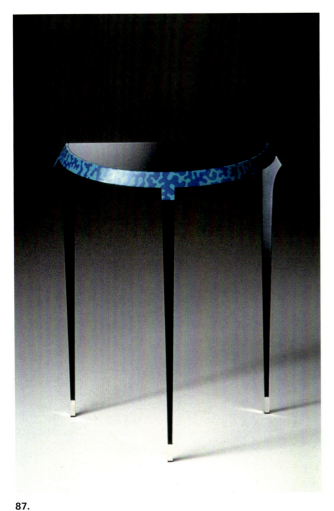

87.

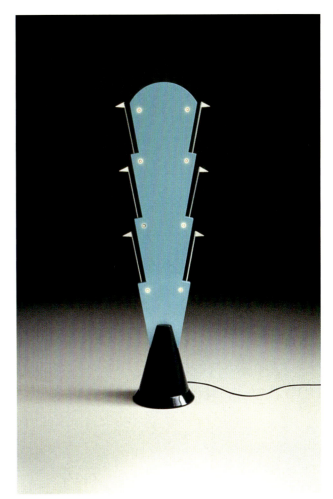

88.

86. *Nuova Alchimia* collection for Zabro (Zanotta), poster, 1984
87. *Agrilo* console, *Nuova Alchimia* collection for Zabro (Zanotta) with Alchimia, Bruno Gregory and Giorgio Gregori, 1984
88. *Atomaria* floor lamp, *Nuova Alchimia* collection for Zabro (Zanotta) with Alchimia, Bruno Gregory and Giorgio Gregori, 1984
89. *Zabro* chair/table, Nuova Alchimia collection for Zabro (Zanotta) with Alchimia, Bruno Gregory and Giorgio Gregori, 1984

89.

OBJECTS WITH ART AND SOUL: THE DESIGNER AS PAINTER

90.

91.

92.

90. *Cipriani* bar/cabinet for Memphis, 1981
91. Gold and hematite watch and jewellery for Türler, 1988
92. Gold and hematite watches for Türler, drawing, 1988

OBJECTS WITH ART AND SOUL: THE DESIGNER AS PAINTER

93.

94.

93. *Stelline* chair for Elam Uno, drawing, 1987
94. *Stelline* series, chair with armrests for Elam Uno, 1987

OBJECTS WITH ART AND SOUL: THE DESIGNER AS PAINTER

95.

96.

95. *Stella*, drawing, 1990
96. *Gallinella*, drawing, 1990
97. *Gallinella*, sculpture, Spiritelli Alchimia collection, 1990

CHAPTER 6

97.

OBJECTS WITH ART AND SOUL: THE DESIGNER AS PAINTER

98.

98. Decoration for the Renault *Super 5* car, 1985
99. *Design Pittorico* (Pictorial Design) drawing for the Zabro (Zanotta) sideboard with Alchimia, 1986
100. *Lampada di Milo* floor lamp, Segno, 1988, reissued by Codice Icona, 2022
    overleaf: Groninger Museum, study for the pavilions of Ancient, Contemporary, Decorative and Regional Art, drawing, 1990

99.

100.

OBJECTS WITH ART AND SOUL: THE DESIGNER AS PAINTER

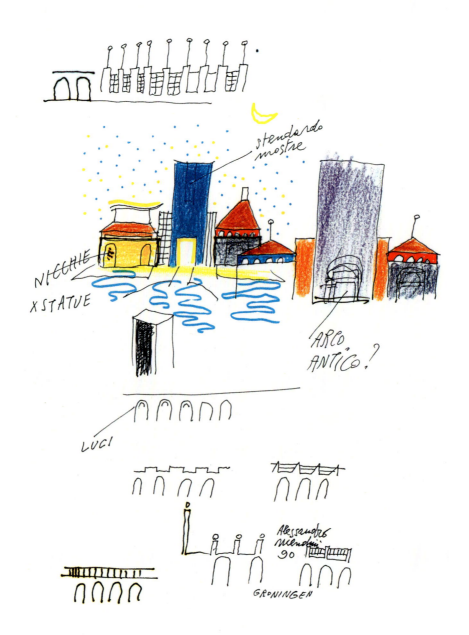

LEARNING A NEW UTOPIA: FROM LAS VEGAS TO GRONINGEN

LEARNING FROM LAS VEGAS: THE AGE OF GLOBALIZATION

Imagine a positive and critical use of these terms: hybrid, contorted, ambiguous, compromised, corrupt, conventional, accommodating, redundant, incoherent, equivocal. Embrace these 'genres' as deep, conscious materials for design. And if it's true that 'there's nothing to learn from Las Vegas,' we certainly have much to learn from Learning from Las Vegas *and its authors.*
Alessandro Mendini and Stefano Casciani, 1985[1]

In the long life of Alessandro Mendini, 1985 stands out as a pivotal year, professionally and artistically, as well as culturally and existentially. Hailed alongside Paolo Portoghesi as one of the fathers of postmodernism, he received many collaboration requests from companies and institutions. This included Aldo Rossi's *Progetto Venezia* (Venice Project) edition of the Venice Biennale, for which architects were asked to redesign parts of the city. Mendini's distinctive, organic and sculptural proposal for a new Accademia Bridge, designed with Studio Alchimia, was conspicuously unrealistic: an ironic nod to the impossibility of continuing to practice architecture in the traditional sense.

In February of that year, among the many requests he received, was another proposal from Venice, this time from CLUVA – a publishing house founded by students at the Università Iuav di Venezia (IUAV) – to write the introduction to the Italian edition of Robert Venturi's book (co-authored with Denise Scott Brown and Steven Izenour), *Learning from Las Vegas*.[2] This work is certainly the most provocative among the American architect's writings and also in the realm of contemporary architectural criticism and theory more generally. Along with Venturi's sophisticated *Complexity and Contradiction in Architecture*[3], it developed a refined analysis of architecture across eras to draw out the 'complexities and contradictions' that Venturi used to define his absurdist method: acknowledging the inconsistencies in the work of architects, in the market and within the architectural landscape, and integrating them into the project rather than pretending they don't exist.

Venturi was among the architects that Mendini had invited to participate in Alessi's *Tea & Coffee Piazza* programme, and it was probably Venturi who suggested to the Italian publisher that Mendini should write the introduction. Having accepted the assignment, perhaps to also get the opinion of a younger designer and to reaffirm the relevance of a text that was already a number of years old, Mendini proposed that I co-write the text with him. At the time, I was no longer part of *Domus*'s editorial team, but our collaborations extended to the activities of Studio Alchimia, Zanotta and others.

In any case, it was the perfect opportunity to grapple with the document that lies at the origins of a new clarity in observing and designing contemporary architecture. Venturi's point of view – realistic about the challenges and contradictions, but also hopeful – had been set out both in his controversial publications and in his buildings, such as the iconic house he designed for his mother in Chestnut Hill, Philadelphia, in 1962. It was also a chance for us to preview the translation of a text that for a long time had been touted as negative and destructive for design – especially due to the famous sentence 'Main Street is almost all right,' which had infuriated many urbanists and city planners, particularly in Italy.[4] They were outraged at the idea itself that one could consider the American strip 'almost perfect', despite it being the result of an uncontrolled accumulation rather than judicious planning, following precise and detailed urban schemes.

However for Mendini, who always remained an architect, both in his way of thinking and in his utopian aspirations, and for me, a writer on architecture and design, it was natural to embrace the lesson of Venturi and his colleagues from *Learning from Las Vegas*. Based on a scientific analysis of the landscape of this sprawling urban agglomeration in the Nevada desert full of the worst aberrations of taste, the tone of the book seemed almost ironic (or even sarcastic). However, in Venturi, Scott Brown and Izenour's refined intellectual analysis, Las Vegas was also full of pointers – new 'rules' towards a design that was sensitive to social reality. All of the above was meant to achieve, as Mendini and I put it:

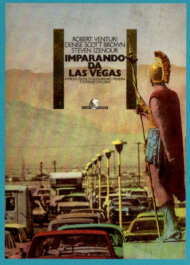

Italian edition of Learning from Las Vegas, 1985

L-R: Alberto Alessi, Achille Castiglioni, Enzo Mari, Aldo Rossi and Mendini in the Alessi factory, Crusinallo, 1989

Mendini and Robert Venturi working on Tea & Coffee Piazza project, 1983

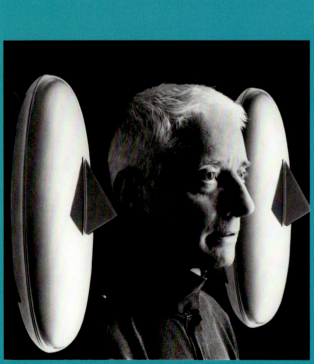

Mendini and the Peyrano box for Alessi, 1990

CHAPTER 7

[...] A 'gentle' architecture: that is, an architecture that is not patronising, that is able to adopt the practice of 'both/and...' rather than 'either/or...'; precise and even serious, but not for this reason forfeiting its ability to be self-ironic, or to incorporate the banality of current signs, so long as they are revisited and reinterpreted in a critical, different manner.[5]

For Venturi, 'elements of architecture have symbolic meaning and convey messages about the environment, making it comprehensible and therefore usable by people in their everyday lives'. In the 1976 exhibition *Signs of Life: Symbols in the American City*,[6] Venturi, Scott Brown and Associates expressed their interest in both the commercial strip and suburban sprawl: places where architectural symbolism has continued and intensified its tradition, contrary to the areas 'controlled by architects, where that tradition has been dispersed or destroyed by the Modernists' attempts to eradicate decoration and historical-symbolic associations from architecture.'[7]

Venturi almost seems to evoke the figure of the classical architect, in his stubborn hypothesis of restoring the integrity of the architectural message. Undoubtedly, his 'Roman years' of 1954–56, when he won the Rome Prize and studied at the American Academy (where most of the figurative world of *Complexity and Contradiction in Architecture* was born), left a methodological and mannerist mark on him, rooted in the Renaissance and Baroque Roman traditions. At times he appeared, as Vincent Scully put it, 'an Italian architect who was part of the great tradition' – but one who sensed the oppressive climate of Italian modernism in the 1950s and returned to the suburbia of the United States to practice his unorthodox anti-modernism in a 'pop' setting.

In Las Vegas, Venturi, along with his partner Denise Scott Brown and their graduate assistant Steven Izenour, surveyed the bad taste prevalent in buildings and neon signs, which were flashy but indispensable in a city that primarily consisted of casinos and other entertainment venues. This was vividly captured in a description by Morris Lapidus, another architect whom Mendini had always viewed with great interest, even dedicating a *Domus* cover to him. The uncontrolled orgy of styles in Las Vegas, as described by Lapidus, included: 'Miami Moroccan, International Jet Set Style, Hollywood Orgasmic Modern Art, Organic Retro, Bernini à la Yamasaki cum Roman Orgiastic, Moorish à la Niemeyer, Moorish Tudor [...] and Hawaiian Bauhaus.'[8]

Yet even within this stylistic chaos and authentic kitsch – so well depicted in its nocturnal, spectacular essence by director Martin Scorsese in the opening scenes of his film *Casino* – the authors of *Learning from Las Vegas* discovered an unusual form of classification, which they would then transform into a working method, however eccentric and intellectual. They described it as follows:

We shall emphasize image – image over process or form – in asserting that architecture depends in its perception and creation on past experience and emotional association and that these symbolic and representational elements may often be contradictory to the form, structure and program with which they combine in the same building. We shall survey this contradiction in its two main manifestations:

1. Where the architectural systems of space, structure, and program are submerged and distorted by an overall symbolic form. This kind of building-becoming-sculpture we call the 'duck' in honour of the duck-shaped drive-in, 'The Long Island Duckling'.[9]

2. Where systems of space and structure are directly at the service of program, and ornamentation is applied independently of them. This we call the 'decorated shed'.

Much like the rest of the book, the authors' conclusion is both surprising and contradictory:

We maintain that both kinds of architecture are valid – Chartres is a 'duck' (although it is a 'decorated shed' as well), and the Palazzo Farnese is a 'decorated shed' – but we think that the 'duck' is seldom relevant today, although it pervades Modern architecture.[10]

So what, then, is the solution to this dilemma (which remains as relevant today as in the 1980s), assuming there is one? Between the 'duck' and the 'decorated shed', which is the most appropriate symbol to express contemporaneity? There is no doubt that the 'ducks' are winning the battle. This book is not the place for a discussion on twenty-first-century architecture, but it is undeniable that so-called 'starchitects'[11] (or those aspiring to the status) have heavily emphasized the formalistic and expressionistic aspects of construction. And even if Mendini agreed in principle with Venturi's rejection of 'ducks' in favour of 'decorated sheds' (which were closer to Mendini's own sensibility and poetics), he would dedicate the last decades of his work with his brother Francesco to working on 'ducks', aspiring – and eventually succeeding – to create an architectural language that was universally understandable in a global cultural and market context.

At the end of the 1980s, Mendini's design choices took a separate, third route. Without rejecting the symbolism of architectural forms, he opted for a method that favoured teamwork, and for two techniques borrowed from the historical avant-garde: the collage and the 'exquisite corpse'. This approach first manifested in his significant *Casa della Felicità* (Happiness House) project for Alberto Alessi in Italy and then evolved and developed naturally into his masterpiece, the Groninger Museum in the Netherlands. Even there, he nodded strongly to the idea of the 'decorated shed', in details such as in the pedestal at the end of the section of the museum designed by Coop Himmleb(l)au – a large surface entirely clad in Abet *Proust* laminate, a feature he employed in many of his later projects and buildings in South Korea.

Despite his rebellious iconography, Mendini emerged as one of the best interpreters of Venturi's thinking, especially in terms of its democratic and liberal ambitions, which the American critic Aaron Betsky described as part of a long wave of social realism that has continued and, paradoxically, is perhaps better appreciated in the present day then when it was written:

The political dimensions of what Venturi maintained for so many years have remained obscured because his work became strangely associated with conservative tendencies in culture [...] But they do ring true to us today. Venturi was arguing for an architecture that drew on the history of architecture around the globe, despite his focus on the West, and wanted to make an architecture that would be open and responsive to the diversity of culture.[12]

ARCHITECTURE BETWEEN AVANT-GARDE COLLECTIVES AND KITSCH

On a spring day in 1987, I met with Alessandro Guerriero in an office on Via Fratelli Gabba in Milan – the location of *Domus*'s pre-war newsroom. Alchimia was temporarily based there, and Mendini used the space to work on his designs while he waited to open a new studio with his brother Francesco for their return to architecture projects. Sometimes it was possible to also find Pierre Restany there; he occasionally used the space as a studio when he visited Milan for the magazine and his art projects. It was a creative hub, revolving around Mendini and his friends.

On that occasion Guerriero asked me to prepare a presentation on Mendini's work for Frans Haks, the director of an unspecified Dutch museum. A few weeks later, Haks came to the studio for the presentation (which was put together with 35mm slides) and he proved as keen and enthusiastic about Mendini's work as he was unaware of it. In particular, he wanted to learn more about his architectural ideas and projects, such as the *Casa della Felicità* for Alberto Alessi and family, which was under construction at the time.

Seduced by the mysterious charm of Mendini's drawings and images, a rarity in Italian architectural production in the late 1980s, Haks (who would go on to become one of the greatest connoisseurs and enthusiasts of Mendini's work) wanted

Mendini to design the new building for Groningen's Groninger Museum in the Netherlands. Groningen is a small city with an important history and a remarkable cultural tradition, largely thanks to its university. And the museum's collections were eclectic: it held many Chinese and Oriental porcelain objects, local traditional silverware and a collection of exotic curiosities gathered by Jan Albert Sichterman, a wealthy seventeenth-century official of the Dutch East India Company. Sichterman became known as the 'King of Groningen' after he brought his collections back from Bengal, along with Clara, his pet rhinoceros.

The Netherlands' architecture and design scenes were still fairly provincial despite a strong Modernist design tradition that included the artist and architect Gerrit Rietveld, a great master and innovator. (This would, of course, change in the 1990s, with the rise of design companies like Droog and the international media coverage of Rem Koolhaas, who Mendini had presciently featured in *Casabella* in the 1970s).

Haks's decision to ask a Radical Italian architect to design and build a large new museum therefore felt both eccentric and visionary. Mendini, despite his fame, hadn't built a structure in decades and, unlike some of his successors at *Domus*, he hadn't taken advantage of the magazine to promote himself as an architect, choosing instead to focus on the philosophical and cultural aspects of design. It was only after stepping away from the world's most important design magazine – perhaps as a reaction to the radical and unexpected split – that he threw himself, with great commitment and energy, into the physical construction of architecture, alongside his brother Francesco and many collaborators.

In the 1995 book *Alessandro & Francesco Mendini! Philippe Starck! Michele De Lucchi! Coop Himmelb(l)au! in Groningen*, Haks talks about the project's origins in great detail in a lengthy interview with journalist Corien Lugtenberg.[13] Beyond the immediate respect and affinity he had for Mendini as a person, once they had met, Haks understood that among Mendini's many inspirations was the idea of collaborative work involving many hands – and, more importantly, many minds. Mendini believed that in a creative group individual nature and expression are not diluted, but rather highlighted, through collaboration.

Naturally, this method of working requires a highly skilled leader, and Mendini seemed the ideal person for the role, with his extensive experience participating in, and leading, groups of creators, from Nizzoli Associati to Studio Alchimia. The latter (with the special contribution of Giorgio Gregori) would soon start collaborating with the Mendini brothers on the Groninger Museum project after the success of their group architecture experiment *Casa della Felicità*.[14]

Alberto Alessi asked Mendini to design the house in Omegna, on Lake Orta, in 1983, and the project was completed in 1988. Mendini created a floorplan more like the composition of a painting and commissioned different architects to look after the various sub-buildings. Originally conceived according to Mendini's belief that 'the use of colours, the shape of spaces and symmetry could directly influence quality of life', the house gradually became a more conventional dwelling. The plans, which evolved over the course of the project, included several disparate principles, which nonetheless coexisted harmoniously. One key concept was to reflect the charm of rural villages or traditional architecture: where a house becomes a miniature city that includes a home, workspace, orchard and spaces for play and relaxation. Everything is integrated into the environment, with small additions that respect – but don't strictly follow – the existing structures.

There was no hierarchy between the different buildings. Each stood on its own, yet in relation to the others. It was as if different people, or different personalities, inhabited the different spaces – so the scientist or artisan might live in Aldo Rossi's tower/observatory/laboratory, and the collector or bibliophile or writer might live in Robert Venturi's library, relaxing in front of the fireplace designed by Ettore Sottsass. There was also no traditional facade. Paradoxically for such an aesthetically driven project, the functions of the house were given precedence over its exterior appearance, almost as if there were a deliberate effort to maintain privacy and keep life inside discreet.

Under Mendini's leadership, the house was born and developed in the same way a person brings together different items, memories, or dreams in their own home. This collaborative design process fostered

Casa della Felicità by Alessandro and Francesco Mendini: library design by Robert Venturi, Orta lake, 1983

Casa della Felicità by Alessandro and Francesco Mendini: living room with fireplace designed by Ettore Sottsass, Orta lake, 1983

a dialogue between the client and the lead designer, who also acted as a kind of 'conductor' for the other designers. The result was a unique living collage, an early manifesto of furnishing as a way of existing, an existentialist project that was as collaborative as possible.

In the first book about Atelier Mendini – the multidisciplinary design studio he founded in 1987 with his brother Francesco and many young collaborators that would become not only his workspace, but also a part of his life – Mendini himself explained the motivations behind his choice to work in groups and the value of the collective project:

> *As a solitary person, someone who loves to root my work in intimate experiences, I have nonetheless always worked in groups, with others [...] The group doesn't just embody the structuralist principle of the whole being greater than the sum of its parts. The group fills the void, the abyss that surrounds the individual's design idea; it satisfies the need for discussion and doubt and acts as a form of validation even before the result is achieved: it therefore anticipates the outcome of the work, presenting the final result more as a question than an answer.*[15]

Mendini's constant pursuit for dialogue with other minds and voices continued at Atelier Mendini, where he put the feedback he'd gathered by working in teams to fruition. Over the years Alessandro and Francesco were joined by many collaborators – graphic designers, designers, artists, journalists, psychologists and architects – among whom Bruno and Giorgio Gregori, the co-founders of Studio Alchimia,[16] were a constant and important presence. As great visualizers of ideas and projects at all scales – from objects to interiors and buildings – at a time when architectural drawing was not yet dominated by computers, the two brothers, while maintaining their collaboration with Alchimia, had the opportunity through Atelier Mendini to see several architectural projects realized, most notably the Groninger Museum.

ATELIER MENDINI

The address where the Atelier would be based from 1988 onwards was significant. After a brief spell during which Alessandro's collaborators gathered in a repurposed commercial space on Via Rossini – across from the studio he had shared with Nizzoli Associati, where he had maintained a small office – his brother Francesco found an opportunity to refit a large former workshop on Via Sannio, in Milan's Lodi-Porta Romana area. For many years, it had been part of the nearby Italian-Swiss company Asea Brown Boveri (ABB), a large metalwork factory founded in 1867, which initially made electrical motors and generators, and later ovens, trolleys, trams and trains.

It was an exemplary case of the 'industrial archaeology' trend which had garnered critical acclaim in Italy during the 1970s but had lost much of its appeal by the 1980s. The transformation of the former workshop into a large architecture studio aimed not only to create a spectacular office in terms of size, colour scheme and spatial qualities but also a space suitable for developing major projects like the Groninger Museum. For a variety of reasons, Mendini decided that it was the right time to join forces with Francesco to acquire the new space.[17] They initially divided the space between them, but it was united under the common name of Atelier Mendini, where they worked together, both bringing their respective visionary, cultural, and technical-executive expertise to the table. Over time, key collaborators joined the team, including architects Gerda Vossaert, Carla Ceccariglia, Pietro Gaeta, Alex Mocika, Andrea Balzari, graphic designer Massimo Caiazzo and later, the Gregori brothers.

On the upper floor of the large space, Mendini also created his own residence, from which he would descend into the studio via a metal staircase every day until the final weeks before his passing. For over thirty years, the Atelier was a place of intense creative energy, a testament to the intertwining of life and work that for Mendini had always overlapped.

Atelier Mendini on Via Sannio, Milan, 1989

Atelier Mendini design group, Milan, 1994

Atelier Mendini on Via Sannio, Milan, 1989

CHAPTER 7

THE MUSEUM AS ARTISTIC UTOPIA

After the initial decision of opting for a collaborative project, the process of bringing the Groningner Museum to life was long and complex. For both Frans Haks and Mendini, this was the project of a lifetime, a rare and unique opportunity to build from scratch a place entirely dedicated to an artistic utopia that became a shared vision for both. Haks quickly dismissed the idea of renovating the existing museum, and instead started the search for the best location for a new building, which had been made possible by a generous contribution from NV Nederlands GasUnie (Dutch Gas) of roughly $14 million (around $30 million today). The final decision was to place the new construction in the water of the Verbindingskanaal, in front of the central railway station. This would make it immediately visible from the station and create a landmark for the city, as both city hall and the sponsor wanted – though it also created significant technical challenges, such as the necessity for a new connecting bridge.

The plan for the project called for four main structures, entrusted to Mendini, Philippe Starck, Michele De Lucchi and Coop Himmelb(l)au. The latter inherited the pavilion initially assigned to the American artist Frank Stella, whose participation fell through due to disagreements about the project's direction. The final design incorporated some of Stella's ideas, such as a translucent roof which granted the pavilion plenty of natural light.

Amid technical difficulties and shifts in design choices, seven more years passed from the project's initial start. But as Haks recalled, in this case the delay ended up being an advantage: 'The final design turned out to be much richer than I would ever have imagined, in that respect the length of time the process took is a blessing.'[18] At the museum's inauguration on 29 October 1994, in the presence of the Queen of the Netherlands and a vast crowd in awe of the unexpected construction, a shy and emotional Mendini concluded his speech by referring back to the concept that guided the project, which had been enthusiastically embraced by the museum's director since the beginning:

> *We designed a floorplan with an archaic, symmetrical and rigorous shape: seen from above, the museum almost looks Egyptian. At the centre of this system, we placed a golden tower which houses a storage area for the artworks, which we conceived as a treasure trove of artistic knowledge. Around the tower we assembled a scene of architectural spaces that are very different from one another, which were designed to contain every aspect of the visual arts: very ancient objects together with very new ones, big and small, craft, industrial design, installations, documents on art from every corner of the world. It's a system of spatial relationships devised to make the visitors' experience fascinating and dynamic. These are, in short, the principles that guided us. We hope to have given the residents of Groningen something positive. We admire the Netherlands, which wisely keeps dotting its land with new museums. On behalf of all designers I want to thank the Netherlands for giving us a unique and truly unrepeatable experience. We dedicated ourselves to it with the utmost commitment.*[19]

The Groninger Museum wasn't spared accusations of Formalism, which, of course, was precisely what Mendini was pursuing in the majority of his architectural projects. This very definition – or accusation (which in Soviet Russia could have dire consequences for the accused, particularly if they were an artist, poet, musician, or architect, often leading to artistic silence, opposition and marginalization) – actually originates from the literary movement of Formalism, specifically Russian Formalism. It began in the 1920s with authors such as Vladimir Propp, whose *Morphology of the Folktale* (1928) created the basis for the structural analysis of texts. These ideas went on to influence the research of anthropologist Claude Lévi-Strauss and linguist Roland Barthes.

This kind of semiological analysis suited Mendini, who was a refined designer-intellectual and a critic of the status quo, even when designing a grand monument to Western culture like a museum. To borrow a concept from Russian Formalism, one could say that the Groninger

Museum represented the ideal blend of story (*fabula* or Фабула in Russian) and structure (*intreccio* or Субъект). The museum's *fabula* is artistic but also solid, durable, monumental on the outside and organic on the inside; its *intreccio* is how it is organized conceptually and spatially. This is reflected in the mix of De Lucchi's neoclassicism with Coop Himmelb(l)au's deconstructivism, Starck's frivolousness with the sturdiness of Mendini's tower, cutting-edge design with historical craftsmanship and the high-end Bisazza glass mosaics with the low-tech Abet *Proust* laminate.

As a prime example of Mendini's theories – from the importance of teamwork and embracing unexpected outcomes, to a post-kitsch aesthetic that disregards traditional notions of beauty or ugliness – the Groninger Museum can still teach us lessons many years later. The disciplines of art and architecture might find themselves at the most dramatic crossroads in their millennia-long history, facing the risk of disappearing into the language of digital design, yet Mendini managed to find a way to reconcile function and narration in form. Here, he found room for a sustainability that goes beyond mere mathematics or rhetoric, bringing formal innovation and a touch of controversy (where needed), and allowing designers to reclaim their artistic identity through a blend of technical and humanistic approaches.

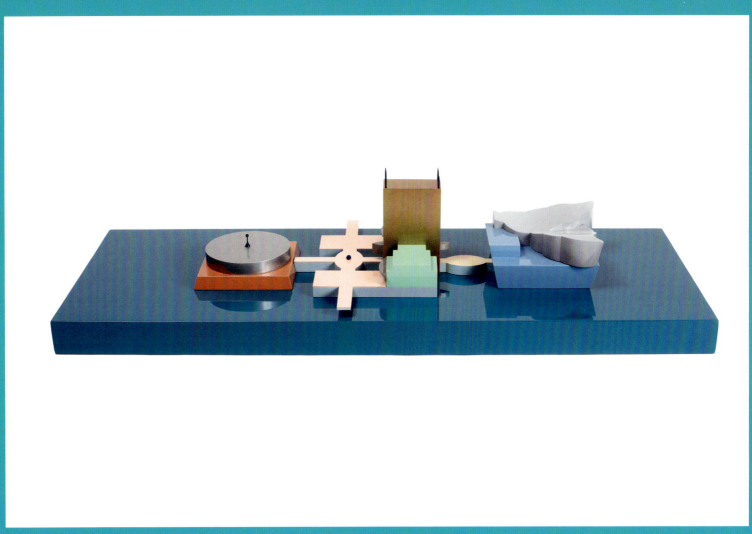
Model of the Groninger Museum, featuring the unrealized Ancient Art pavilion by Frank Stella on the right, 1988

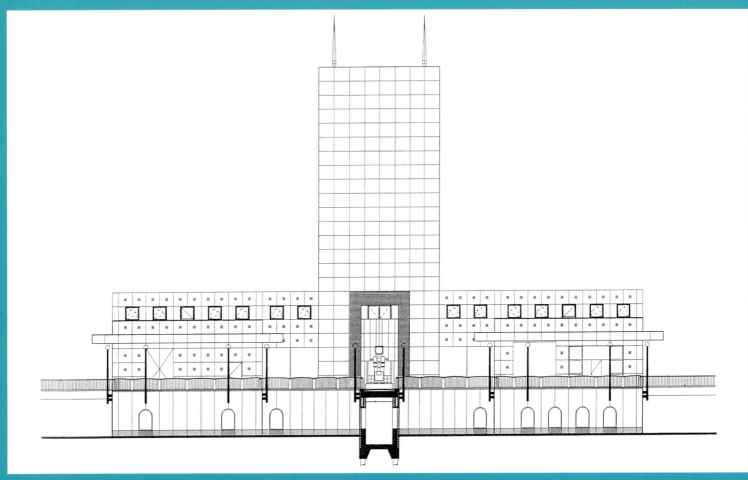
Drawing of the gold storage tower and entrance facade of the Groninger Museum, 1988

LEARNING A NEW UTOPIA: FROM LAS VEGAS TO GRONINGEN

101.

101. Design for the new Ponte dell'Accademia (with Alchimia) for the Architecture Biennale, Venice, 1985
102. Casa della Felicità: garden plan, painting, 1988
103. Casa della Felicità: garden plan, study for painting, 1988

CHAPTER 7 170

102.

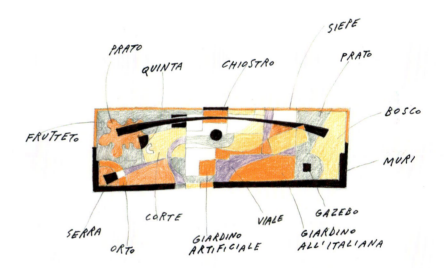

103.

LEARNING A NEW UTOPIA: FROM LAS VEGAS TO GRONINGEN

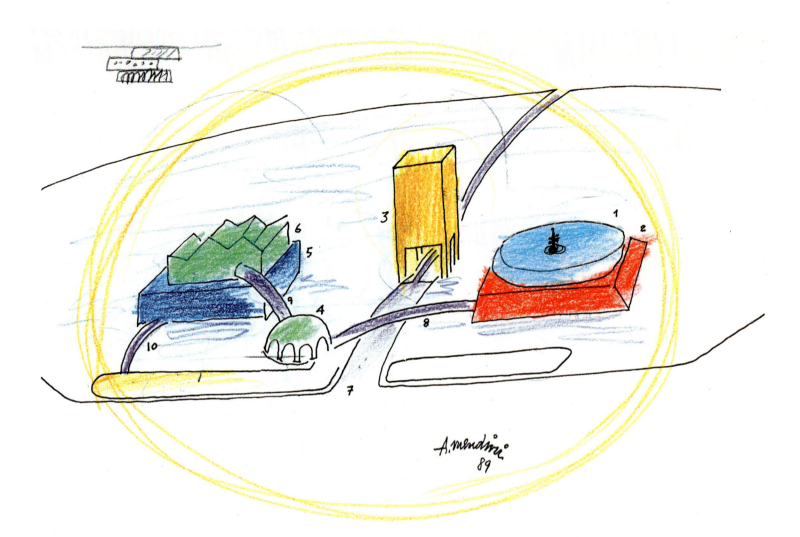

104.
104. Groninger Museum, drawing, 1989
105. Groninger Museum: East Pavilion with the lower section designed by Mendini clad in the *Proust* motif and the upper section designed by Coop Himmelb(l)au, Groningen, Netherlands, 1988-1994

105.

LEARNING A NEW UTOPIA: FROM LAS VEGAS TO GRONINGEN

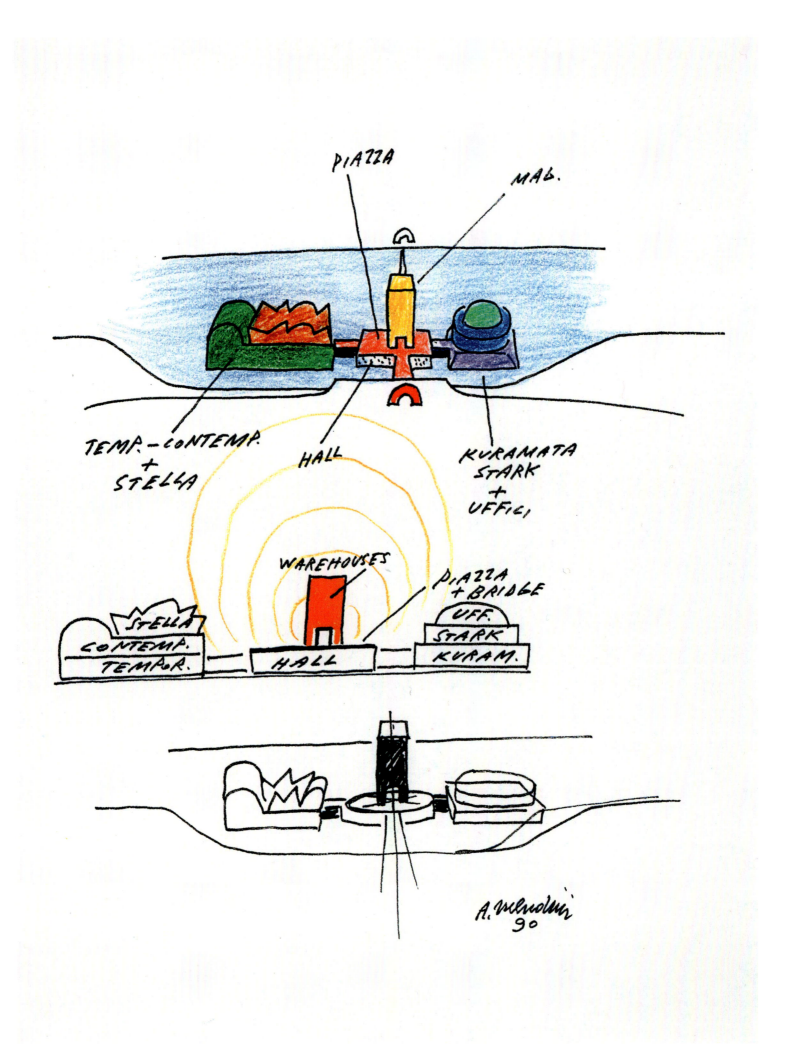

106.

107.

108.

106. Groninger Museum, drawing, 1990
107. Groninger Museum, Alessandro and Francesco Mendini with Alchimia, Michele De Lucchi, Philippe Starck and Coop Himmelb(l)au, Groningen, Netherlands, 1988-1994 (renovated 2010)
108. Groninger Museum, Decorative Arts Department, interior design by Philippe Starck, Groningen, Netherlands, 1994

LEARNING A NEW UTOPIA: FROM LAS VEGAS TO GRONINGEN

109.

109. Groninger Museum: *Tutto di oro?* (Everything in gold?), study for the pavilions of Ancient, Contemporary, Decorative and Regional Art, drawing, drawing, 1990
110. Groninger Museum: connecting square leading to the East Pavilion, Groningen, Netherlands, 1994
111. Groninger Museum: gold storage tower and museum entrance, Groningen, Netherlands, 1994

CHAPTER 7

110.

111.

LEARNING A NEW UTOPIA: FROM LAS VEGAS TO GRONINGEN

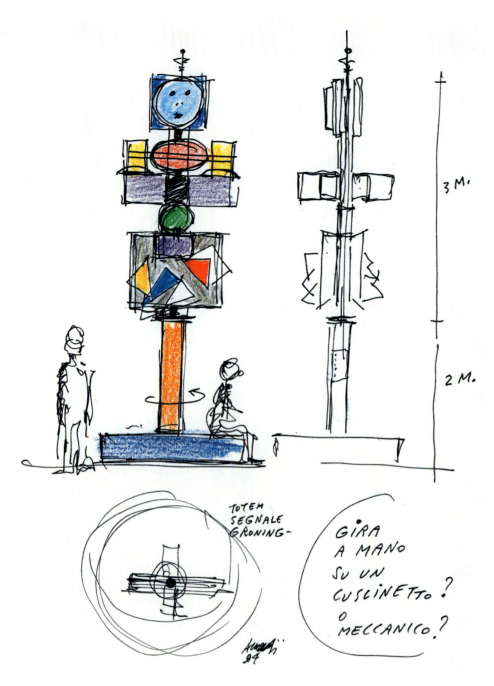

112.

112. Groninger Museum: sculpture, drawing, 1994
113. Groninger Museum: sculpture by the entrance to the museum, Groningen, Netherlands, 1994
114. Groninger Museum: drawing for the Pavilion of Ancient Art by Coop Himmelb(l)au, 1990
115. Groninger Museum: central staircase connecting the pavilions of Contemporary Art and Ancient Art, Groningen, Netherlands, restyled 2010

113.

CHAPTER 7   178

114.

115.

LEARNING A NEW UTOPIA: FROM LAS VEGAS TO GRONINGEN

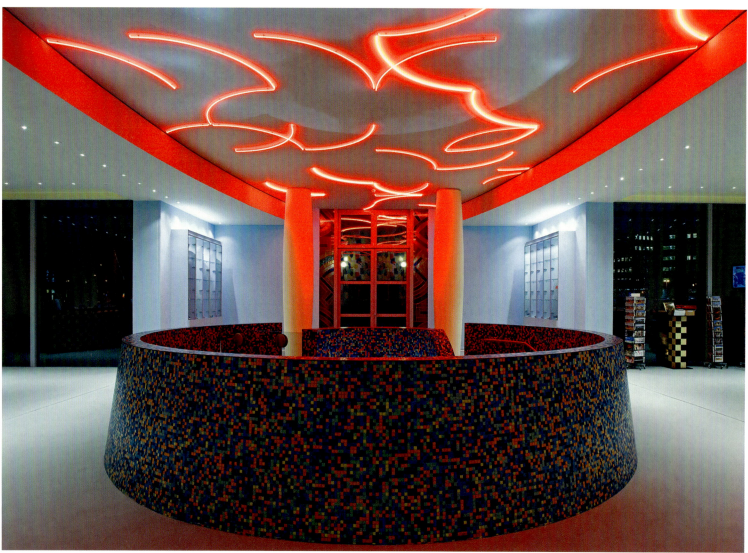

116.

116. Groninger Museum: entrance hall by Alessandro and Francesco Mendini, with Bisazza mosaic staircase and light installation by François Morellet, Groningen, Netherlands, restyled 2010
117. Groninger Museum: Bisazza mosaic staircase by Alessandro and Francesco Mendini, Groningen, Netherlands, 1994
overleaf: *Lots of Dots* wristwatch with *Proust* pattern for Swatch, drawing, 1990

117.

THE GOLDEN DESIGN AGE: SWATCH TO BISAZZA AND BEYOND

TAKING ARCHITECTURE BY THE HAND

In 1989, the Olivari brothers – third generation of a family of metal industrialists who were geographically, culturally and personally close to Alberto Alessi and his company[1] – turned to Mendini to embark on a broad collaboration, from designing new products to redefining the company's overall image. At that time, Mendini had developed a more radical yet poetic vision of design. He recognised that while it might not be possible to revolutionize the world through design (the not-so-secret aspiration of almost every avant-garde), there was still immense value in combining craftsmanship and industry to create beauty in everyday objects. This beauty emerged from simplicity and was transformed through imaginative forms, colours and materials.

In this dreamy but realist approach, Mendini believed it was crucial to create a synthesis between industry, designers and everyone else involved in the production. A company could define its cultural identity through a relentless pursuit of quality at every stage – from conception to material realization through to consumption. Mendini applied his unique 'non-method' design approach, refined over years of thinking about drawing, production and sales, and influenced by his own theory of 'the banal' to a series of door handles for Olivari. He saw the handle as a 'miniature' that 'belongs to the history of fashion and holds the same aesthetic significance for a home as jewellery does for the human body.'[2]

His 1992 *Tebe* handle, which carefully combined a perfectly-proportioned cone, sphere and brass spindle, evoked his signature zoomorphic motifs – it is perhaps reminiscent of a bird's beak – while remaining balanced and ergonomic. In the 1994 *Aurora* handle, he tackled the challenge of combining glass and brass, achieving a lightness that remains unmatched and demonstrating that he was 'an unyielding dreamer of perfect forms.'[3]

Between 1991–92, Mendini also conceived a new design for Olivari's offices and factory – a project with Pietro Gaeta and Dagmar Trinks which largely focused on preserving the company's historical memory. Mendini proposed a small handle museum, meant to bring order and identity to a collection of pieces produced by a group of high-quality designers, with a coherence rarely seen in other productions. While the new headquarters ultimately didn't come to fruition, Mendini's involvement left a significant mark on the company's history.

I was entrusted with curating and writing a book on the history of design for Olivari, a similar undertaking to what Mendini had done for Alessi with *Paesaggio Casalingo* (Homely Landscape). The title of the resulting book, *L'architettura presa per mano* (Architecture Taken by Hand),[4] was a reference to the close, 'anthropological' relationship between objects, spaces and the people who live in them, and it included many prominent designers, from Marcello Piacentini, Gio Ponti and Marcello Nizzoli to Paolo Portoghesi and the young Massimo Iosa Ghini.

FROM VICENZA TO HIROSHIMA AND BACK AGAIN

Mendini's collaboration with Bisazza, a leading producer of glass mosaic tiles, began in 1989, with the construction of the Paradise Tower in Japan – a celebratory building rich in symbolism. Together with his brother Francesco and architect Yumiko Kobayashi, Mendini designed the 55-metre-high tower on its star-shaped piazza covered in Bisazza's blue mosaic tiles as part of Hiroshima's *Sea and Island Expo*. Made of polished steel, the tower's shiny exterior reflects the sky, while its spire disappears into the blue. Inside the structure and throughout the surrounding area, an electronic system broadcasts music composed by Davide Mosconi,[5] one of Mendini's comrades from the days of his Radical adventures. The music features sounds taken from nature and is at its strongest at the centre of the tower, where there is a multifaceted Swarovski crystal sphere (the biggest in the world): a symbol of purity. Built by Mitsubishi Heavy Industry, the tower represents a pivotal moment in Mendini's career, blending Western light-based aesthetics with Eastern ideas rooted in shadow and penumbra.

Much like his relationship with Alessi, where he became a close friend and chief consultant to Alberto Alessi, Mendini gradually infused Bisazza with a passion for expressing ideas through colour. Bisazza's founder Renato and, later, his children Piero and Rossella, saw Mendini's work as more than just a professional collaboration – it was a gateway to architecture through thoughtful creativity. From defining colourways and combinations to designing objects big and small for iconic late-century brands like Swatch and Alessi,[6] to creating urban monuments at Rome's Termini Station and for the Naples Metro, Mendini's collaboration with the Bisazza family produced new visions of interiors, architecture and even urban planning at the turning point between two millennia.

It's no coincidence that the most complex, emotionally charged and utopian project among these collaborations was the design of the Naples Metro stations. Brought to life with the contribution of dozens of artists, invited and coordinated by the renowned critic Achille Bonito Oliva, and supported by the engineers of the Naples Metro led by Egidio Silva,[7] these stations – particularly Salvator Rosa and Materdei, overseen by Mendini and his brother Francesco – became a manifesto for contemporary Italian art and a prototype for public space as cultural enrichment for the wider public. Bonito Oliva referred to them as 'compulsory museums'[8] – they were symbols of the potential cultural revival of the banal city through a mutual understanding between artists, industry and society at large.

The design and realization of the Salvator Rosa and Materdei stations stand as the most significant demonstration of Atelier Mendini's architectural capabilities. Having already tested urban intervention in Naples with the redevelopment of the city's Villa Comunale park, the Metro Art initiative offered the studio another chance to integrate art and architecture.

The programme, which started in 2001 and continued until the completion of the Duomo Station designed by Massimiliano and Doriana Fuksas in 2021, assigned different stations to different designers. Mendini's case was unique: he designed the exits of the Materdei and Salvator Rosa stations using a mix of elements that seamlessly integrated with interventions by artists invited by him and Bonito Oliva – both above and below ground. In Mendini's view, 'metro stations, just like public squares, streets, markets and stalls should be considered aesthetic works, like fragments of outdoor theatre.'[9]

No doubt the unique monumental character of Naples, its theatrical nature enhanced by a historically rich yet structurally chaotic urban fabric, supports this artistic approach. For the Salvator Rosa station, Mendini and Bonito Oliva chose a number of Neapolitan artists including: Renato Barisani (enamelled steel sculptures and mosaic facade); Lucio Del Pezzo (bronze sculpture and Amalfi ceramic walls); Nino Longobardi (bronze columns); Ugo Marano (marble mosaic and ceramic panel); Mimmo Paladino and his uncle Salvatore (sculpture and children's play equipment in the San Salvator Rosa square and a multi-material restoration of a pre-existing facade); Augusto Perez (bronze sphinx); Gianni Pisani and Ernesto Tatafiore (mosaic facades); Perino & Vele (papier-mâché sculptures) and Anna Sargenti (large painting along a train track). More artistic interventions were completed by Enzo Cucchi, Alex Mocika, Fulvia Mendini and Mimmo Rotella.[10] At the Materdei station, Italian artists were joined by international creatives: Robert Gligorov, George Sowden and Sol LeWitt intervened with photographs, panels and sculptures, and other works were contributed by Sandro Chia, Anna Gili, Innocente, Luigi Ontani, Denis Santachiara, Luigi Serafini and Ettore Spalletti.

Across the twelve stations, completed by other creatives such as Gae Aulenti, Dominique Perrault, Karim Rashid and Oscar Tusquets, the sheer number of artworks along Naples Metro Line 1 is unmatched in Europe.[11] Despite changes in local government, the municipality remained committed to the idea of infrastructure as more than something purely functional. The Naples Metro management supported the project from the start and allowed Mendini to realise one of his unspoken utopias: to return as a key player in the design and reconstruction of Italian cities without being constrained by real estate interests, free to choose intervention sites and even rehabilitate problematic areas. His ultimate goal was 'that these stations, these new "transit architecture" events would become aesthetic spaces, art walks.'

The Naples Metro project also enabled an experimental workshop for Bisazza, which, through its collaboration with several of the artists involved in the stations, produced other, more 'personal' works. Among

Casa Bisazza showroom, Milan, 1994

L-R: Casciani, Mendini and Italo Lupi, Milan, 1991

Mendini, Casciani and the Metropolitana Napoli artists, Naples, 2001

Mendini at the opening of Fondazione Bisazza, 2012

Salvator Rosa metro station, Naples, 2001

them was the large mosaic *Bagnanti* (Bathers) by Sandro Chia, initially created for the brand's Milan showroom, designed by Fabio Novembre, and now displayed at the Fondazione Bisazza in Alte. For many reasons, this mosaic served as a bridge between a great ancient tradition and a modern one: it references the icons of ancient Roman sportsmanship and the monumentality of Italian Modernist artist Mario Sironi, with a touch of the grace of Gino Severini. The piece heralded a new phase for Sandro Chia, who was already a painter of the Transavanguardia, where mosaic became an essential element of his new expressive direction.

Mendini's strategic consultancy sparked a wave of artistic collaborations for Bisazza, involving both experimental and established artists. Over the years I personally had multiple opportunities to realize projects, ranging from sculptures for the Foundation Jacqueline Vodoz and Bruno Danese in Milan, to the decoration of the Montenapoleone Metro station in Milan[12] with Mimmo Paladino, which provided an account of our everyday life to passersby. Other notable contributors included Ettore Sottsass, Enzo Cucchi, Studio Job, Jaime Hayon, Isao Hosoe, Marcel Wanders, Patricia Urquiola, Jan Kaplický, Massimiliano Fuksas and many others. Whether through simple sketches or fully realized projects, they all contributed to creating a vibrant new landscape.[13]

This 'mosaic city' first envisioned by Mendini would later recur in many of his buildings, where he employed the multi-coloured mosaic palette to blend private and public spaces, minimalism and monumentality, space and architecture. Bisazza continued to work closely with Mendini during his later years, when his research was increasingly inspired by sculpture. This was particularly evident in his major solo exhibition, *Mosaico Mendini* (Mendini Mosaic), staged at Milan's Triennale in April 2011, where he showed the huge, mosaic equestrian statue *Il Cavaliere di Dürer* (Dürer's Knight).

Industry and the architect-artist entered the history of design together, inspiring new ideas, designers and clients alike. They found that they could use materials, techniques and a chromatic language with great evocative power to make works that sat between the rationality of functional design and the freedom of cultural inspiration.[14]

DIVERSIFIED SERIES FOR LOW-COST COLLECTING

The phenomenon of low-cost mass collecting, and its less sophisticated counterpart – the compulsive purchasing of the same object, particularly fashion accessories such as celebrity-endorsed sneakers – cannot be understood without considering the logic of post-industrial consumption. Mendini was a keen observer and interpreter of a society based on fetishized commodities, and he had long foreseen how this phenomenon would evolve in a hedonistic direction. Thanks to his artistic intelligence he found himself in the role of pioneer, on the cusp between mainstream 'pop' taste and the 'democracy' of consumption, at times even gently bordering on kitsch. This was evident during his many years of collaborating with Swatch, the Swiss watch company that radically transformed both the market and consumer preferences.

The collaboration began in 1990 with the design and production of watches such as *Metroscape* (derived from a drawing of a city by Alchimia), *Cosmesis* (featuring the *Galla Placidia* pattern) and *Lots of Dots*, which applied the *Proust* armchair pattern to the surfaces of the already famous plastic watch that had become an object of fanatical collecting. This collective consumer frenzy, something of an 'epidemic', is largely the outcome of a strategy that Nicolas Hayek, a marketing guru, had begun to formulate at the beginning of the 1980s. In 1983 he oversaw the merger of Swiss watch companies ASUAG and SSIH into SMH, which under the name ETA, began producing a plastic watch that would evolve into Swatch.

Swatch, short for 'second watch', was intended by its creators to be a high-quality but low-cost product. With half the number of components of a traditional wristwatch, it could be produced at a greatly reduced cost without compromising quality. This meant they could be easily purchased and used as a second watch, perhaps as an everyday alternative to a more precious model, and passed down from generation to generation, gaining sentimental value alongside monetary worth.

Even so, the success of the Swatch as a compulsively collectable object (at a low cost) wasn't inevitable. The first Swatch models were strictly black and/or white. These were followed by a collection of 12 multi-coloured models, but it was only thanks to Hayek's marketing genius, and specifically his push towards more variety in the models, that the Swatch collecting phenomenon was born. Throughout the 1980s and 1990s, the scale of this collective frenzy was remarkable: long queues formed outside shops whenever a new model was released and there were collector's clubs all around the world. Together with the regular series models, the brand's limited editions led to the production of 20 million units in 1990 alone.[15]

After a number of years collaborating with Swatch, Mendini took over from Matteo Thun to become the brand's art director in 1993. Once again, the idea of a 'collection' of products – which once belonged only to fashion, and then expanded to design and particularly furniture, thanks to Studio Alchimia and Memphis – was perfected and pushed to the extreme. Many different creatives were invited to design their own Swatch. This included artists such as Mimmo Paladino (who became friends with Mendini and dedicated the portrait *Un chioschetto con amicizia* to him in 2005), Mimmo Rotella, and Bruno Munari, who in 1987 was 80 years old and whose ironic *Tempo Libero* (Free Time) Swatch was one of his last works. Collaborators and designers close to Atelier Mendini were also included, such as the cartoonist Massimo Giacon and the graphic designer Massimo Caiazzo, who also produced some iconic promotional images for the company, including a pineapple made of watches.

But in order to keep the appeal – or rather, the charm – of the collections and their accelerated rhythm alive, the company needed to sell a Swatch 'mood' to the collector and the simple buyer alike. To this end, Mendini chose to reintroduce the decorative lexicon he had previously developed with Alchimia, his Atelier and alone. His communication projects, installations and large exhibitions – such as *Swatch Emotion*,[16] staged at Turin's Lingotto in 1993 – were both a chance for Mendini to research but also apply his updated stylistic approach. This style had seemingly been softened and enriched by simpler figurative elements (such as animals and people) that were easy for a large – or even very large – public to recognize and identity with.[17] It was an aesthetic encyclopedia that was best exemplified in the design of the shops that Alessandro and the Atelier Mendini worked on, together with Francesco and with the collaboration of Bruno and Giorgio Gregori.

These so-called 'monobrand' stores were the idea of Franco Bosisio, who was in charge of restructuring SMH Italia. Bosisio had been tasked with restructuring SMH Italy, which he led to become the most important component of the group in Europe, in terms of market share and revenue with Swatch. Until 1995, he was also Mendini's primary interlocutor. The two built a close relationship in order to reach the marketing plan's objectives, and they were in mutual agreement on the company's many different needs, including the idea of working with an entire group and not just its leader. As Bosisio himself put it in the 1994 book about the Atelier:

> *Mendini demonstrated that authority could be paired with freedom and that it does not necessarily mean speaking 'from command.' Mendini's case is one where authority is based on cultural and even affectionate relationships, where the credit he is given stems from the freedom recognized in ideation and creation.*[18]

Certainly, the collaboration with Swatch – which continued until 2000 – was a truly collective endeavour, which required all the diverse skills within the Atelier. Mendini served as the strategic planner and director and he involved other producers in the construction of displays and shops, such as Bisazza for mosaic flooring and glass surfaces. The goal was to give the monobrand stores – the point of direct contact with consumers – an increasingly delicate and luminous image, with new and iridescent colours and pop graphic-design inventions.[19]

Mendini also invited other artists and designers to intervene on particular occasions, such as the *Swatch Art Clock Towers* created for the 1996 Atlanta Olympics, for which Swatch was one of the sponsors.

Ron Arad, Javier Mariscal, Marc Newson, Verner Panton and other authors of the as-yet still young and vibrant avant-garde of New International Design designed 8-metre-high clock towers, which were later reproduced in a smaller scale, as limited-edition sculptural objects. Thus, the great nebula of creatives orbiting around Mendini for Swatch expanded, along with the numerous collaborators from his own Atelier. Among those that were most continuously active, it's worth giving a special mention to Giorgio Gregori. Not only was he a great visualizer using traditional hand-drawing tools, but also a true designer of objects and spaces in close synergy with Mendini, who remembered him with these moving words in 1997, two years after Gregori's premature death:

> *I had a 'calligraphic–emotional' relationship with Giorgio Gregori. Over many years we engaged in a continuous dialogue, a duet, a silent and conniving symbiosis, almost devoid of words, played out entirely through the line of a pen, the only tool of visual transmission we used to express the initial ideas for a work [...] After our parallel experiences at Alchimia, Giorgio and I found that we had the same handwriting [...] so much so that sometimes there was confusion about the authorship of certain drawings. But while I avoided and betrayed the humble, fundamental work of the Carthusian monk, Giorgio did nothing but draw and draw: his loving and virtuous care was single-mindedly devoted to visualizing things with an expert, admirable, inspired hand. As an artist, Giorgio was a delicate, sensitive energy in drawing [...] a silent stylistic illustrator of architectural fables, a rare interpreter of aesthetic mirages, a gentle spirit who traversed the sharp turbulence of New Design unscathed.*[20]

Over the following years, due to the ebbs and flows of history – including that of design – the winning formula of Swatch's diversified series idea progressively lost its cultural relevance and became just another marketing phenomenon. Nevertheless, interest in Mendini's design approach remains strong. For Swatch, he poured all his intellectual energy into portraying the consumer society at its most spectacular within the Swiss brand's image and its 'authentically fake' products. These products were genuine but not naive, self-aware of their primarily cosmetic nature. They were never destined to change the world, but rather to offer a colourful, joyful and optimistic image of it.[21]

Young design team of Swatch Lab art directed by Mendini, Milan, 1994

Mendini with his collection of Swatch watches, 2016

Mendini and Ettore Sottsass, Venice, 1993

Swatch Corner Fiorucci, Milan, 1994

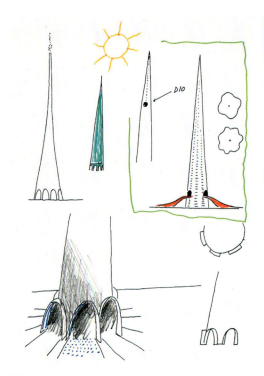

118.

119.

118. *Torre Paradiso* (Paradise Tower), drawing, 1989
119. *Torre Paradiso* (Paradise Tower), model, 1989
120. *Torre Paradiso* (Paradise Tower) steel tower, project with Yumiko Kobayashi realized for Expo Hiroshima, Hatoba Park, Hiroshima, Japan, 1989

120.

THE GOLDEN DESIGN AGE: SWATCH TO BISAZZA AND BEYOND

121.

121. *Swatch Emotion* exhibition at the World Trade Center Singapore
by Alessandro and Francesco Mendini, drawing by Bruno Gregory, 1994
122. *Swatch Emotion* exhibition at the World Trade Center Singapore
by Alessandro and Francesco Mendini, 1994
123. Swatch Shop by Alessandro and Francesco Mendini, Via Montenapoleone,
Milan, 1994

122.

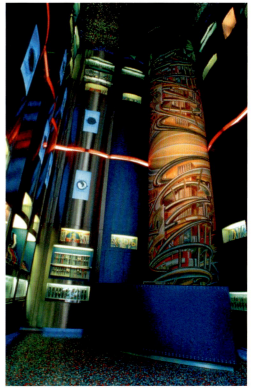

123.

THE GOLDEN DESIGN AGE: SWATCH TO BISAZZA AND BEYOND

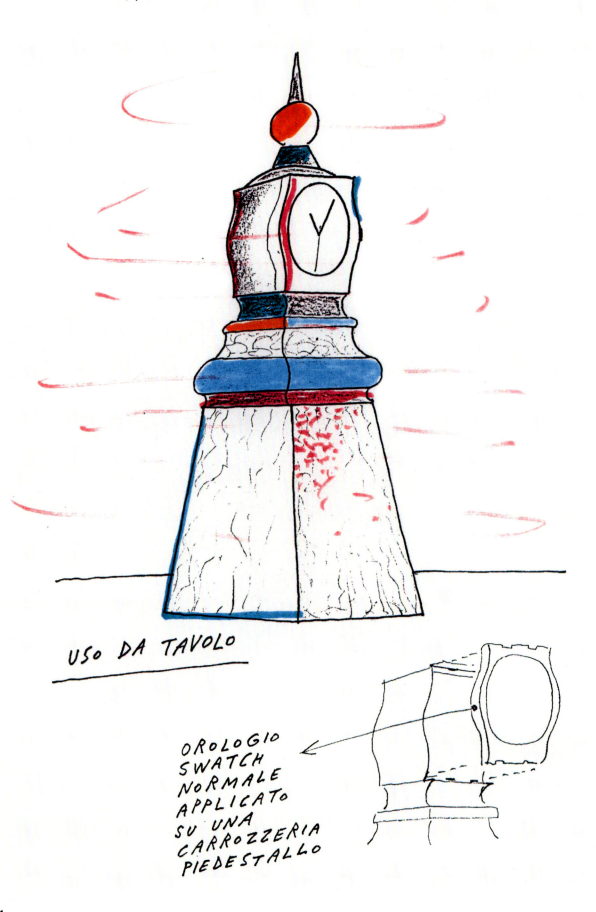

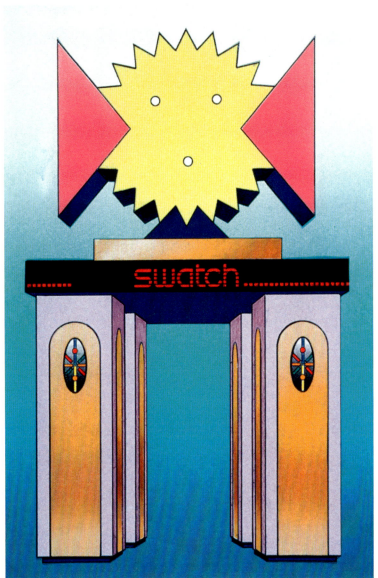
125.

126.

124. *Little Monument to the Swatch*, table clock for Swatch, drawing, 1990-1991
125. Display piece for Swatch installation by Alessandro and Francesco Mendini, drawing by Massimo Caiazzo, Bruno Gregory, Annalisa Margarini, 1994
126. Display piece for Swatch installation by Alessandro and Francesco Mendini, drawing by Massimo Caiazzo, Bruno Gregory, Annalisa Margarini, 1994

THE GOLDEN DESIGN AGE: SWATCH TO BISAZZA AND BEYOND

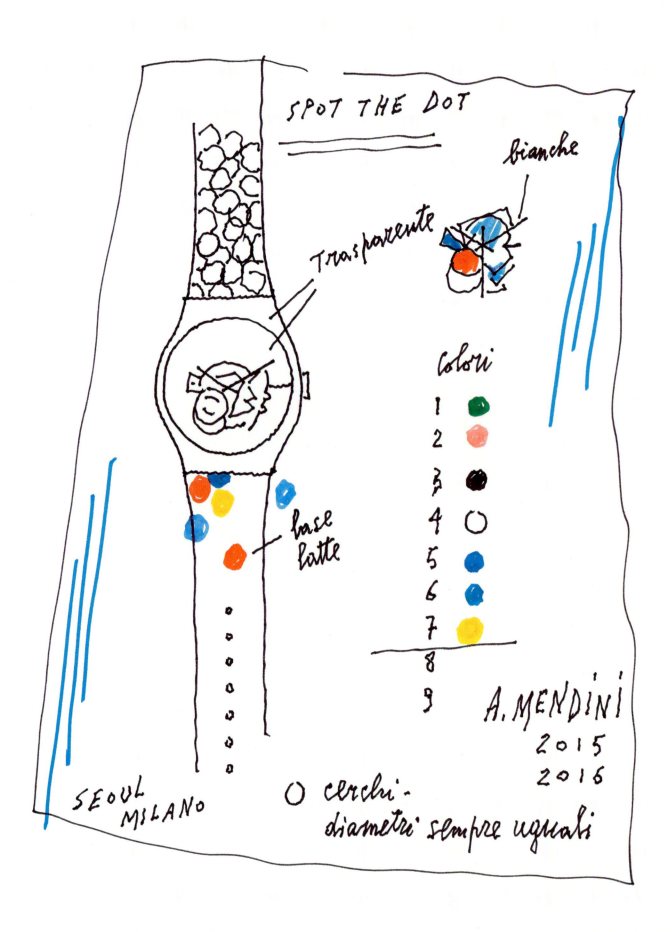

127.

128.

129.

127. *Spot the Dot* wristwatch with *Proust* decoration for Swatch, drawing, 2015-2016
128. *Spot the Dot* wristwatch for Swatch, 2016
129. Swatch Lab wristwatches, Spring/Summer and Fall/Winter collections 1994-1995.

THE GOLDEN DESIGN AGE: SWATCH TO BISAZZA AND BEYOND

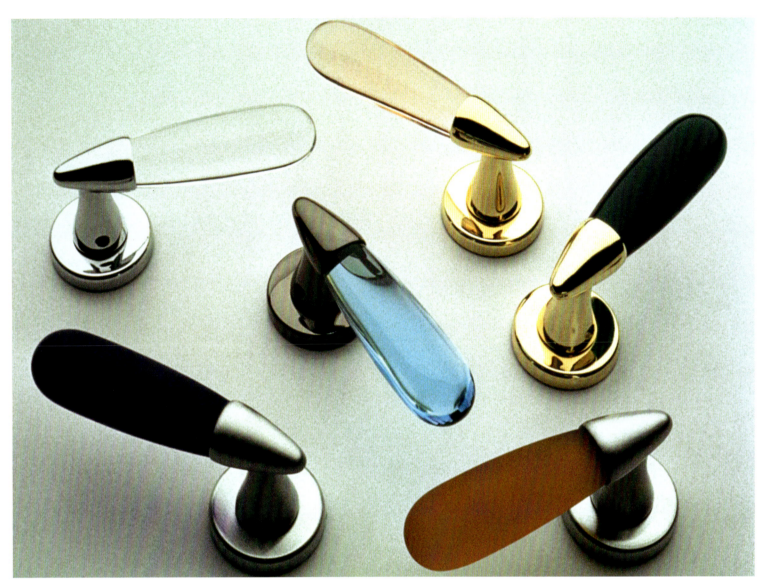

131.

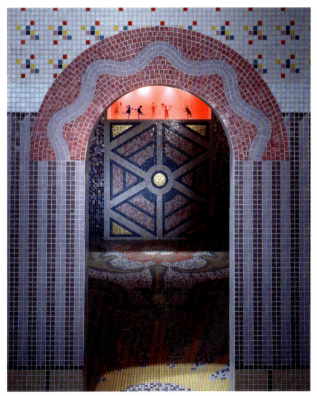

130. *Venere* door handle series for Olivari, drawing, 2001
131. *Aurora* steel and coloured glass door handle series for Olivari, 1994
132. *Chiesa del Vasaio* (Church of the Potter), entrance to the small structure made from Bisazza mosaic for *Artinmosaico: The Bisazza Collection*, Scuderie di Palazzo Reale, Naples, 1996

132.

THE GOLDEN DESIGN AGE: SWATCH TO BISAZZA AND BEYOND

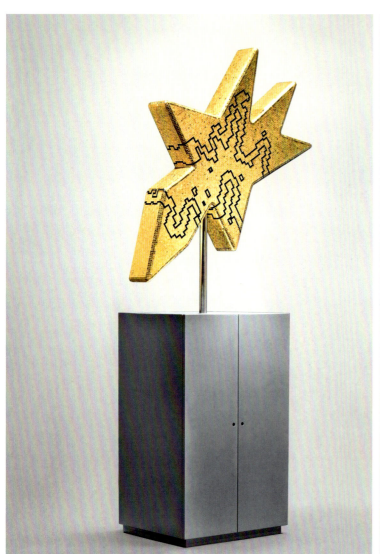
133.

134.

133. *Mobili per uomo* (Furniture for Man): *Stella* (Star) storage unit and mosaic sculpture for Bisazza, 2002
134. *Mobili per uomo* (Furniture for Man): *Guanto* (Glove) storage unit and mosaic sculpture for Bisazza, 1997
135. *Mobili per uomo* (Furniture for Man): *Testa* (Head) storage unit and mosaic sculpture for Bisazza, 1997

CHAPTER 8

135.

THE GOLDEN DESIGN AGE: SWATCH TO BISAZZA AND BEYOND

136.

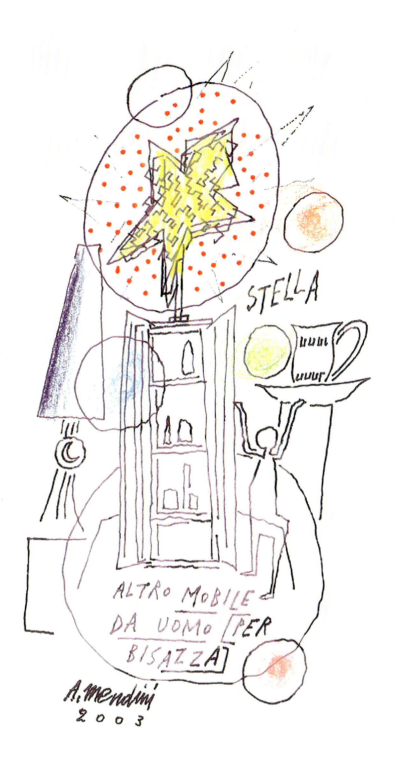

137.

138.

136. Stuttgarter Bank: Bisazza mosaic mural in the entrance hall by Alessandro and Francesco Mendini, Stuttgart, Germany, 1996
137. *Mobili per uomo* (Furniture for Man): *Stella* (Star) for Bisazza, drawing, 2003
138. *Stella* (Star) Bisazza mosaic sculpture in the grounds of the Sieger family castle, Schloss Harkotten, Germany, 1999

 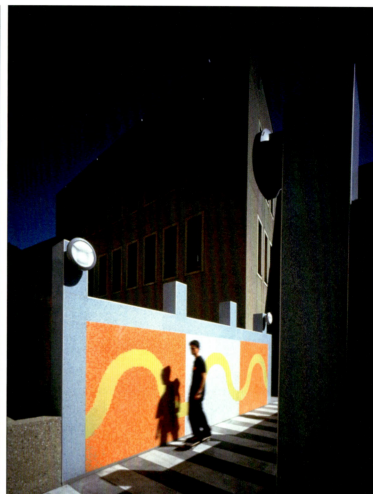

139.
140.

139. Maghetti District: redevelopment of the district by Alessandro and Francesco Mendini using Bisazza mosaic, Lugano, Switzerland, 1998-1999
140. Maghetti District: redevelopment of the district by Alessandro and Francesco Mendini using Bisazza mosaic, Lugano, Switzerland, 1998-1999
141. Salvator Rosa metro station, Naples Metro Line 1, Exit 2 by Alessandro and Francesco Mendini with ceramic piece *Napoli Città Madre* by Ugo Marano, 2003
142. Salvator Rosa metro station, Naples Metro Line 1, Exit 2 by Alessandro and Francesco Mendini with ceramic pieces by Enzo Cucchi and facade by Mimmo Paladino, 2003

141.

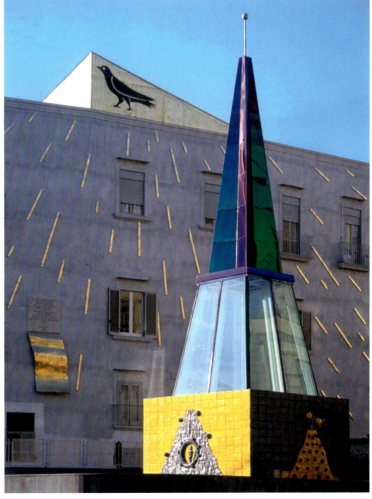
142.

THE GOLDEN DESIGN AGE: SWATCH TO BISAZZA AND BEYOND

143.

CHAPTER 8

144.

145.

143. Salvator Rosa and Materdei metro stations, Naples, drawing, 1999
144. Università metro station, Naples Metro Line 1, by Karim Rashid, Alessandro and Francesco Mendini, Naples, 2010
145. Materdei metro station, Naples Metro Line 1, lift entrance by Alessandro and Francesco Mendini with ceramic pieces by Lucio Del Pezzo, Naples, 2003

THE GOLDEN DESIGN AGE: SWATCH TO BISAZZA AND BEYOND

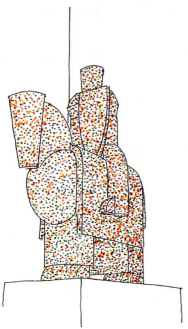

146.

147.

146. Cavaliere di Dürer (Dürer's Knight), drawing with *Proust* decoration, Bisazza, 2010
147. Cavaliere di Dürer (Dürer's Knight) sculpture in Bisazza mosaic with Delft colours, Bisazza, 2010
148. Cavaliere di Dürer (Dürer's Knight) in Delft colours, drawing, Bisazza, 2010
    overleaf: *I am Mr Ciao* sculpture for SPC Group, drawing, 2015

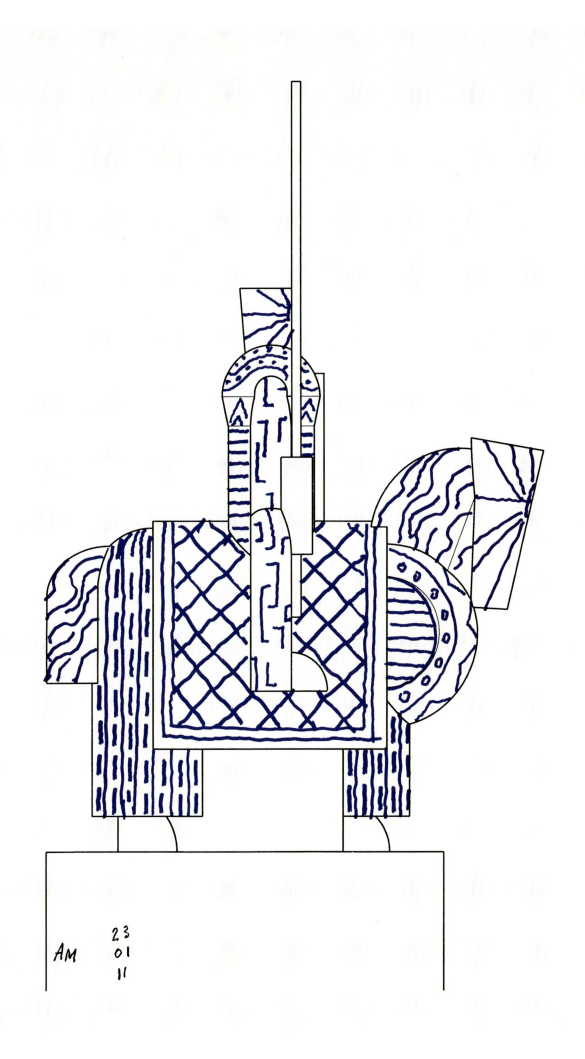

148.

THE ALESSI CORKSCREW AND THE GLOBAL CITY

RETURN OF THE REPRESSED: ALESSI OBJECTS, SAME BUT DIFFERENT

In a little-known text – a transcript of a talk given at the conference *Il design e le sue prospettive disciplinari* (Design and its disciplinary perspectives) held at CentroKappa in 1977, which doesn't appear in the archives of his extensive body of work – Mendini revealed his deep-seated aversion to objects, especially when forced to design them. It's an autobiographical and sentimental account that still reflects his 'political' and radical spirit, even though it's expressed in the polite and detached manner typical of his lighter conversations, where his tone was ironic, sometimes caustic, but ultimately kind toward people and things.
Speaking of the 'heroic' design of the post-war years, he said:

If I divide my life into decades, I've not been a good witness to design, to the design object. Of the 1940s, I remember a series of radio stations that transmitted very dramatic output, ranging from Mussolini's speeches and war bulletins to partisan messages and Radio Londra. Of the 1950s, I recall a lamp by Menghi, a lamp that was shown in an exhibition. The lamp had a pendulum and two little feet that attached it to a table. It was always broken and was held together by a kind of sticky tape. I was told not to touch it because it could give you an electric shock. The design of the 1950s, which originated in Italy, spread with overwhelming force. This activity was a spark, but also a kind of boomerang, because after that dry and experimental era we ended up with consumerism and productive hedonism. Let's just say it started well but ended badly.[1]

Curiously, this conference took place more or less at the same time that Mendini met Alberto Alessi. Both the entrepreneur and his company provided the ideal context for Mendini to rethink his objectives. Alessi was a historic company, but one that needed to refresh its identity, pushing Mendini to reconsider his skeptical views.
In an important Alchimia catalogue from 1987, a decade after the CentroKappa conference – which had been attended by Milan's greatest design masters – Mendini felt ready to express his most mature contradictions. He did so with a series of *Telegrammi al Designer* (Telegrams to the Designer),[2] in the tradition of the aphorisms, which can be traced back to his editor's letters for *Casabella*, his texts for *OllO* magazine, and through to our co-editorship of *Domus* for the *Nuova Utopia* (New Utopia) series. The premise of the *Telegrammi* was a clear, ruthless and relevant analysis of the context in which design is born and develops:

the moral hypothesis of the traditional industrial system was to spread wealth through technology and thus achieve the utopia of widespread well-being stop

the phenomenon of inequality has instead increased and irreversible violence is a constant feature of humanity stop

Methodological instructions – if any can be found – were mostly poetic, with a touch of mysticism:

there is no development but circularity between past present and future which eternally redesign themselves stop

the new designer will no longer create real, certain and valid things for eternity stop

loving design opposes functional design stop

earthly paradise was a perfect place its characteristic was the total absence of architecture objects organisation planning Even today the optimal hypothesis of the world is to exist without designing stop[3]

GLOBAL COSMETICS: 100% MAKE-UP

Faced with these somewhat dreamy concepts – better suited to the painterly and metaphysical explorations of the Alchimia laboratory than to the research and development centres of a factory – Mendini found a kindred spirit in Alberto Alessi. Indeed, it wouldn't be an exaggeration to describe Alessi as a patron, as he was eager to support Mendini's intellectual leaps whether they led to mass production, unique objects or diversified series.

In 1989, Alessi and Mendini started to dream up what would go on to become arguably the most complex diversified series ever attempted. Its title, *100% Make-Up*, pointed to the fact it was a cosmetic project, though it also contained elements of the alchemical and metaphysical, with numerological undertones in its commercial execution. The concept was to produce a first edition of 100 units of 100 variants of the same vase, each decorated by a different artist, resulting in a total of 10,000 pieces that were at the same time identical but also unique – and all sold at the same price.

The archetypal shape of the vase was designed by Mendini, with a conical lid that made it resemble an urn. If, however, one imagined the vase upside down and without its lid, its shape resembles that of ancient Chinese vases, with a widening curvature that narrowed before re-opening as a truncated cone. But these nods to ancient traditions were not the only enigmas of the *100% Make-Up* vase. Under each vase of the first edition, Mendini wrote:

> [...] The names of all authors stamped in alphabetical order, numbered from one to ten thousand. The identity of each author is indirect but specified by the numerical sequence.[4]

Whether the name of the author was recognizable or not seemed to be of little importance. The whole project felt like an attempt at artistic communism – an egalitarian totalitarianism in which each author followed the rules, or rather, the exercise, of imagining their own visual identity within the constraints of a single form. An interesting historical precedent can be found at the onset of the Soviet era when the Imperial Porcelain Factory of St Petersburg, which had produced exquisite tableware for the Tsars in the 19th century, became the State Porcelain Factory. Undecorated plates from the company's vaults and, eventually, newly produced ceramics were used for remarkable compositions by the likes of Sergei Chekhonin, Ilya Chashnik, Kazimir Malevich, Nicolaj Suetin, Alexandra Shchekotikhina-Pototskaya and others, in a hypothetical attempt to teach the values of the Revolution to the masses.[5] However, between the Russian Revolution and the *100% Make-Up* project lies not just some 70 years of history, but the evolution of capitalism and its commodities – a system of strict rules amongst which cultured exceptions like Alessi could still find a place.

Mendini's own operation became a small census of designers (and artists) who were willing to embrace his rules. Partly inspired by the form of the vase he conceived, many of the decorations referenced ideas close to Mendini's heart, such as human features and bodies. In addition to the vase by Mara Voce (one of Mendini's own pseudonyms), those elements could be found in Yong Ping Huang's vase, which featured an acupuncture chart; the vases decorated by Gabriel Bien-Aimé and Mark Kostabi, both of which had human figures; and also in Riccardo Dalisi's stylised *Pulcinella*.

There were plenty of stand-out patterns: Alighiero Boetti's mix of abstract and figurative marks in *Tutto* (Everything), and many ethnic and neo-ethnic ones by both famous and lesser-known authors including Emmanuel Ekefrey, Aussi Jaffari, Kamba Luesa, Esther Mahlangu, Kivuthi Mbuno, Chéri Samba, Valente Ngwenya Malangatana, Randi Kristensen, Sybilla and many more. Even Robert Venturi expressed himself through a multi-coloured decoration that suggested references to Native American art. However, the project didn't end with the production of the first 10,000 pieces – in a sketch for an exhibition, Mendini envisioned displaying all of them together, highlighting the 'unified vision of a complete industrial series in all its entirety'.[6] He described the process of making the series as an 'aesthetic factory' where the production of pieces was intended as a 'multiplication of their soul, like a sequence of original and similar aesthetic creatures – not mere technical replicas.'[7]

The collection of 100 vases was indeed presented at many exhibitions, first at Florence's Fortezza da Basso, then at the Internationale Frankfurter Messe – the vertical arrangement was designed to highlight the

Alberto Alessi pushes the Standard trolley by Enzo Mari with 100% Make-Up vases, 1992

Ettore Sottsass, Enzo Mari, Andrea Branzi, Mendini and Vico Magistretti in Domus, April 2004

Mendini with his brother Francesco, Milan, 1999

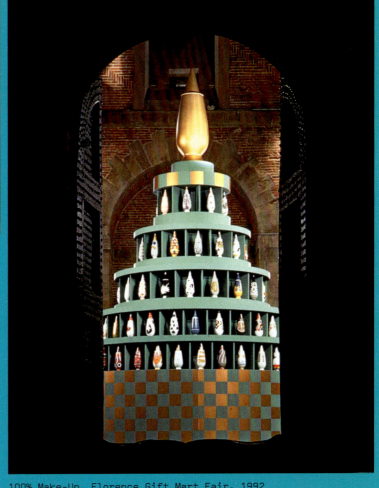

100% Make-Up, Florence Gift Mart Fair, 1992

THE ALESSI CORKSCREW AND THE GLOBAL CITY

monumental nature of the collection. But it was also a turning point for Alessi, marking the company's entry into the porcelain tableware market. The sector was full of possibilities but also challenges: its manufacturing techniques meant it was impossible to ensure consistent high quality across all porcelain pieces in a single production. Yet this didn't deter Alessi. The company produces plates and tableware sets to this day, some of which are still decorated by the same artists and designers who contributed to *100% Make-Up*.[8]

As Mendini envisioned, the project continued to develop. Those vases that had sold the most continued to be produced in an endless series: including designs by Alighiero Boetti, Riccardo Dalisi, Nicola De Maria, Milton Glaser, Michael Graves, Aussi Jaffari, Mark Kostabi, Shiro Kuramata, Kamba Luesa, Sybilla and Robert Venturi, as well as Mendini himself. This series of vases had different prices, despite the fact that they all had been decorated with the same decalcomania technique – Mendini's, which was decorated in pure gold, was the most expensive. But the somewhat arbitrary pricing structure aligned with the spirit of the 'aesthetic factory': if different objects had the same form and were made in the same way, their value lay in their decorative variety. This fusion of theory and design practice created a kind of short-circuit between a Marxist practice/theory relationship and Mendini's vision of a decorative world.[9]

In 2021, on the occasion of the company's centenary (and to mark 90 years since Mendini's birth), as well as to celebrate the importance of *100% Make-Up* in the history of Alessi design, the company produced a version of the vase with the *Proust* armchair pattern in 999 copies, under the supervision of Atelier Mendini. The pattern was still multi-coloured but featured mostly shades of blue and was taken from a drawing made by Mendini in his final years.

FROM THE MILK JUG TO THE CITY: TEA & COFFEE TOWERS

Mendini continued leading design groups all the way into the noughties. At the 2002 Venice Architecture Biennale, he participated in a dual role: as the curator of the *Tea & Coffee Towers* exhibition for Alessi at the Arsenale and as a featured artist in another exhibition on the Naples Metro, an important section of the *Next Cities* exhibition in the Central Pavilion at the Giardini, which I curated. The opportunity for these simultaneous exhibitions arose thanks to Deyan Sudjic, who was the editor-in-chief of *Domus* at the time, as well as the director of the architecture exhibition at the Venice Biennale that year. Sudjic, having conceived of an exhibition that smartly focused on concrete achievements, including details of buildings at a 1:1 scale, suggested that I create space for an Alessi/Mendini exhibition on the theme of the city. Alessi and Mendini accepted our invitation, and for the occasion, they presented part of the results from a second version of *Tea & Coffee Piazza*, which they rebranded *Tea & Coffee Towers*.[10]

Mendini invited 22 architects from different generations, and with different formal styles, to participate in the show. The group consisted of William Alsop, Wiel Arets, Shigeru Ban, Ben van Berkel + Caroline Bos (UNStudio), Gary Chang, David Chipperfield, Denton Corker Marshall, Dezsö Ekler, Massimiliano + Doriana Fuksas, Giorgio Grassi, Jan Kaplicky (Future Systems), Zaha Hadid, Toyo Ito, Tom Kovac, Greg Lynn (Form), Thom Mayne (Morphosis), MVRDV, Juan Navarro Baldeweg, Jean Nouvel, Dominique Perrault, Ricardo Scofidio + Elizabeth Diller and Kazuyo Sejima + Ryue Nishizawa (SANAA). Some of them (including Chipperfield, Massimiliano + Doriana Fuksas and Ito) went on to become successful new designers for Alessi.

The theme chosen for the exhibition was the tower, or high-rise building. Eight towers roughly 8 metres tall were displayed at the Arsenale for the duration of the Biennale, from 8 September to 3 November 2002. In addition to being a successful way to convey Alessi's identity – a model cultural industry that contributed to the global success and reputation of the Italian economy, and could be thought of as the postmodern Olivetti – also marked a small personal victory for Mendini. It challenged the notion that an object cannot have an architectural identity, that architecture is primarily a technical and economic matter, and that emotion – or even aesthetics – cannot exist in its function and symbolic form.[11]

Both the Naples Art Metro project and the exhibition about it for *Next Cities Italy* represented an opportunity for Mendini to quash his image as a mere theoretician and 'imaginist', who was able to conjure up visions but not quite turn them into reality. In fact, several buildings were constructed to his design under the auspices of Atelier Mendini, overseen by both Alessandro and Francesco, who was almost his brother's alter ego: capable of combining overall vision, execution and construction techniques. The *Casa della Felicità* and the Groninger Museum were among their first and most well-known works, but there were plenty of others: the new offices and renovation of the Alessi factory (1993–96), the redevelopment of the Mosaic School in Spilimbergo (1997), the Casino in Arosa (1997), the Quartiere Maghetti in Lugano, Switzerland (1998), the refurbishment of the Ala Mazzoniana at Termini Station in Rome (1999), as well as many commercial and exhibition spaces for Swatch, Bisazza and Safilo, an eyewear company.

THE OBJECT AS AUTOBIOGRAPHY OR SELF-PORTRAIT

Just as every literary work can be seen as an autobiography, so too can we say that over the decades, Mendini's designs increasingly came to represent their creator. Though they were created in a different time, his early sketches and self-portraits reappeared in later years like benevolent ghosts, helping him rediscover his identity through drawing – a medium that for Mendini held the same significance as the written word.

So when Mendini reached the point in his career where he became a designer of bestsellers for Alessi, he chose to make a very personal reference by naming a character after himself, *Alessandro M*, in the form of a corkscrew. It may be one of the more mundane table tools, yet it's filled with imagination and anticipation – after all, it grants access to a bottle's secrets, unlocking them from the well-aged cork that guards them.

Mendini had already made one successful corkscrew in 1994, a lever model in the shape of a stylized woman with arms that lifted up to open the bottle.[12] Named *Anna G* in an obvious reference to Mendini's designer friend Anna Gili, the original design continues to be a popular product. Over the years Mendini has designed many variants, including special *Anna Etoile* editions made from materials (and sold at prices) more associated with jewellery than with tableware.

But it was the *Alessandro M* that truly allowed Mendini to embody his ironic take on his own existence through a potentially infinite series of disguises. The basic model had a body in zamak/resin with a quirky chrome face and hat, and it came in a variety of colours and amusing personalities – another instance of Mendini encouraging low-cost collecting.

From 2003 onwards the *Alessandro M* corkscrew was produced in versions such as *Proust*; *Ghost*, which came complete with sheet and chain; *Delft*, with blue and white Dutch ceramic motifs; *Scozzese* (Scottish) with a tartan kilt and *Pechino* (Peking) with Chinese ideograms. Other designs included *Pinocchio*, *Africa*, *New Age*, *Spaziale* (Space), *Sommelier*, *Svizzero* (Switzerland) and many more. As Mendini noted in a sketch, these were an extension of the ideas he'd had with Swatch and with the *100% Make-Up* project. But with the added self-irony of a designer who was able to present himself as an 'everyday superhero', capable of many disguises. He was a bit like the title character from James Thurber's short story, *The Secret Life of Walter Mitty*: an ordinary man who escaped his everyday routine by daydreaming of being a fighter pilot or a great surgeon, only to find himself in truly adventurous situations.

Mendini's decade-long series of designs and drawings for the *Alessandro M* corkscrew can be read in multiple ways, much like a complex novel. It could be seen as an artistic representation of people's aspiration to be something different from who they are while knowing they are still 'trapped' in their own role, or more prosaically, it could simply be an attempt to increase the iconic value (or the commercial success) of a product by offering it in as many variations as possible.[13] Only Mendini, with his love/hate relationship for objects and design, lightened by his natural sense of humour and an ability not to 'take himself too seriously' (something the great Achille Castiglioni used to warn him about in a friendly way) – and thanks to the steadfast support of Alberto Alessi – could have successfully pulled off such a project and struck such a delicate balance between fun and kitsch.

SMALL, LARGE, EXTRA LARGE

Even though, in the spring of 2018, he was already sick, Mendini kept travelling the world for his professional engagements in the Far East. Yet he could feel that time was slipping by, so he planned two final exhibitions: a great solo show offered to him by the Groninger Museum, which would ultimately open after he died in 2019,[14] and another, perhaps even more important, curated by Aldo Colonetti (in collaboration with Alchimia and his brother Francesco) dedicated to his architecture.

At this second exhibition, which took place in the Sala delle Colonne at Milan's Triennale, visitors were greeted with a Lilliputian city of Mendini's buildings in which they could feel like Gulliver on his travels to unknown and unsettling worlds. The designs in the exhibition included some that had been built as well as others that had been simply hypothesized or fantasized about. The miniature and colourful buildings, resting on bizarre pedestals adorned with 'optica' graphics from the *Merletto* pattern that Mendini had designed for Abet Laminati (the exhibition's main sponsor) were more like parts of a vintage toy train than traditional architectural models.[15]

The forms, colours and materials of the small constructions – acrylic, painted wood and applied graphics, some in neon tones – didn't conform to the neutral, sterile aesthetic codes or the technical and representative language of 'normal' models. They were buildings built 'to scale' but also miniature architectural projects with their own life and function, regardless of whether they had been built or not. They were three-dimensional but projected towards a fourth dimension – or perhaps an altogether different space-time continuum. Their independent, complete meanings could only be deciphered in light of Mendini's sophisticated aesthetics and his many long years of work.

This exhibition brought to mind Aldo Rossi's description of his experience of visiting the statue of San Carlo (the Colossus of San Carlo Borromeo) in Arona, which he repeatedly portrayed in his drawings. Rossi, who had a relationship of 'continuously interrupted conversation' with Mendini, wrote about it in his wonderful book, *Autobiografia Scientifica* (A Scientific Autobiography) – the ideal testament of a left-wing, intellectual architect of a similar calibre to Mendini:

As with the Homeric horse, the pilgrim enters the body of the saint as he would a tower or a wagon steered by a knowing technician. After he mounts the exterior stair of the pedestal, the steep ascent through the interior of the body reveals the structure of the work and the welded seams of the huge pieces of sheet metal. Finally, he arrives at the interior-exterior of the head; from the eyes of the saint, the view of the lake acquires infinite contours, as if one were gazing from a celestial observatory.[16]

Enlarging and shrinking – themes used, of course, by Jonathan Swift in *Gulliver's Travels* – are both powerful narrative devices. In Mendini's own ideal 'scaled-down' world at the exhibition at the Triennale, drawings, buildings, objects, containers and contents, signs and symbols, all met and clashed democratically. Some of Mendini's sculptural pieces (such as the *Lassù* chair and the *Proust* armchair) were also on display in miniature versions that, paradoxically, increased their monumental and symbolic weight. Conversely, models of his buildings often looked like 1:1 prototypes of utensils or furniture: the stunning Fincantieri ferry models are perhaps the best examples of this. These models helped define a relationship of reciprocal usefulness between the different scales of design: what Rem Koolhaas called, unironically, *S, M, L, XL* (Small, Medium, Large and Extra Large) in his 1995 book of that title.

In this sense, there's a curious coincidence in the text that appeared in *Casabella* in 1997 in which Mendini distinguished Italy's aesthetic attitude ('of beauty and

Tea & Coffee Towers for Alessi by Alessandro and Francesco Mendini, Triennale di Milano, 2003

La Punta pavilion by Alessandro and Francesco Mendini for the Seoul Design Fair, Seoul, South Korea, 2010

Render of La Punta pavilion, 2010

THE ALESSI CORKSCREW AND THE GLOBAL CITY

of ritual') from the 'miniaturist' mode of representation that was historically more prevalent in the East than the West. An example of this attitude can be seen in a quote from Orhan Pamuk's 1998 novel, *Benim adım Kırmızı* (My Name is Red), set among the Turkish miniaturists of the 16th century, in which the reader can literally enter the meanings of the images: 'I don't want to be a tree, I want to be its meaning' says a painted miniature tree, one of the book's many narrators.[17] But it's not the same for Mendini's 'volumetric miniatures'.

Like his drawings, which often were only isometric or frontal, Mendini's models concealed a concave dimension that was inaccessible to the physical senses and reserved for the imagination. This content was precious precisely because it was unreachable. The models were more like Wunderkammer oddities (a concept that Mendini held dear), or 'locked room mysteries', the always fascinating trope of crime and noir novels. Their secrets were impossible to access because the entrances to these models were so small that once again they brought to mind Gulliver or, better still, *Alice in Wonderland*.

THE GREAT KOREAN SEASON

Mendini's relationship with South Korea was complex and fascinating. Over the last years of his life, the country played host to most of his activity as an architect, and partly also as an ironic and playful industrial designer. Most of the significant building commissions he designed in South Korea were based on a delicate balance between physical reality and sensory perception. This balance was also visible in *Tender architecture,* one of the first 'scaled down' architecture models made by Mendini in 1982 with Studio Alchimia (as an installation for Alcantara, at the Contemporary Art Pavilion in Milan). This was both a reminder of the importance of so-called 'primary design'[18] and of how much light and colour – often blended – were crucial in attracting and convincing clients.

Beyond the obvious importance of his reputation as an established master of 'Made in Italy' design, one reason his work successfully took root in such a different context can be explained by certain shared traits between his aesthetic of the 'banal' and the local design culture. One such example is the custom of meeting in *bangs*[19] (Korean for 'rooms'): small spaces rented by the hour, widespread in big cities, where people meet with friends and their wider family. Set in buildings of all kinds, the facades of these *bangs* are punctuated with colourful neon, which – just like one of Venturi's decorated sheds – indicates the purpose of the space within: social gathering (*da-bang*), karaoke (*norae-bang*), sauna (*jjimjil-bang*), cinema (*video-bang*), and so on. These spaces are important from both a financial and societal point of view, and they also represent an ambivalence typical of Korean society: on the one hand, a desire to protect the intimacy of family and domesticity, but on the other, a need to externalize one's identity.

Mendini's buildings were also often photographed only from the outside. With the exception of the Groninger Museum and a few other buildings, it is rare to find images depicting their interiors. This was also true of the projects built in South Korea, where this 'masking' of architecture took on a peculiar connotation. The tendency to liquify, distribute and externalize the living space that can be observed in the *bang* is typical of traditional Korean architecture.[20] It is interesting in this sense to compare the traditional Western courtyard – a 'solid' with clear outlines and a noticeable division between interior and exterior – with the equally traditional and corresponding space of the *madang*, an 'expandable fluid' that is more dynamic and blurred at the edges. Mendini's Korean projects combine these two characteristics. Like his models – or Western courtyards – they are closed and clearly contained volumes, but like the *madang* and *bang*, their contents – whether easy or complicated, immediate or profound – spill outwards, opening themselves up to free variations and associations of meaning, creating stories, dreams, signs, colours and references in their shapes and their facades.

For instance, the models for the projects built in Korea can appear as things as diverse as: a playful arrangement of letters and stackable volumes (as in the headquarters for the Triennale di Milano, Incheon, 2009); a kaleidoscope that references Ferrara's Palazzo dei Diamanti (as in *La Punta*, Olympic Stadium, Seoul, 2010); a lift to the moon (as in

Panoramic Tower, Suncheon Bay National Garden, Suncheon, 2018); or an anvil disguised as a harlequin (the office building for Fursys Furniture Company, Chung Ju, 2018). Extracting meaning from them was a game of continuous variation, like trying to interpret the shapes of passing clouds. Through his reflective and self-reflective texts, Mendini fuelled the myth of his own work as a great, moving 'unreal and dusty nebula',[21] where design is, above all, thought ('the designer's goal should not be to design objects, but rather to think about them').

Geographically far but intellectually close to home, even in his mid-eighties Mendini went on long journeys through Korea, because he was irresistibly attracted by the possibility of pushing his design research to its limits.[22] One could say that he turned his decorative and compositional poetics inside out, as if he was removing an intricate, multi-coloured glove. Meanwhile, he delved deeply into both the Western tradition of modern architecture, offering organic, angular shapes, exposed to the blinding light of his spectacular vision, and also the world of dreams and memory that exist between shadow and half-light in Asian culture.

In summary, he put forward his own New-New International Style. In some ways, this was reminiscent of what Sottsass and Memphis had attempted thirty years before, but they never succeeded in turning it into reality by building real architecture. Mendini's 'Korean' language, by contrast, was perfect for the globalization – and therefore the banalization – of the contemporary world, as a homage, or rather a reinterpretation, of Robert Venturi's 'decorated shed'. In doing so, Mendini closed a semi-secular circle between the West and the East, bringing him back to the future to his golden expressive era of the 1980s – but this time triumphantly on an urban scale.

149.

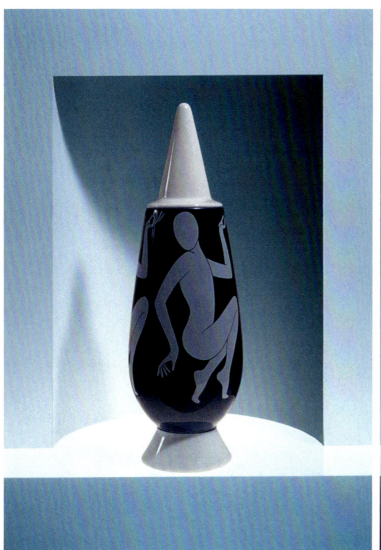

150.

151.

149. *100% Make-Up* vase for Alessi Tendentse, decoration by Mendini, 1992
150. *100% Make-Up* vase for Alessi Tendentse, decoration by Mark Kostabi, 1992
151. *100% Make-Up* vase for Alessi Tendentse, decoration by Robert Venturi, 1992

152.

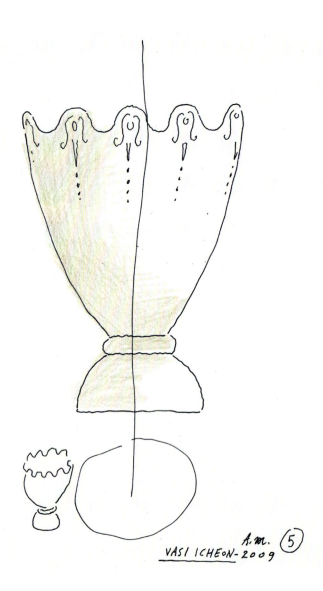

153.

152. Icheon vase, Celadon ceramic vase, Interart Gallery Seoul, South Korea, 2009
153. Icheon vase, drawing, 2009
154. Icheon vase, Celadon ceramic vase, Interart Gallery Seoul, South Korea, 2009
155. *Vaso Utopico*, white ceramic vase with pure gold decorations, 1994

154.

CHAPTER 9

155.

156.

157.

156. Headquarters of the Triennale di Milano (now offices and headquarters of a Korean television broadcaster), Incheon, South Korea, drawing, 2009
157. Cha Bio Complex: entrance to the Cha Health Systems Hospital by Alessandro and Francesco Mendini, Seoul, South Korea, 2015

158.
158. *La Punta* pavilion for the Seoul Design Fair,
 Olympic Stadium, Seoul, South Korea, model, 2010
159. *La Punta* pavilion for the Seoul Design Fair, drawing, 2010

159.

160.
161. *Alessandro M & Anna G Orchestra*, musical carillon for Alessi, 2003
162. *Alessandro M & Anna G* corkscrews for Alessi, new colourways, 2021

160. Outfit variations for the *Alessandro M* corkscrew for Alessi, drawing by Giovanna Molteni, 2009

161.

162.

THE ALESSI CORKSCREW AND THE GLOBAL CITY 233

163.

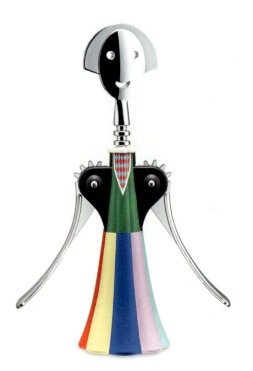

164.

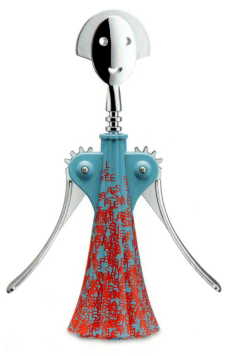

165.

163. *Anna G: Arborea* corkscrew by Mendini (2014) decorated by Fulvia Mendini for Alessi, 2024
164. *Anna G: Parade* corkscrew by Mendini (2014) decorated by Arthur Arbesser for Alessi, 2024
165. *Anna G: Liquid* corkscrew by Mendini (2014) decorated by Studio Temp for Alessi, 2024
166. *Alessandro M: Arborea* corkscrew by Mendini (2014) decorated by Fulvia Mendini for Alessi, 2024
167. *Alessandro M: Parade* corkscrew by Mendini (2014) decorated by Arthur Arbesser for Alessi, 2024
168. *Alessandro M: Liquid* corkscrew by Mendini (2014) decorated by Studio Temp for Alessi, 2024

166.

167.

168.

THE ALESSI CORKSCREW AND THE GLOBAL CITY 235

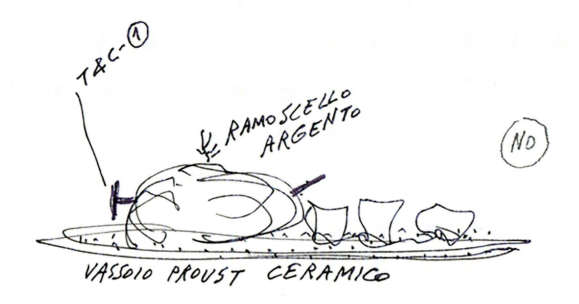

169.

170.

171.

169. *Tea & Coffee Towers* for Alessi, drawing, 2002
170. *Tea & Coffee Towers* for Alessi, drawing, 2002
171. *Tutta* office chair for Iloom, drawing, 2015-2016

THE ALESSI CORKSCREW AND THE GLOBAL CITY

172.

173.

172. *Linea* cabinets for Porro, 2015 (released 2023)
173. Dormitory for furniture company Iloom-Fursys by Alessandro and Francesco Mendini, Chung Ju, South Korea, model, 2018
174. Office building for Iloom-Fursys by Alessandro and Francesco Mendini, Chung Ju, South Korea, model, 2018
175. Decoration for the facade of the Iloom-Fursys headquarters by Alessandro and Francesco Mendini, Chung Ju, South Korea, render, 2018

CHAPTER 9   238

174.

175.

THE ALESSI CORKSCREW AND THE GLOBAL CITY 239

176.

176. *The Bird of Flower* sculpture for Suncheon Bay National Garden, South Korea, drawing, 2016
177. *Torre Panoramica* (Panoramic Tower) for Suncheon Bay National Garden, South Korea
by Alessandro and Francesco Mendini, model, 2018
overleaf: *Margaret and Thomas More: Utopia Island*, drawing, 2015

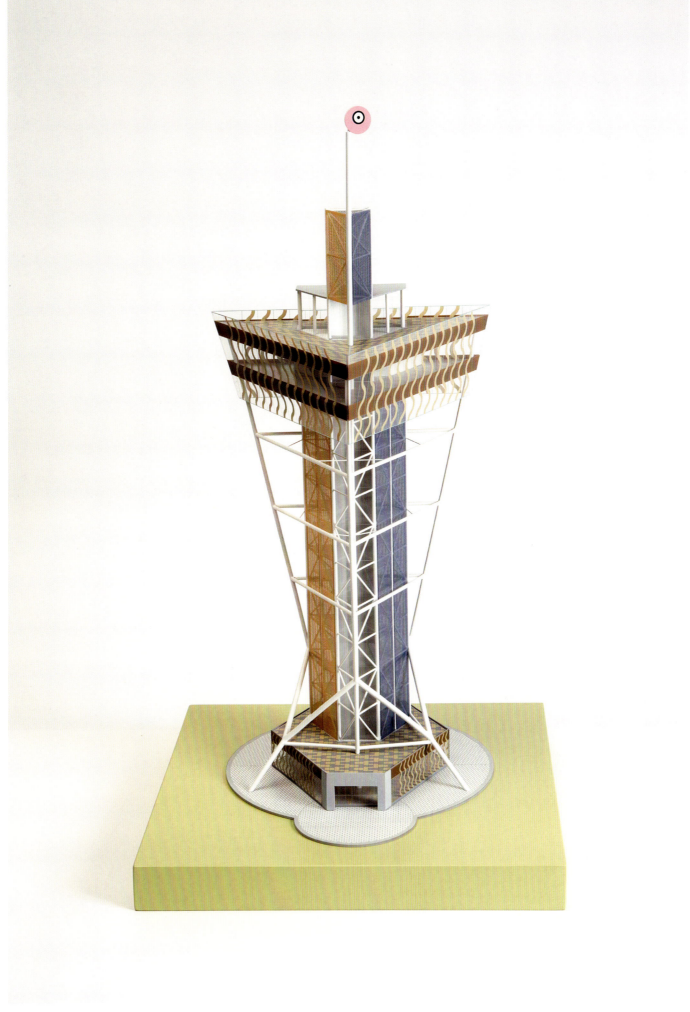

177.

THE END AS AN ETERNAL RETURN: LIGHT, COLOUR AND BACK TO DOMUS

AT THE END OF THE PATH, LIGHT AND COLOUR

It is said that Johann Wolfgang von Goethe's last words were *Mehr licht* (More light). Whatever his actual reasons for uttering them – whether a simple request for another candle in his room or as a last wish to enter the divine light – it is tempting to read those words as a reflection of Goethe's talent and his intellectual curiosity about both human experience and the physical universe. His genius is, after all, what led him to become both one of the founders of the psychological novel when he wrote *Die Leiden des jungen Werthers* (The Sorrows of Young Werther) and also the author of a foundational theory of colours.[1]

Similarly, one could say that in his final years, Alessandro Mendini pursued greater clarity, both in expression and presentation. His yearning for 'more light' was not just philosophical but also physical, embodied in his most significant artistic medium: colour. Mendini revisited colour throughout his projects – albeit more practically than theoretically – right up until his last days.

A progressive Italian intellectual with Mitteleuropean influences, Mendini was also a sharp critic of Western society and its conventions. Over a long career that spanned countless theories and practices, he explored everything from political analysis to urban planning, and from painting to striking aphorisms. Yet, as the years went by, his work became increasingly autobiographical and introspective. Like Proust, he constantly reinterpreted both his craft and his life, channeling the insights he gained into his works, especially his artistic works, which became extensions of his personal identity.

This is why the multicoloured *Proust* pattern, used across his works, took on symbolic significance beyond any commercial value. Mendini playfully distorted it, stretched it to the extreme, shrank it, and explored all possible brushstroke variants and permutations – all to create new vibrations of luminous colour. Even when he was working on the surfaces of buildings or on artistic compositions, such as in his collaborations with Peter Halley (notably for the 2013 exhibition at New York's Mary Boone Gallery), Mendini chose to 'paint' with just a few large fields of colour – a restraint reminiscent of the principle of colour that he had long been experimenting with for the *Proust* patterns.

To define the value and meaning of this continuous experimentation, and to explain the prominence of colour in his work, Mendini engaged in a deeper reflection for an interview/essay that acted as a foreword to *Alessandro Mendini: 30 Colours*[2] – the sample book which he asked me to curate (together with Atelier Mendini) for AkzoNobel, a Dutch paint manufacturing company. The volume was not only a project about colour but also a book-object: the pages perfectly replicated the finishes of the colour range, which had been conceived by Mendini, and served as a practical tool – though the preciousness of the book would almost certainly prevent its readers from tearing out a page to show a decorator.

Mendini named the colours after various inspirations: places he had visited (Sinai Grey, Africa Red, Hollywood Pink); artists he admired (Shama Yellow,[3] Malevič Black) and cherished projects (Galla Placidia Blue, Groningen Gold, Proust Lilac). They were accompanied by quotes and poetic verses that Mendini and I chose together and which evoked the feelings the hues evoked for us, as well as ideas of how they might be used. For instance, Shama Yellow had a fitting quote from Theo Van Doesburg and Cornelis van Eesteren:

We have established the true and rightful place of colour in architecture and thus we declare that painting without architectural construction (which is to say, easel painting) no longer has any reason to exist.[4]

Nor was the dramatic dimension of artistic work missing from Mendini's references. He didn't shy away from confronting it directly; as colour for Van Gogh expressed deeper emotions, here Mendini's Meteora Black speaks to that same intensity:

You will notice that this combination of red-ochre, green darkened by grey and black markings around the edges evokes something of the anxiety of those who, like me, are prey to this fate, and it's called red-black.[5]

It was the design and production of the *Proust* armchair that had given Mendini his initial insight into the infinite possibilities of the chromatic spectrum. This helped shape the relationship of his design poetics to colour, a theme that he discussed explicitly in the foreword to the book:

> *Q. In your research from the 1970s onwards, during the so-called 'radical' period, your projects focused on conceptual tones that essentially excluded colour. At a certain point though, colour exploded into your work – particularly with the* Proust *armchair, which became a sort of 'manifesto' for your new poetic and practical approach. How much was this transition planned?*
>
> *A. The first time I really engaged with colour was in fact with the* Proust *armchair. It coincided with the creation of furniture inspired by Kandinsky, which were made in the same month along with the Kandissi sofa. So Kandinsky, Cubism and Futurism were all involved in the sofa; Divisionism and Pointillism for the* Proust *armchair. It's true that this piece became a sort of manifesto, not only for the use of colour, but also for a particular design approach. On the one hand […] it proved that my approach is more literary than formal, but on the other hand it's a sort of kaleidoscopic, atmospheric attempt: it's about considering the object not as a complete thing but as an element among other elements, and about relying more on the sensations of light, on material systems and colour systems than on precise compositional design elements.*[6]

This 'atmospheric' concept of design, often described as a 'cloud' or 'nebula', was a recurring feature in Mendini's thoughts and writings. When he donated 2,469 of his drawings to the Triennale di Milano, the exhibition of them was fittingly titled *Pulviscoli* (Particles).[7] The term aligns with the meticulous images Mendini created on his famous A4 sheets, usually with his favourite Tratto pen. The word also brings to mind the question – famous and fundamental to physics – of why light seems to act like both a particle and a wave.

> Every project, drawing and object designed by Mendini can be viewed as part of a vast fractal system. Fractals, which can be found in many places in nature – from mountain ranges to Romanesco broccoli – are geometric shapes that repeat the same way on different scales. Zooming in on any detail reveals a form similar to the original. In essence, his vast, almost Borges-like body of drawings could be seen as a miniature universe (or perhaps part of a multiverse), composed of these 'particles' through which Mendini redefined his world – a world where light and colour played a central role.

At the height of his career, when the world's top luxury brands – from Swarovski and Bisazza to Venini and Cartier – commissioned pieces from him, his finest work was that which explored the theme of light and colour. His collaborations with Bisazza on both surface design and sculptural objects were perhaps the best-known and longest-lasting on the topic. But even when working with Swarovski, Mendini managed to craft objects that, through precise cutting – a technique patented by founder Daniel Swarovski in 1892 – achieved an intrinsic, multicoloured brilliance.

> His limited-edition 1988 centrepiece, the most imposing piece among those he designed for the Austrian crystal house, was a kaleidoscope in itself, thanks to its infinite facets. After all, what is crystal if not a material that concentrates and refracts light?[8] Its remarkable physical quality generates colour in its entire spectrum and Mendini harnessed this in various projects. A prime example is the iridescent sphere he designed, which was first shown inside the Torre Paradiso in Hiroshima and later added to the collection of the Groninger Museum.

Unlike other industrial or artisanal materials, crystal cannot be poured, cast, moulded or shaped; it can only be sculpted from a single block through the long, patient work of the master cutter. This quality of craftsmanship fascinated Mendini and is beautifully reflected in his Swarovski pieces, which prompted the designer to rethink manual craftsmanship and challenged observers to grasp the sometimes blurred boundaries between industrial and artisanal production.

Mendini with Morris Lapidus at the Futurists of Today conference, Miami, 1999

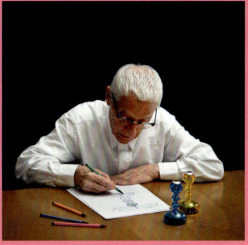
Mendini sketching with Campanello Ramun, Milan, 2015

Mendini with Enzo Mari, Milan, 2010

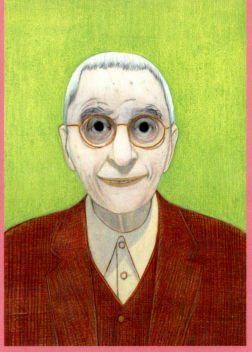
Mendini portrait by Lorenzo Mattotti, 2011

Mendini's relationship with Venini started in 1988 and lasted almost 30 years, until his last design for them in 2016: another centrepiece, this time for the Byblos Art Hotel. The company presented him with the opportunity to explore glass's expressive potential in an interweaving of technique and colour. His work for them ranged from classic vases to elaborate compositions for floor and suspension lighting fixtures such as the 1993 *Galassia* (Galaxy) series, each of which evoked an imaginary celestial body, and the luminous *Colonne* (Column) in 2013.[9]

This exploration of materials and light extended to his collaboration with Cartier, where he created large-scale sculptures for themed exhibitions at the Fondation Cartier pour l'Art Contemporain in Paris. In the late 1990s, Mendini forged a mutual admiration and cultural connection with Hervé Chandès, the refined intellectual who became the director of the institution in 1994. The foundation, housed in a building designed by Jean Nouvel, became a space for artistic and design experimentation, independent of Maison Cartier's collection (as extensive as that was). Instead, it gave space to great authors with different kinds of expertise, from fashion designer Issey Miyake to philosopher Paul Virilio.

The first exhibition that Chandès entrusted to Mendini was *Fragilisme* (Fragility)[10] in 2002, in which Mendini was joined by two younger artists, Vincent Beaurin – who would become a close friend and collaborator – and Fabrice Domercq. At such a great scale, Mendini's works and ideas stood out: after all, he was both the inspirer and protagonist of the theme of fragility. For the occasion, Bisazza produced a giant mosaic version of the *Proust* armchair as well as the *Chiesetta* (Little Church), which had previously been presented in Naples for Arteinmosaico in 1996. Meanwhile, Venini crafted the *Guerrier de Verre* (Glass Warrior) sculpture: a large anthropomorphic head in red glass, adorned with gold and diamond inlays, in a limited series of 36 pieces that were all shown at the Fondation.

In 2010, the sculpture, with some formal variations and in a more delicate colour scheme, was reissued by Venini in an edition of nine copies and renamed *Angelo Guerriero* (Warrior Angel). Its mysterious physiognomy (and gender-fluid decorative elements, such as the first head's gold hoop earrings, and the second head's stone pendants) remained and increasingly returned in the last years of Mendini's work, acting as a continuous portrait – or self-portrait – in the name of colour. The material itself became less important: these 'portraits' could even be made of papier mâché, like his *Neo Malevic* head from 2008, which deliberately referenced the chromatic compositions of faceless human figures from the later works of the father of Suprematism. Mendini himself was capable of transitioning seamlessly between ordinary and precious materials, much like the secret of the alchemist described by Jung:

The material which contains the divine spirit is everywhere, even in the human body. It is cheap and you can find it everywhere, even in the most repulsive matter.[11]

In 2009, Cartier asked him to create a sculpture for the important contemporary art fair Art Basel. The *Colonne Cartier* was shown in the *Salon Precieux* curated by the Atelier. It was over 2.3 metres tall and was made from production offcuts, including precious stones: diamonds, emeralds, sapphires, rubies, tourmalines, amethysts, garnets and other gemstones, chosen and arranged by their colour, were set inside crystal cylinders framed by gold edges (23 kg of gold in total) at a total weight of 720 kg and inestimable value. The *Colonne Cartier* could be seen as another huge kaleidoscope, an object/space of colour and light that reflected a painterly artistic soul, just as Mendini would have liked to be remembered.

BACK TO DOMUS: THE NEW UTOPIA

At the beginning of the 2010s, the cultural identity of the new millennium was struggling to take shape. Fears about the approach of the year 2000 – digital collapse, the end of the Internet, and the end of the world – had been proven unfounded, but the global economic crisis of 2008 upended both markets and social life. The subprime mortgage crisis, the collapse of Lehman Brothers and the resulting recession created a chain reaction which forced governments and businesses alike to rethink their financial prospects.[12]

In Italy, the impact of this global crisis was delayed due to various factors, but the need for a new cultural perspective still felt pressing. In the context of a world where the viral dominance of social media had not yet taken over, the idea of relaunching a print magazine like *Domus* – which had successfully navigated the turbulent waters of the 2000s – was important not only for the Editoriale Domus company but for the wide professional and cultural audience that the magazine catered to – from industries to architects, designers and decision-makers.

Among the publisher's options was the decision to appoint a new editor-in-chief, a role that typically lasted about five years. However, given the economic uncertainty of 2010, there seemed to be room for a shorter, more experimental relaunch of the magazine. This led to the exceptional, if not unique, case of a former editor, Mendini, being called back to lead the magazine at an advanced age. I served as his deputy editor (a role I had held since 2000), supported by a highly professional editorial team[13] eager to collaborate with a master of both design and publishing.

Mendini's vision for this new series, which was slated to last only for 11 'collectable' issues, from April 2010 to March 2011, can be summarized by its subtitle 'The New Utopia', which appeared on the cover underneath the historic *Domus* logo. For Mendini, it was a recurring theme of reflection during those years. He drew inspiration from the dramatic figure of Thomas More, the greatest philosopher and humanist of the English Renaissance, a writer and the inventor of this most cited and debated imaginary place in modern and contemporary history: Utopia. More's unwavering commitment to his beliefs led to his execution under King Henry VIII, in 1535.

With a bold shift of perspective, Mendini, in a 2015 essay, imagined Thomas More as an urban planner[14] (a tragic figure even 500 years ago) for his detailed descriptions of Utopia, which was inspired by the ideal of an egalitarian and just society and which had been illustrated in More's book with a map by Hans Holbein. More's vision of an ideal, egalitarian, and just society was less a matter of censorship for its anti-monarchic stance than a disagreement over religious issues, which were, at the time, deeply political. Less dramatically, when reflecting on the ideal of a contemporary utopia, Mendini summarized its meaning in an interview with *la Repubblica* newspaper a year later:

> *History has often challenged and spectacularly disproved the realization of utopias. But not the idea of utopia itself. To achieve something meaningful, we must aim for an unreachable goal. This is utopia. We need to have the sensitivity to reach far in order to get closer. It's not a grand theory. I'd call it more of a method.*[15]

This 'method' – along with his professionalism and vast experience in leading magazines – formed the basis of Mendini's cultural statements and operational guidelines for developing the new edition of *Domus*. In his handwritten notes and reflections, always penned on A4 sheets in his familiar handwriting, he outlined his 'Theoretical Guidelines' as follows:

Languages for a romantic utopia
Search for   *Authors*
                   Things
                   Situations
                   Products
                   Researches that have:
                             meaning
                             availability
                             a thought
                             a utopia
Humanistic Ideals
Psychology of Living

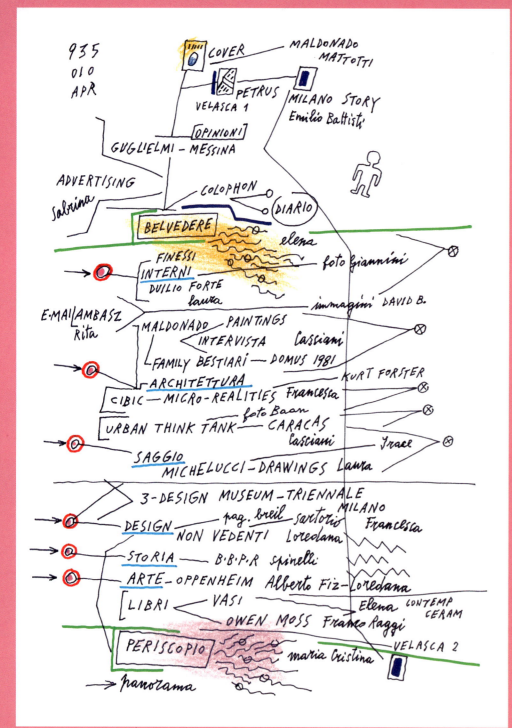

Plan for Domus issue 935, drawing, 2010

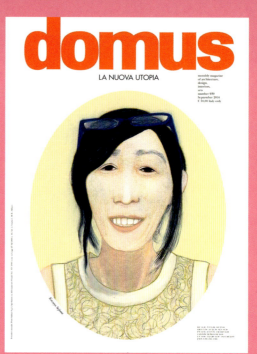

Kazuyo Sejima portrait by Lorenzo Mattotti on Domus issue 939, 2010

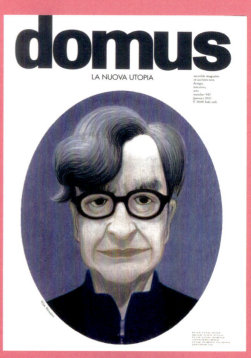

Wim Wenders portrait by Lorenzo Mattotti on Domus issue 943, 2011

Mendini developed the magazine's new graphic design with *Domus*'s longtime art director Giuseppe Basile,[16] who had extensive experience in transforming the magazine quickly and effectively. He proposed essentially lightening the visual layout, making it more fluid and less cluttered in order to provide a broader reading experience, as follows:

> *Start with the current design with the aim of decluttering it*
> *Reduce the number of themes and images*
> *Use wide white margins and only full bleed images as an exception*
> *Incorporate black-and-white images*
> *In general, shorten the length of texts*[17]

The cover was the feature that had the most continuity with Mendini's editorship from the 1980s. Each issue featured a portrait by the artist and illustrator Lorenzo Mattotti – most of which were of an author, architect, artist, designer or other creative that I had interviewed inside the magazine.[18] Mattotti, who had been recommended by Giuseppe Basile and approved by Mendini, was known for his ability to capture both a realistic likeness and a person's character.

The portrait series opened with Tomás Maldonado[19] (who had already appeared on one of Mendini's *Domus* covers in the 80s) on issue 935, followed by Jean Nouvel, Odile Decq, Sigmund Freud, Kazuyo Sejima, Andrea Zittel, Riccardo Dalisi, Peter Cook, Wim Wenders, Nathalie Djurberg and Maurizio Cattelan. These individuals were more than just well-known names: their interviews and features in the magazine delved into their work and its impact on design culture. Together, they represented a balanced snapshot of the artistic landscape of the 2010s and beyond, with a notable inclusion of women creatives, a few legendary masters, and occasional forays into other fields. That was the case with the long interview with Wim Wenders,[20] which focused on the relationship between his cinematic vision, the city and the buildings he considered to be protagonists in his films (for example, the Centre Pompidou in *The American Friend*).

The magazine's new edition was a huge success, both in terms of increased advertising revenue, and also among its readership. The idea of a 'collector's item' as the editor's promotion described it, was attractive to both long-time, loyal readers of *Domus* and new ones, who both appreciated the development of its content, its grasp on a rapidly changing world and the pluralism of its opinions. In contrast to the 1980s, when it had been important for Mendini to seek out fresh voices to break away from a stale, overly technical mainstream (particularly in Italy's 'archi-speak' with texts cloaked in deliberately obscure language), thirty years later – amid the chaos of advanced postmodernity, or what could perhaps even be called post-humanity – *Domus* embraced a multiplicity of voices, even dissonant ones.

The magazine's content encompassed everything from emails by long-term friend Emilio Ambasz reflecting on the past and future of architecture, to the refined reflections of Italo Rota, who analyzed projects such as Freud's historical houses in Vienna and Pierre Chareau's Maison de Verre, a house and office for Dr Jean Dalsace. Architect Maurizio Corrado wrote about high-sustainability projects, while Franco Purini, a key figure in 1970s and 80s 'drawn architecture', weighed in on the theme of longevity. Mendini, always open to both external and internal input, played an active role in all decisions, listening attentively to everyone. For the graphic presentation of content, he relied heavily on Giuseppe Basile, ensuring each piece had the best possible design.

For Mendini, this was one of the most exciting and enjoyable parts of his work: in fact, he could often be found at the art desk rather than in his editor's office. The two areas were separated by the large editorial floor, which publisher Giovanna Mazzocchi had redesigned into an open-plan layout. By then 80 years old, Mendini still paced the floor briskly, sometimes stopping along the way to briefly discuss a story with an editor, or simply to make a polite gesture, such as offering the sweets that he brought to meetings with the team.

Mendini combined this old-school, gentlemanly approach to work with deep intellectual reflection on design, which the magazine allowed him to explore. As he jokingly stated in his first editor's letter, he didn't want to 'fall into the trap' of writing editor's letters that could easily sound rhetorical. He preferred to call his contributions his *Diario* (Diary). Here, he would mix personal reflections, psychological themes and memories with statements on the future of architecture and design. In his first *Diario* entry, he offered an explanation on the choice of 'New Utopia':

I asked myself: why, after so many years (30) are you going back to Domus? The answer is: because I am a utopian. That is: my utopia is that us designers should return to being utopian. In order to work seriously on this idea, Domus *is the ideal platform, thanks to its history, its vocation.*[21]

In the January 2011 issue, the third-to-last before stepping down as editor-in-chief, Mendini revisited the theme of utopia in a poetic way by quoting a passage from Oscar Wilde. It was perhaps an unexpected choice for an author known for being critical and sarcastic, but in Mendini's hands it perfectly aligns with the 'languages of romantic utopia' he outlined in his own notes for the new editorial project.

A map of the world that does not include Utopia is not worth even glancing at, for it leaves out the one country at which Humanity is always landing. And when Humanity lands there, it looks out, and, seeing a better country, sets sail. Progress is the realization of Utopias.[22]

During the intense and fast-paced few months at the helm of *Domus*, Mendini had an important opportunity to check the theoretical and critical hypotheses that he had expressed in the magazine against his inclusive design method: the exhibition *Quali Cose Siamo* (The Things That We Are). The show opened in April 2010 at Milan's Triennale, the third in a decade-long cycle curated by then-director of the Triennale, Silvana Annicchiarico.[23]

The exhibition was very different from conventional design shows, which often lack creative flair, due to its strong encyclopedic and humorous character. Encyclopedic, because it gathered around 800 objects – a far cry from the restraint typically employed by museums and curators – sampling Mendini's many intellectual curiosities and the breadth of his connections with designers and producers. And humorous, because Mendini, together with French designer Pierre Charpin, presented a densely packed panorama of pieces from varied origins, democratically juxtaposed without any thematic or stylistic criteria, only guided by his free associations. This approach brings to mind a Freudian technique where the patient of psychoanalysis is asked to relate all ideas and words that come into their mind, without conscious control.

Thus, a plaster mould of Michelangelo's *David* (meant to demonstrate the potential of Italian craftmanship when paired with digital technology) sat next to items such as: a huge Campari bottle designed by artist Fortunato Depero; an oversized woman's shoe by Ferragamo; one of Achille Castiglioni's jackets; and a precious set of sixteenth-century armour from the Museum Poldi Pezzoli (similar to the one we showed at the exhibition *La Fabbrica dell'Arte* at Copenhagen's Louisiana Museum in 1996). There were Lenci ceramic dolls from the late 1920s by Helen Koenig Scavini; a deconstructivist lamp by Gino Sarfatti for his factory Arteluce; a moulded chair by Palomba Serafini Associati for Crassevig; Maurizio Cattelan's large *objet trouvé*/impossible armchair *Rocchetto* for Dilmos; and a nude portrait of Ettore Sottsass painted by Roberto Sambonet. And on it went throughout the halls of the great wing of the Triennale building designed by Giovanni Muzio.

Amusement and enjoyment was guaranteed by the juxtapositions of scale, style, era, authentic paintings like a piece by Felice Casorati, and ambiguous sculptures such as Gianni Piacentino's useless vehicles, an enormous ceramic stove by Thun, and Gaetano Pesce's *Montanara* sofa/landscape. Very famous designers were placed next to the work of those who were barely known or simply forgotten by the official history of design.

Mendini at Wunderkammer Design exhibition curated by Peter Weiss, Neues Museum Nürnberg, Nuremberg, Germany, 2011

The Futurists of Today conference, Miami, 1999

Mendini with grandsons Tommaso and Michele, 2014

THE END AS AN ETERNAL RETURN: LIGHT, COLOUR AND BACK TO DOMUS

Beyond the undeniable, surprising spectacle of the exhibition – which prompted critic Alice Rawsthorn to write in the *New York Times* 'I have lost count of how many designers have hailed *Quali Cose Siamo* as one of the best design exhibitions they have ever seen'[24] – Mendini's deeper intent became clear to those who knew him well. He believed that we are the things with which we have had, or continue to have, a relationship of some kind: functional, emotional or other. And the objects themselves – whether they are industrial products, unique pieces of high value or cheap souvenirs – become part of us, sometimes as part of our living environment, but certainly also our memory and worldview. This was not merely a literary or narrative idea, but one that should be considered when designing or simply narrating the true history and essence of objects, as Mendini tried to do in the final series of *Domus* and his *Diario*.

His last 'non-editor's letter' for the magazine – written on 15 February 2011, and published in issue 945 – was very long, which went against his original prescription. It was undoubtedly an emotional farewell to the readers, to the editorial team ('with no hierarchy, in alphabetical order') and to publisher Giovanna Mazzocchi. But it was also a reaffirmation of the goal to define a New Utopia.

In this final instalment of the *Diario*, Mendini revealed himself. He laid himself bare as he was no longer bound by any fair-play or professional courtesy. He described many of his tics or superstitious habits, which any writer – including myself – holds in high regard.

Now I slowly drink my fairtrade Darjeeling tea, the black breakfast variety in white, unprinted teabags. I am sitting on a chair designed by Mario Botta, made for the 700th anniversary of the Swiss Confederation [...] I need to focus, really focus, I need my brain to work, to understand what to say, to explain what I have done this year at Domus. I have my own psycho-gymnastic technique to slow the rhythm of my thoughts when I need to write [...] It involves walking around the house, doing circuits of the three identical round tables in the living room, kitchen and library, made of lacquered white fiberglass, designed by Eero Aarnio [...] A year ago, I said 'Utopia is the bone that Mickey Mouse dangles in front of Pluto's nose to make him run and dream'. I took the occasion to dangle that bone in front of my readers for a while. I wanted to prioritize a historical perspective over current affairs, perhaps, calling it the New Utopia. A puzzle of utopias devised by many committed scholars and critics. Yes. Now my mind is ready to write, just a little more to go.[25]

ESCAPE AND DESIRE, THE AFTER-ME

In order to make his mark in the highly individualist and competitive world of international architecture and design, Mendini couldn't afford to ignore the construction of his own myth. And he was very successful in this – from his early break with Radical design to his eventual global fame (though not always matched by professional success), he carefully built his reputation.

At the same time, he was driven by a deep desire not to abandon his vocation as a critical, progressive intellectual – a philosophical artist striving to analyze the contradictions of modern and postmodern culture. With sharp, sometimes cynical insight, he sought to understand the reasons and causes behind the unpredictable phenomena he witnessed, despite his sense of powerlessness in the face of society's great transformations.

This bitter lesson had, for almost a century, distracted architects and designers – more Enlightenment thinkers than Modernists – from focusing on the artistic quality of their work. From the Steintor Bus Station in Hannover (1994) to the Naples Metro projects, from redeveloping industrial areas in Milan's Bovisa district (2010), to numerous public buildings in Seoul, Suncheon, and Gwangju (2008–19), Mendini returned to engage with the challenges of the urban landscape, despite the stark differences between Italy and South Korea. The escapism of the 1960s and 70s was replaced by a deep desire for presence, solidified through a close personal and professional relationship with his brother Francesco and the team at Atelier Mendini, particularly Young Hee Cha, who coordinated and co-designed many of the projects in Korea.

In design, one of his final and most successful works was the *Amuleto* lamp, developed and produced by the Korean company Ramun. It was an unusual kind of object: formed of three circles (its base, the middle joint ring and the diffuser that contained an LED light source), it translated Mendini's love of minimalist, two-dimensional drawings into three-dimensional form, enriched with user-focused functionality. It came with a certificate of photobiological safety, attesting to the absence of risk from the light's impact on eyesight, which had been achieved by collaborating with the ophthalmology department of a university hospital. The ring-shaped diffuser minimized shadows while ensuring optimal lighting.

Underscoring the artistic intention behind the project, the *Amuleto* was presented posthumously in 2019, in a special edition of 17 pieces using *Najeon jang*, the Korean mother-of-pearl inlay technique that has ancient origins and that Mendini also used in a number of furniture pieces. Executed by Bang-ung Song, one of the technique's great masters, using more than 1,500 pieces of mother-of-pearl, the inlay highlighted the cosmic symbolism that Mendini had given to the lamp's shape: the three circles represented the sun, earth and moon. The name *Amuleto* was chosen so it could also act as a good-luck charm for Mendini's cultural and familial legacy.

Significantly, the limited edition of the lamp was presented for the first time as part of the retrospective *Mondo Mendini – The World of Alessandro Mendini*[26] at the Groninger Museum, marking the 25th anniversary of its opening. Mendini had started planning the exhibition in 2018 and it opened posthumously in October 2019. The museum's intentions were ambitious: to pay homage to its own designer, making him the protagonist of a major show with more than 130 pieces. Yet Mendini eschewed any self-congratulatory rhetoric and turned the exhibition into a tribute to the artist and designers that had influenced him. The show featured works by seventy individuals who in some way had inspired his work, or who he had crossed paths with in his life: from Alberto Savinio to Riccardo Dalisi, Michele De Lucchi to Fortunato Depero and Gio Ponti to Anna Gili – once again blending art and autobiography.

In contrast with the grand spectacle in Groningen, the exhibition *Piccole Fantasie Quotidiane* (Small Everyday Fantasies) at the Madre Museum in Naples – his first posthumous show in Italy, which ran from October 2020 to May 2021 – was more intimate, yet equally evocative. Naples was a city that Mendini loved deeply and that had greatly influenced him, and he was one of the few Milanese figures able to translate the city's rich culture into a unique aesthetic.[27]

Curated by Arianna Rosica and Gianluca Riccio in collaboration with Atelier Mendini, the exhibition was a rich retrospective of his works, with a focus on their colours and forms. It featured the pinks and blues of his Radical 1970s *oggetti 'impossibili'* ('impossible' objects), the vibrant hues of his twelve *Stoa* polychrome ceramic sculptures for Superego and a *Proust* room with various pieces and a large ceramic panel by Vietri. This panel, painted with brushstrokes inspired by Signac, one of the originators of Pointillism, paid tribute to the craftsmanship of the Campania region.

This show also resonated with Mendini's connection – both real and imagined – to the spaces where his works were displayed, as well as the involvement of other artists who were close to him. For instance, Francesco Clemente's ceramic floors and frescoed room formed the backdrop to Mendini's 1970s Radical *Poltrona di Paglia* (Straw Armchair) and Mimmo Paladino also contributed: these other designers and artists helped transform Mendini's identity into one he cherished and that made him so beloved by others.

An architect, designer, philosopher, artist, painter, sculptor and poet of words and images, Mendini was a true Janus. He looked both north towards Mitteleuropa with its historical avant-gardes and the Northern Italy of the industrial golden age and also south, to Southern Italy and the rest of the world, channeling its anarchic, rebellious and sometimes revolutionary spirit into his works.

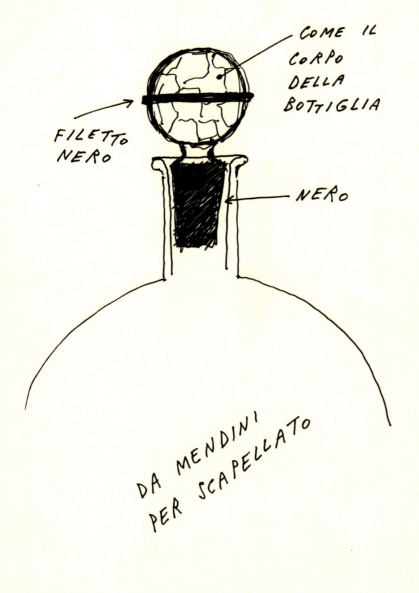

178.

179.

178. Stopper for *Tonda* bottle for Venini, drawing, 1988
179. *Oggetto Meditativo* crystal monstrance for Swarovski, 1999
180. *Dor* Murano glass vase for Venini, 1988
181. *Amboise* Murano glass bottle for Venini, 1990

180.

181.

182.

182. Casa Mendini: *Achernar* Murano glass pendant for Venini and *100% Make-Up* vases for Alessi Tendentse, Milan, 1993
183. Decorations for plates for Venini, drawing, 1988
184. Decorations for plates for Venini, drawing, 1988

183.

184.

THE END AS AN ETERNAL RETURN: LIGHT, COLOUR AND BACK TO DOMUS 259

185.

186.

185. *Cavallino* sculpture for Venini, drawing, 2008
186. *Cavallino* sculpture in blown glass for Venini, 2008
187. *Tête Géant* (Giant Head) and *Visage Archaïque* (Archaic Face) sculptures for *Fragilisme* exhibition at Fondation Cartier pour l'Art contemporain Paris, drawing, 2002
188. *Guerrier de Verre* red incalmo glass sculpture with gold earrings, project with Dorota Koziara for Fondation Cartier Paris, by Venini, 2002

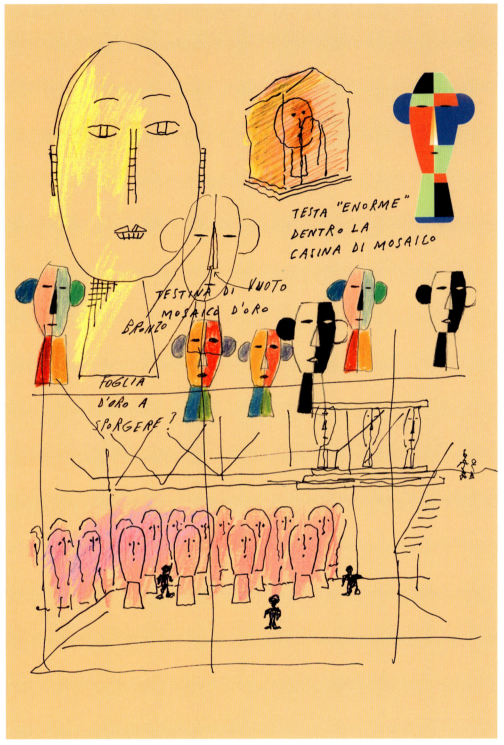

187.

188.

THE END AS AN ETERNAL RETURN: LIGHT, COLOUR AND BACK TO DOMUS

189.

189. *Le Salon Précieux Cartier* for Fondation Cartier pour l'art contemporain, Art 40 Basel, by Alessandro and Francesco Mendini, Basel, 2009
190. *Colonna di Cartier* (detail) for Cartier, Paris, 2009
191. *Fragilisme* exhibition at Fondation Cartier pour l'art contemporain, Paris, 2002
192. Skateboard designs for Supreme, 2016

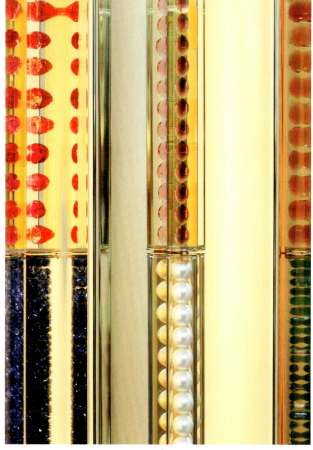

190.

CHAPTER 10   262

191.

192.

THE END AS AN ETERNAL RETURN: LIGHT, COLOUR AND BACK TO DOMUS

193.

194.

195.

193. *Alessandro Mendini and his Artisans: Three*, ceramic sculpture for Superego Design, Vacheron Constantin, Fondation Cartier pour l'art contemporain, Fondazione Cologni, 2013
194. *Alessandro Mendini and his Artisans: Four*, sculpture for Slide, Vacheron Constantin, Fondation Cartier pour l'art contemporain, Fondazione Cologni, 2013 2013
195. *Alessandro Mendini and his Artisans: Nine*, gold-plated brass vase for Cleto Munari, Vacheron Constantin, Fondation Cartier pour l'art contemporain, Fondazione Cologni, 2013

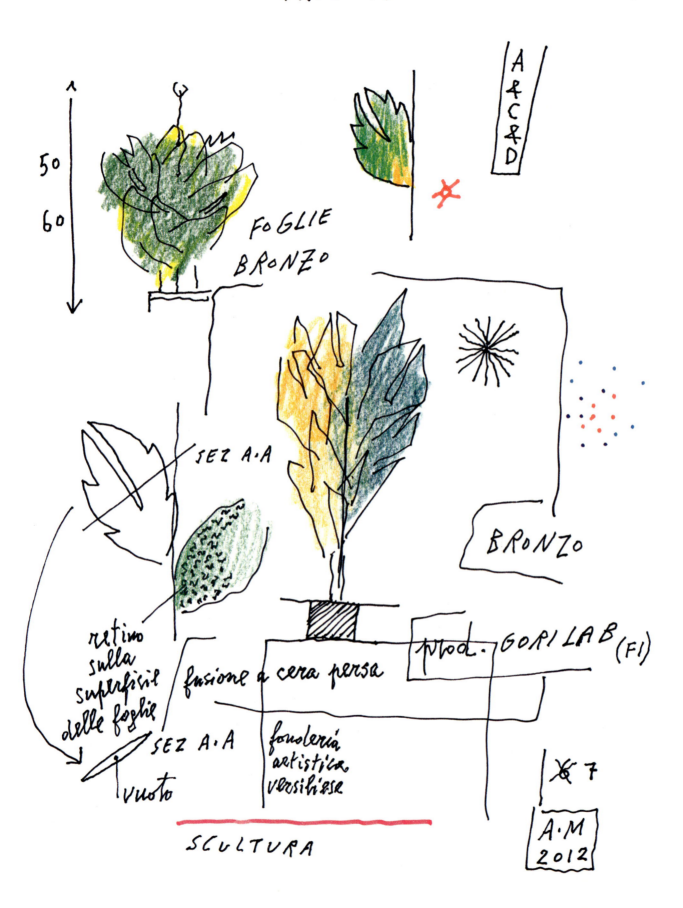

196.

197.

198.

196. *Alessandro Mendini and his Artisans: Seven* sculpture for Gori Lab, Vacheron Constantin, Fondation Cartier pour l'art contemporain, Fondazione Cologni, drawing, 2013
197. *Tre Primitivi: Luna & Sole* (Moon & Sun) storage unit for Alpi, 2018
198. *Tre Primitivi: QFWFQ* storage unit for Alpi, 2018

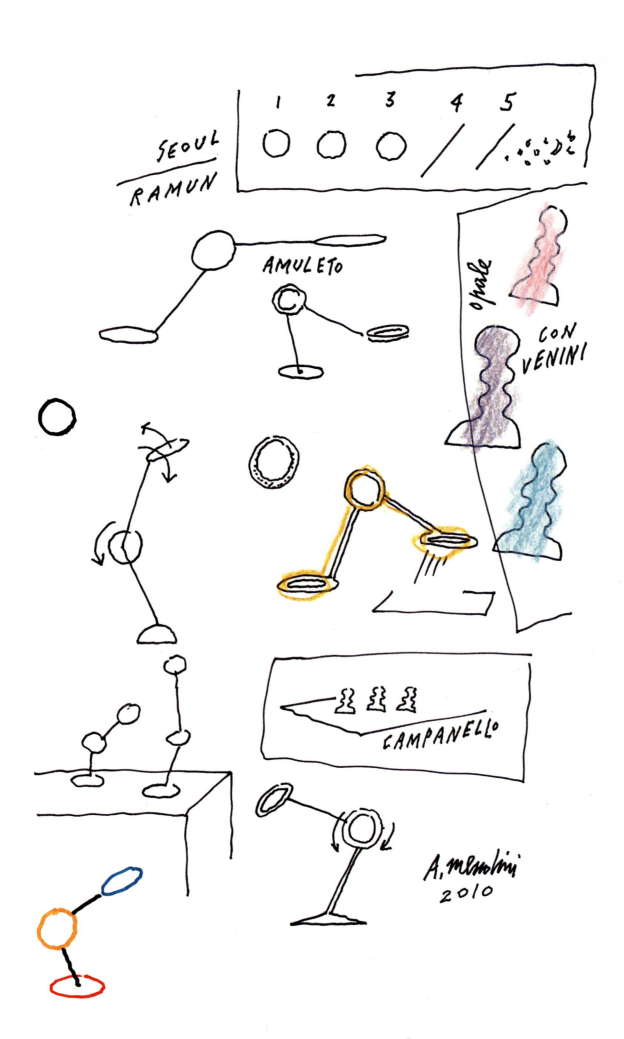

200.

199. *Amuleto* (Amulet) table lamp for Ramun, drawing, 2010
200. *Amuleto* (Amulet) table lamp for Ramun, 2012

THE END AS AN ETERNAL RETURN: LIGHT, COLOUR AND BACK TO DOMUS

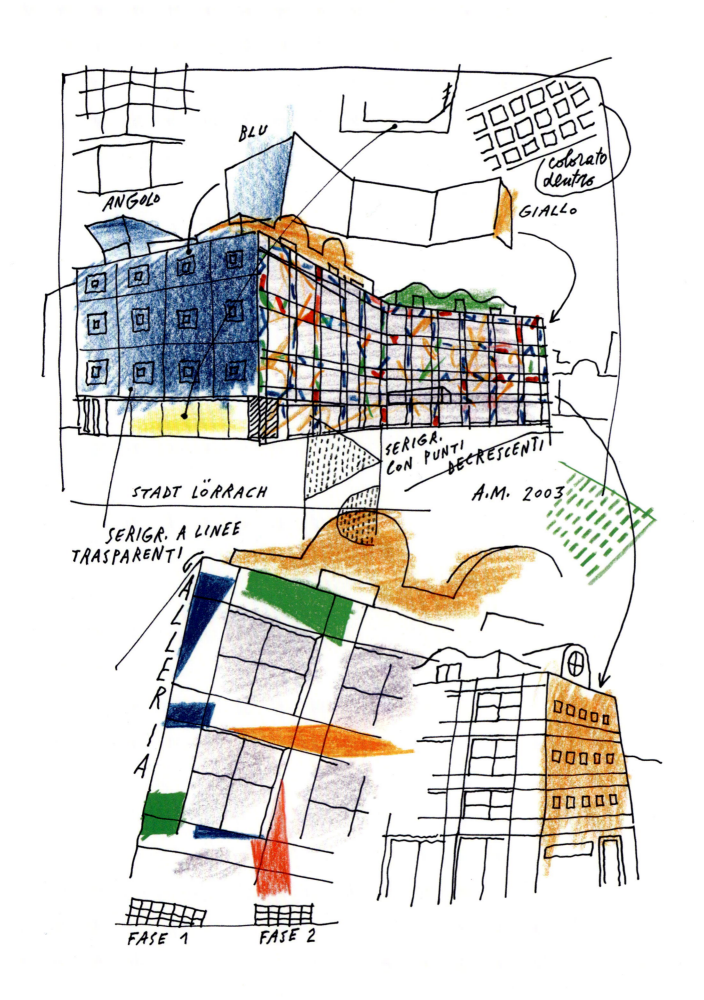

202.

201. Galleria Mendini, multifunctional building for housing, commercial and recreational spaces in Lörrach, Germany, drawing, 2000-2004
202. Galleria Mendini, multifunctional building for housing, commercial and recreational spaces by Alessandro and Francesco Mendini, model, 2000-2004
203. Steintor bus stop by Alessandro and Francesco Mendini, Hannover, Germany, 1992

203.

204.

204. *Piccole Fantasie Quotidiane* (Small Everyday Fantasies) exhibition curated by Arianna Rosica and Gianluca Riccio, *Poltrona di Paglia* in the Francesco Clemente painted room, Madre Museum, Naples, 2020
205. *Piccole Fantasie Quotidiane* exhibition, *Proust* armchair and objects, Madre Museum, Naples, 2020
206. *Piccole Fantasie Quotidiane* exhibition, *Zabro* chair/table and *Kandissi* sofa, Madre Museum, Naples, 2020

205.

206.

THE END AS AN ETERNAL RETURN: LIGHT, COLOUR AND BACK TO DOMUS

273

EPILOGUE

Alessandro Mendini passed away on the night of 18 February 2019 in his home on Via Sannio, just above the Atelier where, for thirty years, he sent out his messages. Whether these were fragile or strong, abstract or figurative, useful or useless, he always sought to be *primus inter pares* – first among equals. These messages were addressed not only to his brother Francesco and his daughters Fulvia and Elisa, but also to the most distant of his collaborators and the many other creators he discovered, promoted, supported or simply loved.

> In this 'group portrait with a postmodern intellectual', his view of himself and of the artists close to him was of individuals, separate but capable of coming together in multiple combinations to work toward both realistic and utopian goals. This remains part of that *pulviscolo* (fine dust) that he used to describe his works and the general state of critical imagination, which also serves as a great prophecy of the future/present of design and the soul it contains, at its best.

If the virtual world has truly become the fifth (or sixth) dimension where much of humanity now prefers to live for extended periods – its most mysterious and looming manifestations being the Internet of Things and Artificial Intelligence, presenting unpredictable futures for humankind – Mendini, with his deep belief in collaboration, foresaw and built an *Internet of Souls*. In this space, dozens, hundreds, perhaps even thousands of creators with diverse, often vastly different inspirations interacted and converged in a common direction, under Mendini's guidance or simply his inspiration. In this way, the waters of good theory and practice, in which he swam for so long and which still carry these creators along, flow toward the beautiful lake of an imaginary Eden of design – a place Mendini would have liked to visit and perhaps has now reached.

> It comforts the author of this book, Mendini's friends who feel his absence and always will, as well as his devoted and ever-growing audience, to think that perhaps from up above, he might occasionally peek out from between the clouds. With his wide eyes, like those of a kind and ancient idol, he might still watch over what has become of his cultural legacy, and see how his family, colleagues, and companions in design, architecture, and art – the art that Mendini always, above all, loved, at least as much as he loved life – are doing.

Milan, 8 January 2024

opposite: Alessandro Mendini, portrait by Mario Ermoli, 1994

IN THE GARDEN OF EDEN:
THE BIGGER PICTURE OF ALESSANDRO MENDINI

p277. *Art of Italian Design* theoretical diagram, drawing, 2008
p278. *La cucina Alessi: Agreste* with Oras, Fores and Valcucine, drawing, 2005
p279. *MicroMacro*, Murano glass vases blown and caged in metal grids for Cleto Munari, drawing, 2003
p280. *Craquelé, Abitare il tempo* installation, Verona, drawing, 2006
p281. *DiADaInConSuPerTraFra*, decorations for cabinet, Zerodisegno, Carlo Poggio, 2007
p282. *Mendinismi*, fibreglass vases and plates for Corsi Design, drawing, 2008
p283. *La cucina Alessi: Sinuosa*, Alessi by Valcucine Italia, drawing, 2005
p284. *Omaggio a Palladio*, sculptures in mosaic for Bisazza, drawing, 2000
p285. *Ebdomero*, bench for Abet Laminati in the garden of the Triennale di Milano, drawing, 2005
p286. *Normali Meraviglie* (Small daily fantasies) for the exhibition in Genoa, capital of European culture, drawing, 2004
p287. *Torre dell'Orologio* (Clock Tower), Gibellina, Sicily, drawing, 1987
p288. Casa a Olda, drawing of the house dedicated to Mendini's daughter Fulvia, Olda Val Taleggio, 2006
p289. *Alessandro: Ciao!*, for Alessi, drawing, 2003

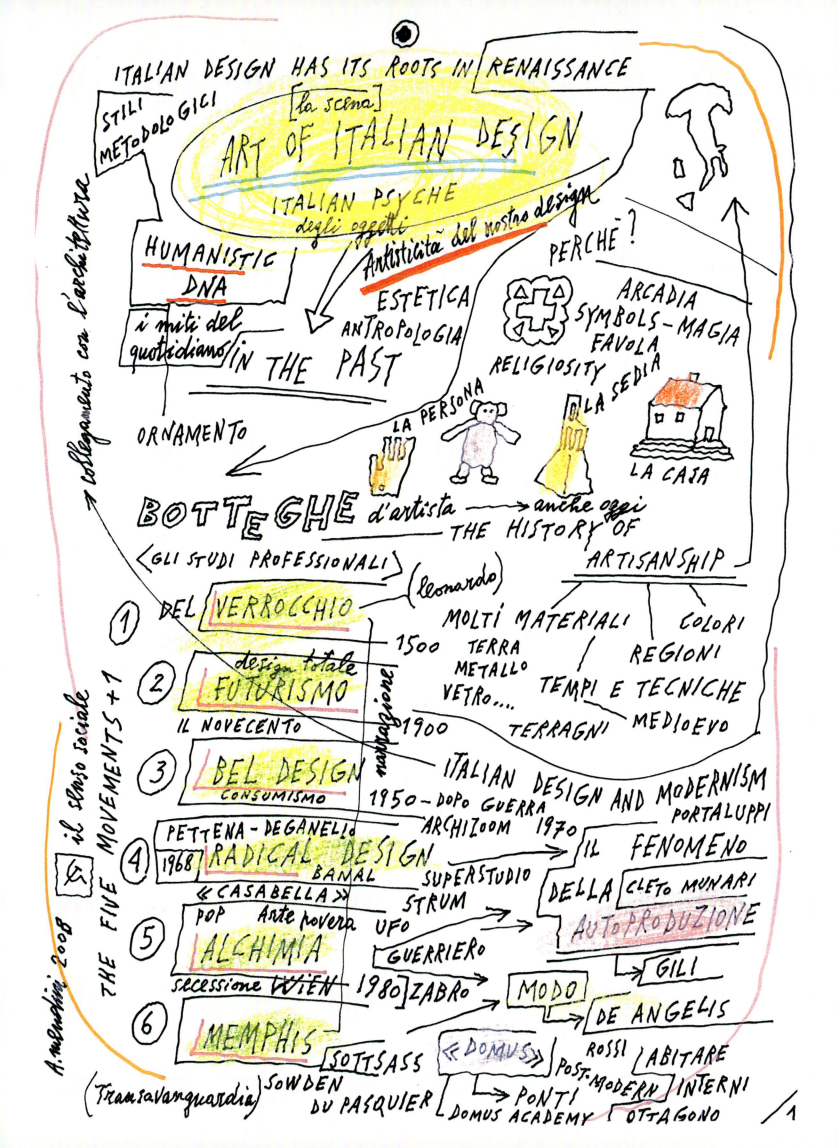

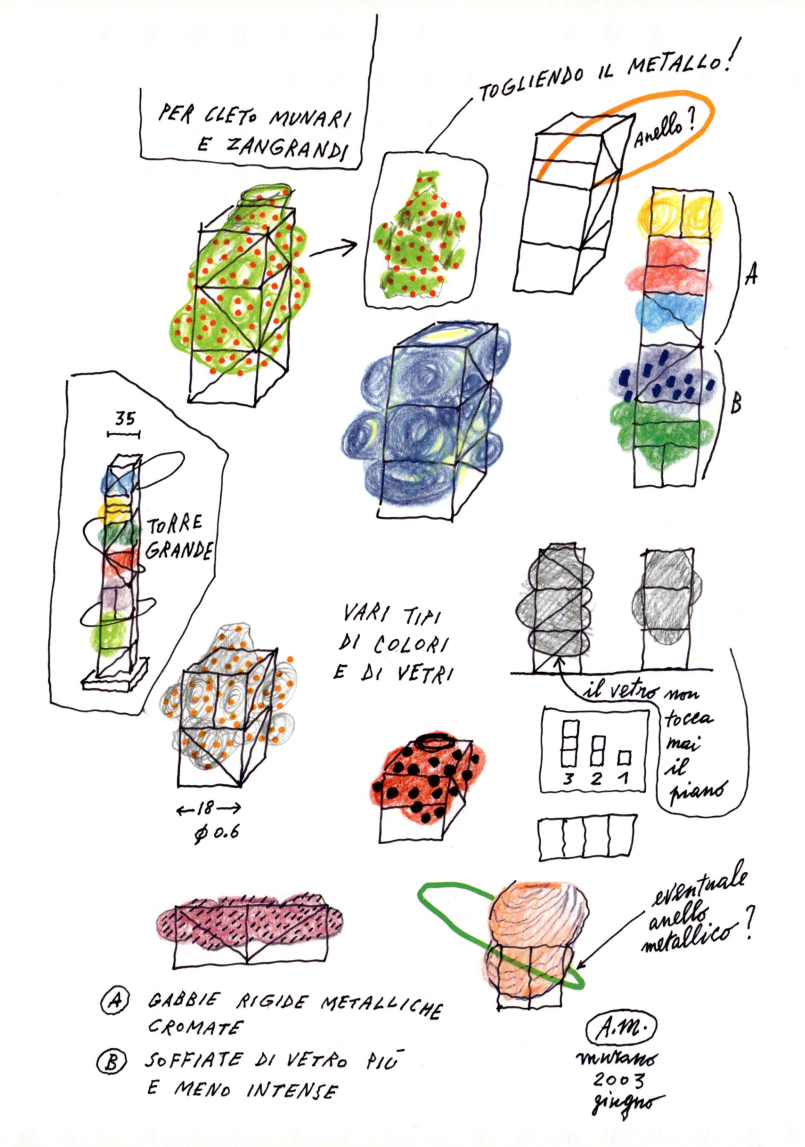

« CRAQUELÉ »

(lo stilema del craquelé)

ARCHITETTURA

OGGETTO

ABITO

ARTE

A. Mendini
2007

ETC.

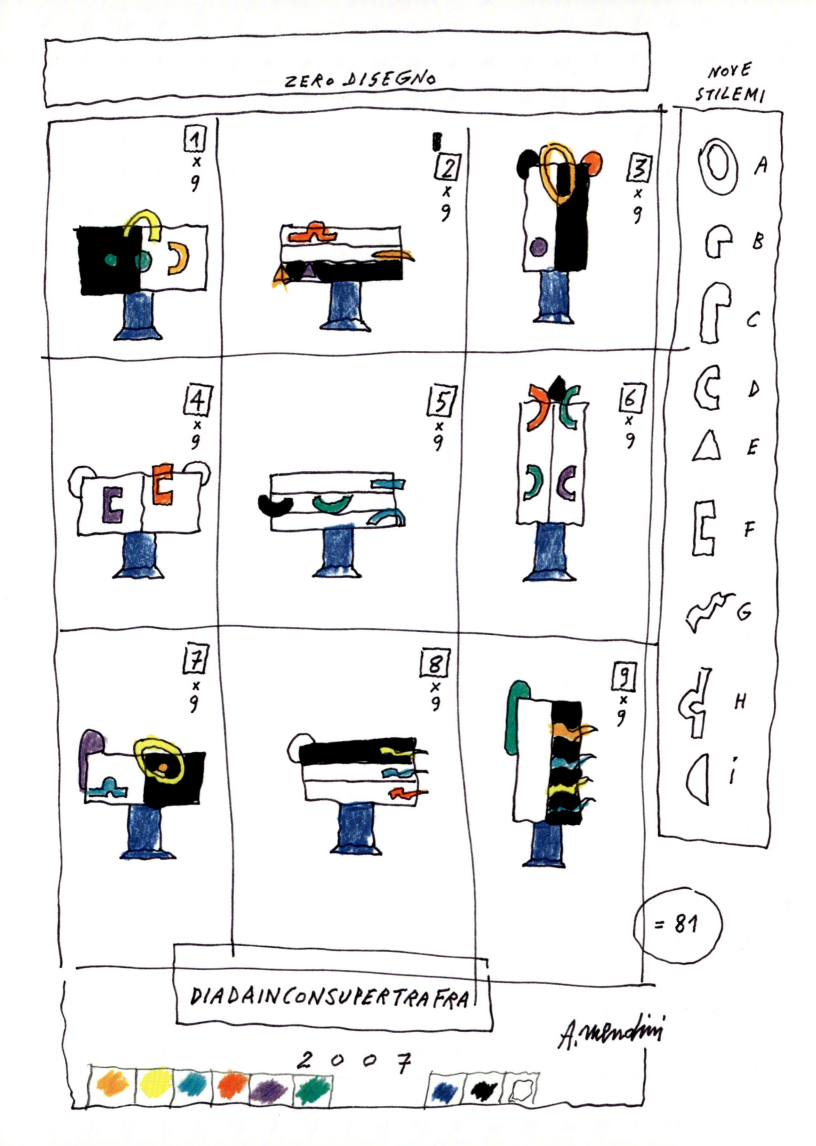

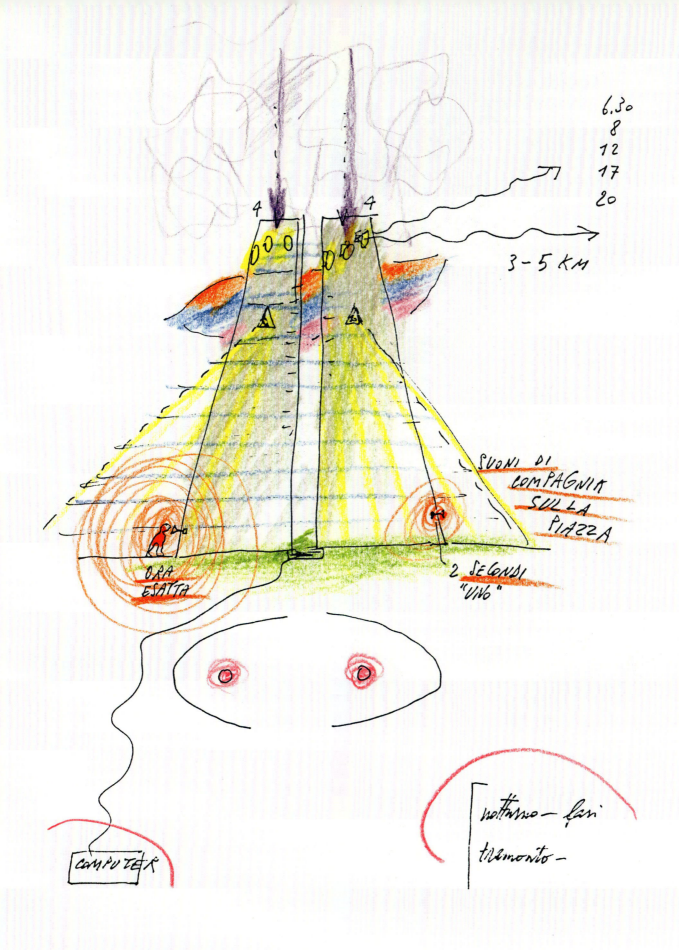

FOOTNOTES

CHAPTER 1: IN SEARCH OF LOST TIME AND SPACE: THE ORIGINS

1. in Mario Brunati, Alessandro Mendini, Ferruccio Villa (eds.), *Antoni Gaudí*, Studio Brunati/Mendini Editions, Milan 1958.
2. Gio Ponti, in M. Brunati and A. Mendini (eds.), *Erich Mendelsohn*, Studio Brunati/Mendini Editions, Milan 1960.
3. In the Mendini archive there is a postcard sent to Mendini in 1947 by Ettore Scola (another famous Italian director, who at the time was drawing for *Marc'Aurelio*), asking him to send some of his cartoons to the editorial office for publication.
4. A. Mendini, 'Il progetto amorale', in *Per un'architettura banale*, manuscript, Oct. 30, 1979, now in Loredana Parmesani (ed.), *Alessandro Mendini, Scritti*, Ambrosetti/Skira Foundation, Milan 2004, p. 68.
5. 'I was born on Via Giorgio Jan in 1931. My grandfather Francesco had commissioned the design of the house from Piero Portaluppi, and the care with which it was designed reveals the deep understanding they had in creating this remarkable residence, one of the architect's most refined. Portaluppi called it a "villa", and its clear inspiration came from the Viennese Secession and Alpine architecture.' A. Mendini, in *Casa Museo Boschi Di Stefano*, Family Album No. 1, notebook 3, Boschi Di Stefano Foundation, Milan 2008.
6. A. Mendini, 'Intervista con Filippo Betto', in *Il secolo veloce*, Skira/Fabrica, 2007, now in Loredana Parmesani (ed.), *Alessandro Mendini, Scritti di domenica*, Postmedia Books, Milan 2016, p. 208.
7. A. Mendini, 'Il meraviglioso pino luccicante crollò sul pavimento. E la festa cominciò', in *Corriere della Sera*, November 30, 2013, now in *Scritti di domenica*, op. cit., p. 31.
8. During the same years, Alberto Savinio – forced to flee in 1943 after learning that he was on a list of suspected anti-fascists – also had a house in Versilia, at Ronchi-Poveromo. It was first devastated by bombings (a bomb fell right in the living room where he painted) and later by raids from German Nazis who had occupied the area.
9. A. Mendini, 'Il meraviglioso pino luccicante crollò sul pavimento. E la festa cominciò', op. cit., ibidem.
10. A. Mendini, *Pane e Progetto*, manuscript, January 4, 2008, Mendini Archive.
11. A. Mendini, *I miei anni '60*, in *Gli anni '60. Le immagini al potere*, exhibition catalogue, Mazzotta Foundation, Milan 1996, now in Loredana Parmesani (ed.), *Alessandro Mendini, Scritti*, Ambrosetti/Skira Foundation, Milan 2004, pp. 30-31.
12. A. Mendini, *I miei anni '60*, op. cit., ibidem.
13. 'In this sense, the role that Scheggi attributes to himself as an "*ideatore plastico*" could be particularly appropriate and prescient,' in 'Ilaria Bignotti, intervista su Paolo Scheggi', in *Alessandro Mendini, Scritti di domenica*, op. cit., p. 304.
14. 'I believe the intermediary for my meeting with Paolo Scheggi was Germano Celant, in 1964 [...] I called Scheggi because we both felt the need to talk, we were constantly trying to theorize what we were doing in architecture, looking for a way to translate the project, the ideas, into words [...] Scheggi was important in this regard for intellectual exchange, for reflecting on architecture, for discussing certain projects [...] I remember interesting words from Scheggi, an intellectual connection, a light but constant presence. His intelligence.' in 'Ilaria Bignotti, intervista su Paolo Scheggi', in *Alessandro Mendini, Scritti di domenica*, op. cit., p. 303.

CHAPTER 2: RADICAL DESIGN: THE GHOST IN THE MACHINE

1. In Gian Mario Oliveri, 'La nostra storia', in Luigi Spinelli (ed.), *G. Mario Oliveri e gli Studi Nizzoli. Architecture and design since 1948*, Editoriale Domus, Milan 2001, p. 65.
2. A. Mendini, 'Metaprogetto sì e no', in *Casabella*, no. 333, February 1969, p. 14.
3. 'Il Lonfo non vaterca né gluisce e molto raramente barigatta, ma quando soffia il bego a bisce bisce sdilenca un poco e gnagio s'archipatta,' Fosco Maraini, *Il Lonfo*, in *Gnòsi delle Fànfole*, De Donato Editore, Bari 1966 and 1978, later in idem, Baldini Castoldi Dalai Editore, Milan 1994.
4. Adolfo Natalini, Cristiano Toraldo di Francia, Roberto Magris, Gian Piero Frassinelli, Alessandro Magris, Alessandro Poli.
5. Dario and Lucia Bartolini, Andrea Branzi, Gilberto Corretti, Paolo Deganello, Massimo Morozzi.
6. Carlo Bachi, Lapo Binazzi, Patrizia Cammeo, Riccardo Foresi, Sandro Gioli, Titti Maschietto.
7. A. Mendini, 'Architettura per l'uomo dimenticato', editorial, *Casabella*, no. 349, pp. 5-6.
8. From a conversation between Emilio Ambasz and the author, May 2023.
9. A. Mendini, 'The Land of Good Design', in E. Ambasz (ed.), *Italy: The New Domestic Landscape. Achievements and Problems of Italian Design*, The Museum of Modern Art, New York/Centro Di, Florence 1972, pp. 370-379.
10. For an account of the 'Bracciodiferro' experience, see Anty Pansera, with Mariateresa Chirico, *Bracciodiferro. Gaetano Pesce – Alessandro Mendini 1971-1975*, Silvana Editoriale, Milan 2013.
11. The Global Tools group published two fanzines: *Bollettino Global Tools*, no. 1, 1974, and *Bollettino Global Tools*, no. 2, 1975. For a complete historical-critical reconstruction, see Valerio Borgonuovo and Silvia Franceschini (eds.), *GLOBAL TOOLS 1973-1975: Quando l'educazione coinciderà con la vita*, SALT/Nero Editions, Istanbul/Milan 2018.
12. Paola Navone, Bruno Orlandoni, *Architettura radicale*, Documenti di Casabella, Milan 1974.
13. Federica Di Castro (ed.), *Sottsass's Scrap-Book*, Documenti di Casabella, Milan 1976.
14. A. Mendini, 'Introduzione', in Federica Di Castro (ed.), *Sottsass's Scrap-Book*, op. cit., p. 5.
15. CentroKappa (ed.), *Il design italiano degli anni '50*, Editoriale Domus, Milan 1980.
16. All quotations by Alessandro Mendini are taken from *Il design italiano degli anni '50*, op. cit.
17. 'In terms of publishing, when *Casabella* was shut down after being acquired by Electa, *Modo* became the new reference point [...] Mendini had been removed, but Electa wanted us to continue it. *Domus* was more international, but *Casabella* was the most culturally advanced. Electa promised us that everything would continue as before and then ousted Mendini, but the editorial team was very united, and everyone followed Mendini. Although I had no other job, I decided to leave and do something else. We didn't earn much, but it was the only steady job I had.' Franco Raggi, interview for the thesis *La disobbedienza nel progetto*, by Aldo Olivero, 2010.
18. A. Mendini, 'Design dove sei?', in *Modo*, no. 1, 1977, now in Loredana Parmesani (ed.), *Alessandro Mendini. Scritti*, Ambrosetti/Skira Foundation, Milan 2004, pp. 555-556.
19. Davide Mosconi, *Concerto. Pezzo per arpa, sgabello, donna e lana* – harp player Ines Klok – costume by Alessandro Mendini and Lidia Prandi. *Pezzo per bandoneon, fisarmonica, armonica e nastro adesivo* – accordionist Davide Mosconi. March 25, 1975, La Tartaruga Gallery, Rome.
20. Lidia Prandi, *I Nuovissimi. 58 designer selezionati da Modo*, RdE, Milan 1989.
21. A. Mendini, 'Appello al ministro della Pubblica Istruzione', in *Modo*, no. 33, 1980, p. 11.

CHAPTER 3: PROUST: A KITSCH REVOLUTION FOR THE COMMON MAN

1. 'We were a nice group that was clearly involved in politics [...] But the most interesting gesture was to give up the degree. We told ourselves it was a bourgeois way to enter society, and that's how my university story ended.' Alessandro Guerriero, in 'Alchimia del Mondo,' interview with S. Casciani, in *disegno. la nuova cultura industriale*, vol.4, SCMD Media e Design, Milan 2014-2015.
2. At Studio Alchymia, Alessandro Guerriero served as art director, his sister Adriana handled the management of the studio, while the technician Stefano Bianchi was responsible for the production of objects and furniture for many years.
3. See Studio Alchymia's untitled catalogue and collection of posters (including Mendini's *tavolino Bara*), Studio Alchymia, Milan 1977-1978.
4. In 1979, the experiment was repeated at Milan's SICOF photography show with the *Stanza Banale* – set up with Franco Raggi and Daniela Puppa, his collaborators first at *Casabella* and then at *Modo* – which exclusively displayed *objets trouvés*, an entire decor made of lowbrow, if not blatantly kitsch, furniture and objects; with the exception of a chandelier by Gino Sarfatti for his company Arteluce, which, despite its strong expressiveness, blended in with the rest of the decor as an additional element of 'visual disturbance'.
5. 'I bought the frame (the wooden structure of the armchair, ed.) in Veneto on a trip I took with Sandro Guerriero, and I had it hand-painted with acrylic colours by two talented young painters, Prospero Rasulo and Pierantonio Volpini [...] Later, Franco Migliaccio, a very skilled painter and art critic from Milan, began to decorate it in Milan on wooden frames and white canvas produced in Lombardy.' A. Mendini, 'History of the Proust Armchair (1976-2001)', in *Alessandro Mendini. Scritti*, Loredana Parmesani (ed.), Skira/Ambrosetti Foundation, Milan 2004, pp. 206-207.
6. A. Mendini, 'History of the Proust Armchair (1976-2001)', in *Alessandro Mendini. Scritti*, op. cit., p. 206.
7. See A. Guerriero, B. Gregori (eds.), *Studio Alchimia. Bau. Haus Art Collection*, Alchimia Editore, Milan 1981.
8. In the domestic setting of the show *Tango Glaciale*, which debuted on January 27, 1982, at the Teatro Nuovo in Naples, directed by Mario Martone and featuring Andrea Renzi, Tomas Arana and Licia Maglietta, all four members of the Falso Movimento company.

CHAPTER 4: FROM POSTMODERN TO NEOMODERN: THE ALESSI AND DOMUS YEARS

1. A. Mendini, 'Marcello Pietrantoni', in *Data*, no. 24, 1976.
2. A. Mendini, *Pane e Progetto*, op. cit.
3. Gianni Mazzocchi, foreword of *Domus* 596, July 1979, p. 1.
4. In the volume *Alessandro Mendini. Scritti*, op. cit., the text is dated to 1976, but the first Global Tools seminar on the body was held in 1975. See Franco Raggi, 'Notes for a Reverse Ergonomics,' in Valerio Borgonuovo, Silvia Franceschini (eds.), *Global Tools. 1973-1975*, SALT/Graham Foundation/Nero, Milan 2018.
5. Town in Molise, a central-southern Italian region where Fiat set up an engine factory in the early 1970s, also to take advantage of government funding through the then CasMez (Cassa per il Mezzogiorno).
6. A. Mendini, *Pane e Progetto*, manuscript, op. cit.
7. The project was ultimately not realized. In the 1990s and 2000s, Russian and Chinese editions of *Domus* were published, but the only entirely bilingual edition remained the Italian one.
8. See Ettore Sottsass, *Formal Exercise No. 2. Catalogue for Decorative Furniture in Modern Style, 1978-1980*, Studio Forma/Alchymia, Milan 1980.
9. See S. Casciani, review of *Design ist unsichtbar*, writings by C. Alexander, G.C. Argan, F. Burkhardt, A. Mendini, A. Hareiter et al., Österreichisches Institut für Visuelle Gestaltung-Locker Verlag, Vienna 1981, in *Domus*, no. 619, July/August 1981, p. VI. See also Angela Hareiter (co-curator of Forum Design), 'Was ist Design?', in *Zwischen Kunst und Design*, in *Kunstforum International*, no. 66, pp. 51-83.
10. François Burkhardt, 'Sull'accettazione del design italiano nella Repubblica Federale Tedesca' in AA.VV. *Möbel aus Italien. Produktion – Technik – Modernität*, ICE (Istituto nazionale per il Commercio Estero) – Kölnisches Stadtmuseum, Milan-Cologne 1980, pp. 155-156.
11. Barbara Radice (ed.), *Elogio del Banale*, Alchymia Studio Forma, Milan 1980.
12. A. Mendini, in *Elogio del Banale*, op. cit., pp. 14-15.
13. Franco Raggi, in *Elogio del Banale*, op. cit., p. 26.
14. Andrea Branzi, 'Il design banale', in *La casa calda. Esperienze del Nuovo Design Italiano*, Idea Books Edizioni, Milan 1984, p. 127.
15. A. Branzi, 'Il design banale', in *La casa calda. Esperienze del Nuovo Design Italiano*, op. cit., pp. 122, 127.
16. Rosa Maria Rinaldi, in AA.VV., *The Modifying Surface*, exhibition catalogue, Centrodomus/Editoriale Domus, Milan 1980.
17. See S. Casciani, 'Alle radici del design italiano V, Ettore Sottsass jr. Una vita per l'industria', in disegno. *la nuova cultura industriale*, vol. #4, SCMD Media e Design, Milan 2014-2015, pp. 74-81.
18. A. Mendini, *Paesaggio casalingo. La produzione Alessi nell'industria dei casalinghi dal 1921 al 1980* (graphic design by Bruno Munari), Editoriale Domus, Milan 1979.
19. A. Mendini, 'Introduzione', in *Paesaggio casalingo*, op. cit., p. 5.
20. E. Sottsass, 'Esperienze con la ceramica', in *Domus*, no. 489, 1970, p. 55.
21. Among others, Lidia Prandi, Alberto Gozzi, Patrizia Rizzi.
22. See Hans Hollein (ed.), *MAN transFORMS. An International Exhibition on Aspects of Design*, exhibition catalogue, Cooper Hewitt Museum, New York 1976.
23. See *Paesaggio casalingo*, *XVI Triennale – Primo ciclo – La sistemazione del design*, exhibition catalogue, December 1979-March 1980, Alessi-Triennale di Milano, Milan 1980.
24. See *Oggetti e Progetti. Objekte und Projecte. Alessi: storia e futuro di una fabbrica del design italiano*, exhibition catalogue, Die Neue Sammlung – The International Design Museum, Munich, Mondadori Electa, Milan 2010.

CHAPTER 5: ENDLESS EPHEMERA: FURNITURE AS FASHION

1. Walter Benjamin, *Parigi, capitale del XIX secolo*, R. Tiedemann (ed.), Einaudi, Turin 1986.
2. From a conversation with the author, 1998.
3. Georg Simmel, 'Die Mode', article for *Die Zeit*, 1895, later in *Philosophy of Fashion*, 1905; Italian trans. *La moda*, Editori Riuniti, Rome 1985.
4. G. Simmel, 'Die Mode', op. cit., p. 25.
5. A. Mendini, 'Cosmesi universale', in *Domus Moda* 1, supplement to *Domus* no. 617, May 1981, p. 9.
6. Dario Bartolini, 'Struttura-Non struttura', in *Domus Moda* 2, supplement to *Domus* no. 621, October 1981, pp. 36-37.
7. With Giorgio and Bruno Gregori, Mauro Panzeri, in Rosa Maria Rinaldi, 'Dal corpo alla città', in *Domus Moda* 1, op. cit., pp. 50-53.
8. 'Only two days before the Memphis event, Alessandro Mendini and Studio Alchimia presented a project whose diversity of themes, protagonists, and intentions anticipated, like an overture, everything that was to become important in design during the 1980s: *il Mobile Infinito*.' Rainer Krause, in Peter Weiss (ed.), *Alessandro Mendini: Designed Painting – Painted Design*, exhibition catalogue for Kunst-Museum Ahlen (Germany), 1997. This volume is an exhaustive examination and documentation of Mendini's work as a designer-painter.
9. A. Mendini, in AA.VV., *Il Mobile Infinito*, catalogue of the performance exhibition at the Politecnico di Milano *Leonardo da Vinci*, 18-25 September 1981, Alchimia Editore, Milan 1981.
10. A. Mendini, *Il Mobile Infinito*, op. cit.
11. AA.VV., *Conseguenze impreviste. Arte, moda, design: ipotesi di una nuova creatività in Italia*, catalogue (3 volumes) of the 'distributed exhibition' in Prato (FI), Municipality of Prato/Electa, Florence 1982.
12. See A. Mendini, 'Interview with Paolo Bettini', in *Domus*, no. 637, March 1983, p. 1.
13. See Carlo Guenzi (ed.), *Elective Affinities. Twenty-one Designers Seek Their Own Affinities*, exhibition catalogue for the show at the Triennale di Milano (Triennale Notebooks), Electa, Milan 1985.

CHAPTER 6: OBJECTS WITH ART AND SOUL: THE DESIGNER AS PAINTER

1. Ennio Flaiano, 'Diario degli Errori. Racconti di New York. (223) The Parker Pen', in Maria Corti and Anna Longoni (eds.), *Ennio Flaiano. Opere*, Bompiani, Milan 1988, p. 359.
2. E. Ambasz, 'Una fiaba: Alessandro J. Mendini regista straordinario e profeta malgrado se stesso', in AA.VV. (E. Ambasz, M. Bobbioni, S. Casciani, G. Di Pietrantonio, F. Irace, A. Mendini), *Atelier Mendini. Una utopia visiva*, Fabbri Editori/RCS, Milan 1994, p. 12.
3. AA.VV., *Atelier Mendini. Una utopia visiva*, op. cit.
4. For a comprehensive overview of Zanotta design, see S. Casciani, *Mobili come Architetture. Il disegno della produzione Zanotta*, Arcadia, Milan 1984 and 1988.
5. See AA.VV. (S. Casciani, B. and G. Gregori, A. Guerriero, M. Panzeri), *Ricerca sull'ambiente*, Milan 1981.
6. Project by A. Branzi, C. Ceccariglia, S. Casciani, from an idea by A. Guerriero; see Rosamaria Rinaldi, 'Mussolini's Bathroom', in *Domus*, no. 627, April 1982, pp. 49-51.
7. See S. Casciani, *Mobili come Architetture. Il disegno della produzione Zanotta*, op. cit., pp. 152-153.

reworking of the text *Cosmesi Universale*, op. cit.

9. See S. Casciani, 'Architetture Luminose. I mobili di Alessandro Mendini per la collezione Nuova Alchimia', in Pier Carlo Bontempi, Giorgio Gregori (eds.), AA.VV., *Alchimia*, Copi, The Hague, Netherlands-Alchimia, Milan 1985, p. 37 and pp. 29-36.
10. Enzo Mari, *Dov'è l'artigiano*, exhibition catalogue, April-May 1981, Electa Florence-Tuscany Region 1981.
11. A. Mendini and AA.VV., *Architettura Sussurrante*, LP 33 rpm, Lacerba Record Industries, Florence 1983.
12. A. Mendini, 'Ogni oggetto è diverso da ogni altro', in *Domus*, no. 648, March 1983, pp. 34-35.
13. A. Mendini, 'Ogni oggetto è diverso da ogni altro, op. cit., p. 34.
14. A. Mendini, 'Perché ho lasciato *Domus*', manuscript, October 1, 1985, Mendini Archive; published in *L'architettura. Cronache e Storia*, no. 360, October 1985.
15. In 2009, the publisher intended to transfer the editorship of *Domus* from architect and designer Flavio Albanese to the young Joseph Grima, already assistant director to Stefano Boeri and strongly supported by him. The handover was then postponed for a year, and Alessandro Mendini was invited to serve as interim editor-in-chief of the magazine (April 2010-March 2011) with me as co-editor. Mendini, already seventy-nine years old, accepted, and I joined him.
16. 'Is there now a real turning point, requiring design to shift from traditional methods to those typical of artistic creation? After the long history of minor and applied arts, and the brief but intense history of industrial design, is this perhaps the era for a kind of design comparable to 'major' art? The SAD group, simply by its formation, answers yes to these fundamental questions [...] It is one of the first teams of professionals who [...] have practiced, since 1985, this new way of setting up "sub species" projects artistically, which is now at the heart of the debate under the name of DESIGN/ART....' A. Mendini, 'For SAD', in S. Casciani, Anna Lombardi, Paolo Scordia, Gabi Faeh (eds.), *SAD Arte e Design per gli anni 90. Kunst und Design für die 90er Jahre*, Campanotto Editore, Udine-Galerie Margine, Zurich 1987, pp. 10-11.
17. S. Casciani, 'Canzoni per la fine del secolo. Alessandro Mendini dal design alla pittura', in S. Casciani, B. Felis, G. Di Pietrantonio, D. Verzura (eds.), *Alessandro Mendini*, Giancarlo Politi Editore, Milan 1989, pp. 21-30.
18. A. Mendini, 'Pittura Progettata e Design Pittorico', manuscript, April 13, 1986, for the *Caravelles, International Design Quadriennale* exhibition, Museé Saint Pierre, Lyon, 1986; now in *Alessandro Mendini, Scritti*, op. cit., pp. 87-88.
19. See S. Casciani, A. Guerriero, A. Mendini (eds.), *OllO Rivista senza messaggio*, no. 1 Giancarlo Politi Editore, Milan 1988; no. 2, L'Archivolto, Milan 1990.

CHAPTER 7: LEARNING A NEW UTOPIA: FROM LAS VEGAS TO GRONINGEN

1. A. Mendini, S. Casciani, 'Questo libro è un manifesto. Il caos simbolico come ordine architettonico', preface in Margherita Rossi Paulis (ed.), Robert Venturi, Denise Scott Brown, Steven Izenour, *Imparando da Las Vegas. Il simbolismo dimenticato della forma architettonica*, CLUVA, Venice 1985, p. 9.
2. R. Venturi, D. Scott Brown, S. Izenour, *Learning from Las Vegas*, MIT Press, Cambridge, MA 1972.
3. R. Venturi, *Complexity and Contradiction in Architecture*, The Museum of Modern Art Papers on Architecture, New York 1966.
4. Bruno Zevi, high priest of modernist criticism, though greatly admiring Mendini, did not spare harsh criticism of the book by Venturi, Scott Brown, and Izenour when its Italian edition was published: 'In the introduction to the volume, Alessandro Mendini and Stefano Casciani emphasize its full relevance "as an explicit project to organize an anti-modern code." [...] Instead, we witness the wearing out of these heretical, playful, and permissive forward escapes, linked to the opulence and wastefulness of the Pop era.' Bruno Zevi, 'Ritornare a Las Vegas', in *L'Espresso*, no. 46, November 17, 1985, p. 202.
5. A. Mendini, S. Casciani, 'Questo libro è un manifesto. Il caos simbolico come ordine architettonico', original manuscript, March 15, 1985, p. 4.
6. See R. Venturi, John Rauch, D. Scott Brown, *Signs of Life: Symbols in the American City*, Renwick Gallery of the National Collection of Fine Arts, Smithsonian Institution, exhibition catalogue, February 26–September 30, 1976, Aperture Inc., New York 1976.
7. R. Venturi, J. Rauch, D. Scott Brown, *Signs of Life: Symbols in the American City*, op. cit.
8. Morris Lapidus, in *Progressive Architecture*, September 1970, p. 120, now in R. Venturi, D. Scott Brown, S. Izenour, *Learning from Las Vegas*, op. cit., p. 56.
9. Illustrated in Peter Blake, *God's Own Junkyard, The Planned Deterioration of America's Landscape*, Holt, Rinehart, Winston, New York 1964.
10. R. Venturi, D. Scott Brown, S. Izenour, 'Alcune definizioni usando il metodo comparativo', in *Learning from Las Vegas*, op. cit., p. 71.
11. The term that later became widely used, often inappropriately, originated from two Italian scholars, Gabriella Lo Ricco and Silvia Micheli, in the book *The Spectacle of Architecture. Profile of the Archistar*, Paravia-Bruno Mondadori, Milan 2003, which also extensively cites Mendini (p. 157-158).
12. Aaron Betsky, 'Learning from Bob Venturi', in *Architect Magazine* (online), September 20, 2018.
13. Corien Lugtenberg, 'A New Policy for a New Museum', interview with Frans Haks, in AA.VV., *Alessandro & Francesco Mendini! Philippe Starck! Michele De Lucchi! Coop Himmelb(l)au! in Groningen*, Groninger Museum, Groningen, pp. 46-51.
14. On this 'situationist' approach in creating groups and shared work opportunities, Mendini wrote in his reflections in later years: 'My relationships with the many creators I worked with (artists, designers, architects) and with industrialists, institutions, artisans and producers began when I was working in magazines, and did not translate into work at the time. Gradually, I began designing with many of them, based on cultural intent affinities. I do not remember ever going to anyone with a proposal drawing in hand. My contacts are left to chance, somewhat like meteors or parables, a patchwork.' in A. Mendini, *Pane e progetto*, op. cit.
15. A. Mendini, 'Frammenti', in AA. VV., *Atelier Mendini. Una utopia visiva*, op. cit., p. 15.
16. Bruno Gregori (b. 1954, now Bruno Gregory) graduated in painting at the Brera Academy and worked with Studio Alchimia and Mendini from 1979 to 1989; he later continued collaborating with Atelier Mendini, always with exceptional skill as a painter, draftsman, and designer. Giorgio Gregori (1957-1995), a sensitive artist, designer, and extraordinarily talented illustrator, worked with Mendini on all Studio Alchimia projects up to the Groninger Museum. He tragically passed away at thirty-eight in a motorcycle accident. The book *Alessandro & Francesco Mendini! Philippe Starck! Michele De Lucchi! Coop Himmelb(l)au! in Groningen*, Groninger Museum 1985, op. cit., is dedicated to him.
17. Among the circumstances that led Mendini to open the Atelier were an increase in professional assignments, some fatigue in his relationship with Alchimia, and the fortuitous coincidence of the inheritance left to him by his uncle Antonio Boschi (1896–1988), which enabled him, along with his brother Francesco, to make the necessary investment to acquire the large former workshop and set up Atelier Mendini for both of their work.
18. C. Lugtenberg, 'A New Policy for a New Museum,' interview with Frans Haks, op. cit., p. 51.
19. A. Mendini, 'Discorso inaugurale del Museo di Groningen, 29 ottobre 1994,' in *Alessandro Mendini, Scritti*, op. cit., p. 167.

CHAPTER 8: THE GOLDEN DESIGN AGE: SWATCH TO BISAZZA AND BEYOND

1. The Alessi and Olivari factories are about 20 km apart in a region rich with waterways – essential for the area's many metalwork and finishing workshops dedicated to the production of household goods: primarily steel for Alessi items and brass, aluminium and bronze for Olivari handles.
2. A. Mendini, 'Introduzione', in S. Casciani, *L'architettura presa per mano. La maniglia moderna e la produzione Olivari*, Olivari Spa-Idea Books, Borgomanero-Milano 1992, p. 5.
3. Antonio Olivari, 'Miniatura', in AA.VV., *Atelier Mendini. Una utopia visiva*, op. cit., p. 86.
4. S. Casciani, *L'architettura presa per mano. La maniglia moderna e la produzione Olivari*, op. cit. The volume was followed by an exhibition (Venice Biennale 2010, Milan Triennale 2011) and an accompanying book of the same name *Macchina Semplice*. (S. Casciani, *Macchina Semplice. Dall'architettura al design, 100 anni di maniglie Olivari*, Olivari-Skira, Milan 2010). The cover features a drawing of handles by Mendini.
5. 'The bell towers convey their religious messages to the city, while theatres resonate with the sound of operas and concerts. Their forms are designed with acoustics in mind. The same is true for the Hiroshima Tower, intended to convey the idea of Paradise through both its appearance and sound. Made entirely of steel, the tower resembles a tall trumpet standing upright over the land.' A. Mendini, 'Torre del Paradiso, Hiroshima', manuscript, 1989, now in Loredana Parmesani (ed.), *Alessandro Mendini, Scritti*, op. cit., p. 162.
6. 'Like a set of Russian nesting dolls, sometimes a deep collaboration arises from a work opportunity. This was the case with Bisazza and Atelier Mendini. From the Hiroshima Tower to the creation of floors for Swatch stores, the partnership rapidly evolved: the Mendini brothers have shifted from "players" to "coaches", perfectly aligned with the dynamism and flexibility that characterize this company.' P. Bisazza, 'Caleidoscopio', in *Atelier Mendini. Una utopia visiva*, op. cit., p. 86.
7. Engineer Giannegidio Silva was the first to ensure Mendini could work with expressive freedom while respecting the complex procedures of public construction: 'For architects, clients typically represent an antagonist, with whom they establish a relationship of opposing – even hostile – forces. This attitude becomes particularly exhausting when dealing with public clients [...] In the case of the Municipality of Naples and its subway system, however, an exceptional and positive case emerged, entirely unlike the usual dynamic; an alchemical relationship among all the client stakeholders allowed us architects a rare experience.' Alessandro and Francesco Mendini, in *Metropolitana di Napoli*, manuscript, 2001, now in *Alessandro Mendini, Scritti*, op. cit., pp. 191-192.
8. 'The *Stazioni dell'Arte* are compulsory museums [...] massages for the atrophied muscle of collective sensitivity, compelling visitors to absorb the pervasive aesthetic of the work: they symbolize a possible redemption of the banal city through shared understanding between artists, the infrastructure industry and society.' Achille Bonito Oliva, 'Intervention at the conference on the restoration of the Art Stations, Naples 2023', in *Art Tribune* (online), May 9, 2023.
9. A. and F. Mendini, 'Metropolitana di Napoli', manuscript, 2001, now in *Alessandro Mendini, Scritti*, op. cit., p. 188.
10. 'The metro stations are polycentric and centrifugal places [...] It was thought that this intrinsic fragmentation could give rise to a visual polyphony [...] In particular, the mosaic decoration of large facade surfaces of some buildings overlooking the Salvator Rosa station was envisioned,' A. and F. Mendini, 'Gli interventi degli artisti', manuscript, 2000, now in *Alessandro Mendini, Scritti*, op. cit., pp. 188-189.
11. Due to the significant impact of the *Stazioni dell'Arte* on the city's landscape and urban planning, the exhibition *Napoli*, curated by Alessandro and Francesco Mendini, was held at the VIII Architecture Biennale in *Italy. Next cities*, curated by S. Casciani, Italian Pavilion, Venice 2002.
12. 'ENJOY Y(OUR) LIFE is the phrase Stefano Casciani designed and created for the Montenapoleone metro station, creating a colourful mosaic on three platform pillars, each displaying one word [...] The irony and cleverness of this intervention lie in combining the language of advertising with the classical form of the mosaic.' Giacinto Di Pietrantonio (ed.), *Galleria in Galleria*, exhibition catalogue, Norman-Silvana editoriale, Milan 2005, p. 119.
13. For an overview of Bisazza's work on art and with artists, see AA.VV., *Fondazione Bisazza. Design. Architettura. Fotografia*, Bisazza-Rizzoli, Milan 2019.
14. 'The mosaic, with its rational, angular adaptability for assembly, adjusts to everything like a sophisticated fluid. It ennobles whatever it covers, like a royal cloak. The architect builds, square by square, the kaleidoscopic logic of its rhythm.' A. Mendini, 'La scacchiera lucente', in S. Casciani, *Mosaico Mendini. Progetti e opere dalla Fondazione Bisazza*, Bisazza-Skira, Milan 2011, p. 9.
15. For a history of the origins, development and Swatch collecting, see 'The Turning Point' and other essays, in AA.VV., *Swatch 1983/1992*, Swatch Ag., Biel 1992.
16. See AA.VV., *Swatch Emotion*, exhibition catalogue, Lingotto di Torino, Electa, Milan 1992, later presented in Singapore (1994).
17. 'Looking at the hundreds of "Swatch Collectors" lined up at the entrance of the Lingotto in Turin for the *Swatch Emotion* exhibition (1992), they all seemed thrilled to regress to a childlike state as the encountered the "stations" designed by Atelier Mendini, transforming their journey [...] through Swatch's history and present.' S. Casciani, 'Swatch', in AA.VV., *Atelier Mendini. Un'utopia visiva*, op. cit., p. 162.
18. Franco Bosisio, 'Enciclopedia', in AA.VV., *Atelier Mendini. Un'utopia visiva*, op. cit., p. 91.
19. 'The store on Corso Vittorio Emanuele is the first realization of the new look that will define all Swatch stores [...] Just as the previous concept introduced a playful, artistic and positive vision for Swatch spaces, this project presents a fresh language for the public.' A. and F. Mendini, 'Swatch. Negozi in Via Spiga e Corso Vittorio Emanuele, Milano', manuscript, 1994; now in *Alessandro Mendini, Scritti*, op. cit., p. 255.
20. A. Mendini, G. Gregori, manuscript, 1997, now in *Alessandro Mendini, Scritti*, op. cit., pp. 387-388.
21. For the influence of the Swatch experience on Mendini's design, see S. Casciani, 'Cosmesi globale', in *Alessandro Mendini e Alberto Alessi*, special supplement to *disegno. la nuova cultura industriale*, vol. 9/10, 2024, pp. 22-25.

CHAPTER 9: THE ALESSI CORKSCREW AND THE GLOBAL CITY

1. A. Mendini, in 'Il design e le sue prospettive disciplinari', conference papers for the exhibition *Il design italiano negli anni '50*, September 26–October 30, 1977, Centrokappa, Noviglio-Milan 1977.
2. A. Mendini, 'Telegrammi al Designer', in Pier Carlo Bontempi (ed.), *Alchimia*, Alchimia, Milan 1985, p. 9.
3. A. Mendini, in *Alchimia*, op. cit., ibidem.
4. Mendini continues: 'And then a second phase of the project: when the public's preference for certain authors' vases has been demonstrated, those vases will enter unlimited series production.' A. Mendini, 'The New Romantic Style', in *La Fabbrica Estetica: 100% Make-Up*, Alessi Tendence, Crusinallo (NO) 1992, p. 12.
5. For a discussion on Soviet propaganda porcelain, see Tamara Kudryavtseva (ed.), *Circling the Square: Avant-garde Porcelain from Revolutionary Russia*, Fontanka, London 2004.
6. A. Mendini, 'Disegno installazione con tutti i 10.000 vasi', in *La Fabbrica Estetica*, op. cit., p. 13.
7. A. Mendini, 'The New Romantic Style', in *La Fabbrica Estetica*, op. cit., p. 14.
8. Sets with decorations by Alighiero Boetti, Nicola De Maria and Mendini himself enter serial production.
9. 'Ornament today presents itself as an ethnic and pervasive activity; it develops as a transmission of intimate sensations, as a subjective language, and as a conveyance of dreams, anxieties and myths [...] The decorations are like fish in the sea, they exist even if you don't see them.' A. Mendini, 'The New Romantic Style', in *La Fabbrica Estetica*, op. cit., p. 17.
10. See A. Mendini (ed.), *Tea & Coffee Towers. Ventidue servizi da tè e caffè*, Alessi-Electa, Crusinallo-Milan 2003.
11. S. Casciani: 'What was the criterion for selecting the designers to be involved in this new typological research?' A. Mendini: 'I believe the thinking of these architects is fundamental to the debate on contemporary design: they are designers who convey clear and precise messages about world interpretation through architecture.' in 'Next Object', interview with A. Mendini, *Domusweb* (online), September 3, 2002.
12. 'Stefano Marzano, who was Philips' art director [...] suggested we design small objects together [...] Sandro had the idea of creating a mascot, a good luck charm for the series, and it was precisely the project of a corkscrew. When I saw the drawing, I thought it resembled designer Anna Gili a bit, and I mentioned it to Sandro. So, the

object took the name *Anna G*, and after a while, we paired it with an *Alessandro M*, clearly a self-portrait of Mendini.'
S. Casciani, 'Sandro and Me', interview with Alberto Alessi, in *Alessandro Mendini, Alberto Alessi*, special edition *disegno. la nuova cultura industriale* op. cit., p. 13.

13. S. Casciani: 'Over the years, the *Anna G* and *Alessandro M* operations have become "viral". I'd call it a "mass collecting" phenomenon, similar to what Mendini began with Swatch watches.' Alberto Alessi: 'The difference with other "global cosmetic" projects – Sandro's term starting from the 100 vases in 100% Make-Up – is that here, due to the figurative nature of the design, there's a beautiful autobiographical component, a continuous variation of different characters and personalities – the little ghost, the sweeper, Santa Claus, the cook, the prisoner, the Proust corkscrew...' in 'Sandro and Me', interview with Alberto Alessi, in *Alessandro Mendini, Alberto Alessi*, op. cit., ibidem.
14. 'As all museum employees who worked with him in recent decades have experienced, he was undoubtedly one of the kindest, humblest, and most generous people in the international art world. His passing in February this year deeply shocked and saddened everyone.' Ruud Schenk, 'The World of Alessandro Mendini', in AA.VV., *Mondo Mendini*, catalogue of the exhibition, Groninger Museum, October 2019–May 2020, Groninger Museum, Groningen 2019, p. 9.
15. See the exhibition catalogue: Aldo Colonetti (ed.), AA.VV., *Atelier Mendini. Le Architetture*, Mondadori Electa, Milan 2018.
16. Aldo Rossi, *Autobiografia scientifica*, Pratiche Editrice, Parma 1990, p. 10.
17. Stefano Boeri, 'Mendini the Miniaturist', in *Atelier Mendini. Le Architetture*, op. cit., p. 5.
18. The term, indicating quality, non-traditional materials in products and environments (colour, light, tactility), was introduced in the 1970s by the CDM/Montefibre Design Center group (Andrea Branzi, Clino Trini Castelli, Massimo Morozzi) with articles in Mendini's *Casabella*. See CDM Centro Design Montefibre (ed.), 'Il Design Primario', in *Casabella*, n. 408, 1975, pp. 41-48.
19. In a traditional Korean house, for example, the *sarangbang* is the study or sitting room. In modern South Korea, the concept of *bang* has expanded and diversified, from a mere space enclosed by walls within a home to buildings or businesses in commercial urban spaces.
20. Fabio Dacarro, Chang Bok Yim, 'Comparative Review of Exterior Spaces in the Korean *Hanok* and the Italian *Palazzo*: Spatial Aspects of the *Madang* and the Corte', in *Journal of Asian Architecture and Building Engineering* (online), Taylor & Francis, 2021, pp. 369-382.
21. 'The designer's goal should not be to draw objects, but to think about them.' A. Mendini, *The Proust Chair*, letter to Piero Bisazza for production of the *Proust* giant in mosaic for the Bisazza foundation, July 19, 2005.
22. 'Through work contacts and cultural activities [...] we developed a need for a deeper exploration of the two cultures (Italian and Korean), which led to interesting experiences in industrial design, graphics, and crafts [...] In these various projects, we had the chance to intertwine Western and Eastern mentalities and methods, realizing that this globalized cultural relationship could generate very refreshing formulas for the future of design worldwide.' A. and F. Mendini, in *La Punta: Pavilion for the Seoul Design Fair,* 2010 (online) ateliermendini.it.

CHAPTER 10: THE END AS AN ETERNAL RETURN: LIGHT, COLOUR AND BACK TO DOMUS

1. Johann Wolfgang von Goethe, *Zur Farbenlehre*, J.G. Cotta'sche Buchhandlung, Tübingen 1810; Italian trans.: Johann Wolfgang von Goethe, *La teoria dei colori*, prefazione di G.C. Argan, Il Saggiatore, Milano 1981.
2. S. Casciani (ed.), *Alessandro Mendini. 30 colours*, Akzo-Nobel-V+K Publishing, Bussum 1996.
3. 'Shama', Cinzia Tandoi, artist and designer, collaborated with Mendini on several occasions (*Memory Containers. Progetto Creolo per Alessi*, 1991); she passed away prematurely in 1991.
4. Theo van Doesburg, Cornelis van Eesteren, 'Verso una costruzione collettiva', *De Stijl*, VI, 6/7, 1924, pp. 89-91, now in S. Casciani (ed.), *Alessandro Mendini. 30 colours*, op. cit., p. 18.
5. Vincent van Gogh, 'Letter to Emile Bernard from the Saint-Rémy Hospital', April 1988, in S. Casciani (ed.), *Alessandro Mendini. 30 colours*, op. cit., p. 144.
6. S. Casciani, 'Intervista sul colore ad Alessandro Mendini', in S. Casciani (ed.), *Alessandro Mendini. 30 colours*, op. cit., pp. 4-5.
7. Silvana Annicchiarico (ed.), *Pulviscoli. 2469 disegni di Alessandro Mendini per la Collezione Permanente del design italiano*, Triennale di Milano-Charta, Milano 2005.
8. SeeS.Casciani,'AlessandroMendini.Dentroil colore della luce', in *Swarovsky Magazine*, vol. 3, no. 2, 1989.
9. 'When starting to think of a series of vases for Venini, I felt a sense of awe towards glass, this material – or rather this untouchable "light". I wanted to seek the mystery of archetypes [...] and attempt an interpretation of them. I tried to immerse myself in this tradition and these boundaries, and I hope to have been absorbed by them.' A. Mendini, in Giuliana Duplani Tucci (ed.), AA.VV., *Venini Murano 1921*, Franco Maria Ricci, Milano 1989, p. 81.
10. See A. Mendini, Vincent Beaurin, Fabrice Domercq, *Fragilisme*, Fondation Cartier 2002.
11. CarlGustavJung,*PsychologieundAlchemie*, Walter Verlag, Olten 1972; Italian trans., *Psicologia e Alchimia*, Bollati Boringhieri, Milano 1981, p. 319.
12. 'In1929,thespiritofcapitalismwasharnessed by rules that mitigated its destructive aspects for decades. This lesson was forgotten, and after 2008, attempts were made to bypass the core problem, capitalism's instability, through public debt and money printing. This worked in the short term, but now we see the flaws: low growth and income inequality.' See Mario Pomini, 'Lehman Brothers, la crisi del 2008 ha cambiato il mondo e il capitalismo. In peggio', *Il Fatto Quotidiano* (online), 15 September 2024.
13. The *Domus* editorial team of 2010/2011 consisted of: Alessandro Mendini, director; Stefano Casciani, deputy director; editors: Laura Bossi, Rita Capezzuto, Loredana Mascheroni, Francesca Picchi, Elena Sommariva; graphic team: Elisabetta Benaglio, Franco Miragliotta with art director Giuseppe Basile; secretaries: Miranda Giardino, Isabella Di Nunno.
14. 'Hisheadwasplacedonaswordanddisplayed to the public for a month on London Bridge. His daughter Margaret managed to reclaim it, paying a ransom. The Catholic Church made him a saint. This is also how an urban planner can die, and this is also how a new word can be born. Utopia.' A. Mendini, 'Favola urbanistica (Tommaso Moro)', speech for the presentation of the European Prize for Architecture award 2014, 9 February 2015, now in *Scritti di domenica*, op. cit., p. 20.
15. A.Mendini,inAntonioGnoli,*'Trattoglioggetti come fossero esseri umani, li faccio sorridere'*, interview, in *la Repubblica*, 1 May 2016.
16. Giuseppe Basile (1958-2022) worked for 32 years as art and creative director of *Domus* under all the directors up to Mendini, and for 11 more years, always providing extraordinary creative contributions. Together, over more than 100 issues and supplements of the magazine, we worked on all volumes I published with Editoriale Domus, from *Pierre Restany. Il critico come artista* (2003) to *Un cuore di cristallo per Milano. La nuova Università Bocconi* (2008).
17. A. Mendini, handwritten notes for the *Domus* editorial team, December 2009, author's collection.
18. Interviewer and interviewee are portrayed by photographer Mario Ermoli.
19. Maldonado, an intellectual rival of Mendini, would write a sharply ironic thankyou letter to us: '... others will express their amazement that Tomás allowed himself to be involved in one of Alessandro's issues of *Domus*. I have always maintained that this intolerance is harmful to cultural debate. Because the subject of contention involves issues far beyond the shape of armchairs [...] issues where dialogue between different perspectives is irreplaceable.' Tomás Maldonado, typewritten letter, 20 April 2010, author's collection.
20. S. Casciani, 'Il senso di un luogo sulla mappa delle terre vergini', interview with Wim Wenders, *Domus*, no. 943, January 2011, pp. 37-44.
21. A.Mendini,'Diario'8March,in*Domus*,no.935, April 2010.
22. Oscar Wilde, *Il critico come artista. L'anima dell'uomo sotto il socialismo*, Feltrinelli, January 1995, now in A. Mendini, 'Diario' 27 December, in *Domus*, no. 943, January 2011.
23. See A. Mendini, Silvana Annicchiarico (ed.), *Quali cose siamo. III Triennale Design Museum*, Triennale-Mondadori Electa, Milano 2010.
24. 'What does it all mean? Unsurprisingly, there have been lots of interpretations. One is that *Quali Cose Siamo* is Mr. Mendini's riposte to the textbook history of modern Italian design, which is dominated by famous pieces by famous designers. Another is that he is critiquing the celebrification of contemporary design culture [...] Mr. Mendini agrees with the first and second interpretations.' Alice Rawsthorn, 'An Italian Designer's Homage to His Native Country', in *The New York Times*, 29 August 2010.
25. A. Mendini, 'Diario' 15 February, *Domus*, no. 945, March 2011.
26. See AA. VV., *Mondo Mendini. The World of Alessandro Mendini*, Groninger Museum, 2019, op. cit.
27. 'We are thrilled and happy that it is Naples, in particular, that is hosting the first major exhibition in Italy dedicated to Alessandro Mendini after his passing in February 2019. Naples welcomed our father, inviting him to undertake important projects that, together with his brother Francesco, gave a bold and innovative face to the urban network of this complex and wonderful city.' Fulvia and Elisa Mendini, in Arianna Rosica, Gianluca Riccio (eds.), *Alessandro Mendini. Piccole fantasie quotidiane*, Manfredi, Naples 2020.

EXTENDED PICTURE CAPTIONS AND CREDITS

Every effort has been made to trace the copyright holders and obtain permission to reproduce this material. The publisher apologizes for any errors or omissions and would be grateful if notified of any corrections that should be incorporated in future reprints or editions of this book.

All images are courtesy of Alessandro Mendini Archive unless otherwise stated.

INTRODUCTION

P. 9: Alessandro Mendini and Stefano Casciani at Atelier Mendini, Milan, 2009, photo courtesy Donato Di Bello;

CHAPTER 1

P. 10: Newborn twins Alessandro and Mia Mendini with Savinio's painting *l'Annunciazione*, 2006, drawing, felt-tip pen and coloured pencils on paper, 21×29.7cm, Alessandro Mendini Archive;
P. 15 (top): Cover of the Antoni Gaudí exhibition catalogue, Studio di Architettura Via san Maurilio, Milan,1958, drawing by Mendini, Brunati/Mendini/Villa, Alessandro Mendini Archive;
P. 15 (bottom left): Invitation card to Eric Mendelsohn exhibition with note by Gio Ponti, Studio di Architettura Via san Maurilio, Milan, 1960, Brunati/Mendini/Villa, Alessandro Mendini Archive;
P. 15 (bottom right): Cover of the Eric Mendelsohn exhibition catalogue, Studio di Architettura Via san Maurilio, Milan, 1958, drawing by Eric Mendelsohn, Brunati/Mendini/Villa, Alessandro Mendini Archive;
P. 16 (top left): Mendini and twin sister Mia, Milan, 1931, Alessandro Mendini Archive;
P. 16 (top right): Mendini, Villafranca, Verona, 1935, Alessandro Mendini Archive;
P. 16 (middle left): Mendini's childhood home on Via Giorgio Jan, featuring Alberto Savinio's painting *L'Annunciazione*, Milan, 1982, image courtesy Archivio Gabriele Basilico, photo by Gabriele Basilico;
P. 16 (middle right): Mendini's childhood home on Via Giorgio Jan, architect Piero Portaluppi, Milan, 1929, photo courtesy Fondazione Piero Portaluppi;
P. 16 (bottom): Alberto Savinio (De Chirico Andrea), *Autoritratto in forma di gufo*, 1936, tempera and cardboard on paper applied on plywood, 70×50cm, inv. P/1571, Turin, GAM (Galleria Civica d'Arte Moderna e Contemporanea), image courtesy of the Fondazione Torino Musei;
P. 20 (top left): Mendini and Lidia Prandi, Verona, 1962, Alessandro Mendini Archive;
P. 20 (top right): Mendini and Lidia Prandi, Milan, 1962, Alessandro Mendini Archive;
P. 20 (middle): Lidia Prandi, Pesaro beach, 1964, Alessandro Mendini Archive;
P. 20 (bottom): Mendini's portrait for enrollment at the Politecnico University, Milan, 1949, Alessandro Mendini Archive;
P. 22 (top left): Mendini with his aunt Marieda Boschi Di Stefano, late 1940s, Alessandro Mendini Archive;
P. 22 (top right): Architect Mario Brunati, Milan, 1967, source unknown;
P. 22 (middle left): Mendini as a student, Verona, 1948, Alessandro Mendini Archive;
P. 22 (middle right): Mendini and architect Mario Morganti, Milan, 1963, Alessandro Mendini Archive;
P. 22 (bottom): Mendini with brothers Mia, Francesco and Mario Morganti, Lidia Prandi, Ferruccio Villa, Nicoletta and Luciano Bertolini in the Studio di Architettura Via san Maurilio, Milan, 1963, Alessandro Mendini Archive;
P. 24 (image 01): *Self-portrait,* 1962, drawing, pastel on tracing paper, 100×90cm, Alessandro Mendini Archive;
P. 24 (image 02): *Untitled*, 1960s, drawing, pastel on cardboard, 100×90cm, Alessandro Mendini Archive;
P. 25 (image 03): *Una donna*, 1960s, drawing, black and red pencil, ink on paper, 21×29.7cm, courtesy Archivio CSAC Centro studi e Archivio della Comunicazione – Università degli Studi di Parma;
P. 26 (image 04): *Donna Mappamondo*, 1957, drawing mixed media on cardboard, 36.5×51cm, courtesy Museo del Novecento, Milano-Collezione Boschi Di Stefano, copyright Comune di Milano – all legal rights reserved, Ph Postini;
P. 27 (image 05): *Figura*, 1961, drawing, pastel, pencil on cardboard, 90×100cm, courtesy Archivio CSAC Centro studi e Archivio della Comunicazione – Università degli Studi di Parma;
P. 28 (image 06): *Automobile*, 1960s, drawing, silkscreen printing on cardboard, 60×30cm, Stampe artistiche Centenari Milano, courtesy Archivio CSAC Centro studi e Archivio della Comunicazione – Università degli Studi di Parma;
P. 28 (image 07): *Strada che si avvolge*, drawing, 1960s, mixed media on cardboard, 29.7×21cm, Alessandro Mendini Archive;
P. 29 (image 08): *Un anno soffice su sospensioni SAGA*, greeting card for SAGA Pirelli, 1954, Alessandro Mendini Archive;
P. 29 (image 09): *Pescatore*, drawing, 1960s, marker pen, pastels, pencil on paper, 21×29.7cm, Alessandro Mendini Archive;
P. 30 (image 10): Cover of the Pirelli Information and technical magazine, Year XI, No.6, Dec. 1958, drawing by Mendini, Brunati/Mendini/Villa, courtesy Archivio Pirelli;
P. 31 (image 11): Cover of the Pirelli Information and technical magazine, Year XI, No. 5, Oct. 1959, drawing by Mendini, Brunati/Mendini/Villa, courtesy Archivio Pirelli;
P. 31 (image 12): Drawing for Pirelli by Mendini, 1959 courtesy Archivio Pirelli;

CHAPTER 2

P. 32: Global Tools, first Body Bonds seminar, Milan, 1975, drawing, felt-tip pen on paper, 21×29.7cm, Fondo Alessandro Mendini – Triennale Milano;
P. 37 (top left): Cover of *Casabella* issue 367, 1972, The Gorilla beringei beringei, which appears on the cover, is located in the Akeley African Hall of the American Museum of Natural History in New York, courtesy of Mondadori Portfolio/Electa/Marco Covi;
P. 37 (top middle): Cover of *Casabella* issue 394,1974, *Sedia Paglia* (from the *Oggetti ad uso spirituale* series); courtesy of Mondadori Portfolio/Electa/Marco Covi;
P. 37 (top right): Cover of *Casabella* issue 400,1975, *Do It Yourself Tool-Box*, drawing by Fernando Russo, courtesy of Mondadori Portfolio/Electa/Marco Covi;
P. 37 (middle): Mendini's daughter Elisa and the *Casabella* T-Shirt, 1973, Alessandro Mendini Archive;
P. 37 (bottom): Mendini's daughter Fulvia and the *Casabella* T-Shirt, 1973, Alessandro Mendini Archive;
P. 41 (top left): Paola Navone and Bruno Orlandoni, *Architettura Radicale*, Documenti di *Casabella*, G Milani editrice, Milan, 1974, courtesy of Mondadori Portfolio/Electa/Marco Covi;
P. 41 (top right): *Monumentino da Casa*, sales catalogue, Bracciodiferro srl Genoa,

sales catalogue, Bracciodiferro srl Genoa, 1973, Alessandro Mendini Archive;
P. 41 (bottom): Fanzine *Global Tools no. 1*, 1974, Global Tools group: ARCHIZOOM ASSOCIATI: Andrea Branzi - Gilberto Corretti - Paolo Deganello - Massimo Morozzi - Dario Bartolini - Lucia Bartolini; Remo Buti; CASABELLA: Alessandro Mendini - Carlo Guenzi - Enrico Bona - Franco Raggi - Luciano Boschini; Riccardo Dalisi; Ugo La Pietra; 9999: Giorgio Birelli - Carlo Caldini - Fabrizio Fiumi - Paolo Galli; Gaetano Pesce; Gianni Pettena; RASSEGNA: Adalberto Dal Lago - Ettore Sottsass; SUPERSTUDIO: Piero Frassinelli - Alessandro Magris - Roberto Magris - Adolfo Natalini - Cristiano Toraldo di Francia; U.F.O. : Carlo Bachi - Lapo Binazzi (Patrizia Cammeo, Riccardo Forese) - Titti Maschietto; ZZIGGURAT: Alberto Breschi (Giuliano Fiorenzuoli) - Roberto Pecchioli (Nanni Carciaghe, Gigi Gavini), Alessandro Mendini Archive;
P. 42 (top left): Mendini sets fire to the *Lassù* chair, performance in a field in Segrate (Milan), 1974, Alessandro Mendini Archive;
P. 42 (top right): Almerico De Angelis and Lidia Prandi, Global Tools first seminar on Bonds of the Body, Milan, 1975, courtesy CSAC Archive Study Center and Communication Archive – University of Parma;
P. 42 (middle): Mendini sitting on the *Poltrona di paglia*, 1974, photo by Enrico D. Bona, Alessandro Mendini Archive;
P. 42 (bottom): Global Tools, first seminar Bonds of the Body, Milan, 1975, Mendini and Davide Mosconi with binding *Scarpe Vincolanti* by Franco Raggi, Alessandro Mendini Archive;
P. 45 (top left): Cover of *Sottsass's Scrap-Book*, curated by Federica Di Castro, Documenti di *Casabella*, 1976, drawing by Tiger Tateishi, courtesy of Mondadori Portfolio/Electa/ Marco Covi;
P. 45 (top right): *Modo* issue 6, 1978, cover featuring drawing by Milton Glaser, *Manifesto for an art school*, Alessandro Mendini Archive;
P. 45 (middle): Mendini with the *Modo* editorial staff, CentroKappa, Noviglio, Milan, 1979, seated from left: Maresin Cavagna, Valerio Castelli, Alessandro Mendini, Franco Raggi, Cristina Morozzi, Paolo Carloni; standing from left: Claudia Donà, Paola Bianchi, Agustin Olovarria, Daniela Puppa, Patrizia Rizzi, Valentino Parmiani, photo CentroKappa/Valerio Castelli;
P. 45 (bottom): Mendini's niece Claudia on the *Monumentino da casa* in the living room of Via Giorgio Jan, Milan, 1982, photo by Occhiomagico, Alessandro Mendini Archive;
P. 48 (image 13): Université Libre de Bruxelles project, 1960, Nizzoli Associati: G. Mario Oliveri, Alessandro Mendini, Paolo Viola, Francesco Mendini, Antonio Susini, Studio 1999: Carlo Caldini, Alessandro Casini, Mario Preti, Giovanni Sani, Alessandro Mendini Archive;
P. 48 (image 14): Université Libre de Bruxelles project, 1960, Nizzoli Associati: G. Mario Oliveri, Alessandro Mendini, Paolo Viola, Francesco Mendini, Antonio Susini, Studio 1999: Carlo Caldini, Alessandro Casini, Mario Preti, Giovanni Sani, Alessandro Mendini Archive;
P. 49 (image 15): Alessandro and Francesco Mendini, Diedron, Dancing - Refreshment-Recreation complex, Cappella Cantone, Cremona, 1972, project with Andrea Goldsein Bolocan, Daryouch Hadjian, Antonio Susini, Giorgio Tagini, Pier Achille Barzaghi, Antonio Trotta, courtesy Archivio CSAC Centro studi e Archivio della Comunicazione – Università degli Studi di Parma;
P. 49 (image 16): Alessandro and Francesco Mendini, Diedron, Dancing - Refreshment-Recreation complex, Cappella Cantone, Cremona, 1972, project with Andrea Goldsein Bolocan, Daryouch Hadjian, Antonio Susini, Giorgio Tagini, Pier Achille Barzaghi, Antonio Trotta, Alessandro Mendini Archive;
P. 50 (image 17): *Urbolante: Ricognizione sul paesaggio*, 1970, collage and felt-tip pen on paper, 21×29.7cm, courtesy Fondo Alessandro Mendini – Triennale Milano;
P. 50 (image 18): *Casabella* issue 349 featuring *Urbolante: Ricognizione sul paesaggio*, 1970, courtesy of Mondadori Portfolio/ Electa/Marco Covi;
P. 51 (image 19): *Oggetti ad uso spirituale*: study for *Caverna*, *Calvario*, *Dolmen*, 1970, drawing, felt-tip pen on paper, 21×29.7cm, Fondo Alessandro Mendini – Triennale di Milano;
P. 52 (image 20): *Monumentino da casa*, 1970, drawing, felt-tip pen on paper, 21×29.7cm, Fondo Alessandro Mendini – Triennale Milano;
P. 52 (image 21): *Oggetti ad uso spirituale: Sedia 'Elevazione' oppure 'Erezione'*, 1970, drawing, print on tracing paper, 21×29.7cm, Alessandro Mendini Archive;
P. 53 (image 22): *Monumentino da casa*, monumental chair in wood and coloured tape, 142.9×36.2×196.2cm, 1974, courtesy The Museum of Fine Arts, Houston, Museum purchase funded by the John R. Eckel, Jr. Foundation, 2017, photograph © The Museum of Fine Arts, Houston; Thomas R. DuBrock;
P. 54 (image 23): *Oggetti ad uso spirituale: Tavolo Preghiera*, 1972, drawing, print on tracing paper, 21×29.7cm, Alessandro Mendini Archive;
P. 54 (image 24): *Oggetti ad uso spirituale: Tavolo Voragine*, 1972, drawing, print on tracing paper, 21×29.7cm, Alessandro Mendini Archive;
P. 54 (image 25): *Oggetti ad uso spirituale: Tavolo e Sedia Capitonné*, 1972, drawing, print on tracing paper, 21×29.7cm, Alessandro Mendini Archive;
P. 55 (image 26): *Mobili da meditazione, mobili da guerriglia*, 1960s, drawing, felt-tip pen on paper, 21×29.7cm, courtesy Archivio CSAC Centro studi e Archivio della Comunicazione – Università degli Studi di Parma;
P. 56 (image 27): *Oggetti ad uso spirituale: Poltrona, tomba da soggiorno*, soft polyurethane, Gufram, 1974, Alessandro Mendini Archive;
P. 56 (image 28): *Oggetti ad uso spirituale: Tavolo Domen*, 1972, drawing, print on tracing paper, 21×29.7cm, Alessandro Mendini Archive;
P. 56 (image 29): *Oggetti ad uso spirituale: Sedia*, 1970, drawing, print on tracing paper, 21×29.7cm, Alessandro Mendini Archive;
P. 57 (image 30): *Lampada Letargo*, cast brass, Bracciodiferro Genoa, 1973, Alessandro Mendini Archive;
P. 57 (image 31): *Lampada senza luce*, cast brass, Bracciodiferro Genoa, 1973, Alessandro Mendini Archive;
P. 58 (image 32): *Lassù* chair, partially burnt version 85×85×136cm,1974, Collection Vitra Design Museum, Weil am Rhein, Alessandro Mendini Archive;
P. 58 (image 33): *Sedia Terra*, plexiglass and earth, Bracciodiferro Genoa, 1974, Collection Vitra Design Museum, Weil am Rhein, Alessandro Mendini Archive;
P. 59 (image 34): *Monumentino da casa*, performance, Piedmont hills, 1974, Alessandro Mendini Archive;
P. 60 (image 35): *Sedia Grano*, plexiglass and grain, 1974, Collezione Vitra Design Museum, Weil am Rhein, Alessandro Mendini Archive;
P. 61 (image 36): *Valigia per ultimo viaggio*, cast aluminium, 74×20×52cm, for Bracciodiferro/Cassina, 1974, Alessandro Mendini Archive;
P. 61 (image 37): *Tavolino da salotto*, crystal, 50×170×60cm, unique piece, 1975, Alessandro Mendini Archive;

CHAPTER 3

P. 62: *Untitled*, 1979, drawing, black ink and felt-tip pen on paper, 29.7×21cm, courtesy FFMAAM | Collezione Francesco Moschini e Gabriel Vaduva A.A.M. Architettura Arte Moderna © Eredi Alessandro Mendini | ph Gabriel Vaduva;
P. 67 (top left): Alchimia group, Triennale di Milano, 1986, from bottom to top: Bruno Gregory, Pier Carlo Bontempi, Carla Ceccariglia, Alessandro Guerriero, Adriana Guerriero, Arturo Reboldi, Giorgio Gregori, Alessandro Mendini, on the staircase of the Triennale di Milano, Photo by Alfa Castaldi, courtesy Archivio Alfa Castaldi;
P. 67 (top right): Ettore Sottsass and the *Poltrona di Proust*, during the opening of the Bau-Haus exhibition, Studio Alchimia, Milan, 1979, photo courtesy Santi Caleca;
P. 67 (bottom left): Mendini and Franco Migliaccio painting the *Poltrona di Proust*, 1988, photo by Giuseppe Ragusa, Alessandro Mendini Archive;
P. 68 (top): Poster for Studio Alchimia *Bau-Haus Side One* collection, 1979, Alessandro Mendini Archive;
P. 68 (bottom): Studio Alchimia production, spread from *Architectural Review*, ITALY special issue, 1982, courtesy Stefano Casciani Archive;
P. 70 (image 38): *Diagramma Teorico:* cultural chronology 1968-1978 for *Toilet Paper*, 2013, drawing, felt-tip pen on paper, 21×29.7cm, published in the volume '1968: A Collective Epiphany', *Toilet Paper* by Maurizio Cattelan and Pierpaolo Ferrari, in collaboration with The Deste Foundation, Athens, 2014, Alessandro Mendini Archive;
P. 71 (image 39): Redesign of chairs from the modern movement: *Superleggera* by Gio Ponti, 1978, collection Vitra Design Museum, Weil am Rhein;
P. 72 (image 40): Redesign of chairs from the modern movement: *Sedia Universale* by Joe Colombo, 1978, Collection Vitra Design Museum, Weil am Rhein;
P. 72 (image 41): Redesign of Chairs from the Modern Movement: *Zig Zag* by Gerrit Rietveld, 1975, Collection Groninger Museum, Groningen;
P. 73 (image 42): Redesign of chairs from the modern movement: Thonet *No. 14*, 1978, reissued in 1990 in a limited edition by Antologie Quartett, Germany, Collection Die Neue Sammlung, Munich;
P. 74 (image 43): *Ondoso*, coffee table, wooden top covered in celluloid and painted metal legs, 130×32 cm, Alchimia Bau-Haus Side One collection, 1979, Alessandro Mendini Archive;
P. 75 (image 44): *Kandissi* sofa, lacquered walnut wood, padded back and seat, covered in flamed fabric, 75×193×122cm, 1978, Bau-Haus Side One Alchimia collection, Studio Alchimia Milan, 1979, Collection Groninger Museum, Groningen, ph Heinz Aebi © Groninger Museum;
P. 75 (image 45): Redesign of chairs from the modern movement: *Wassily* by Marcel Breuer, 1978, drawing, felt-tip pen and coloured pencils on paper 21×29.7cm, Alessandro Mendini Archive;
P. 76 (image 46): *Kandissone*, patchwork tapestry in shiny and matt cotton with grosgrain and silk satin applications, 250×187cm, made by Lidia Prandi, 1978, *Bau-Haus Side One* Alchimia collection, Studio Alchimia Milan, 1979, Collection Museum of Fine Arts Boston;
P. 77 (image 47): *Poltrona di Proust*, 1978, armchair in carved wood and hand-painted fabric, 108×104×90cm, exemplar painted by Claudia Mendini, Ph Carlo Lavatori;
P. 77 (image 48 left): Pattern study for a variant of the *Proust* texture,1994, Alessandro Mendini Archive;
P. 77 (image 48 right): *Proust*, laminate, Abet Laminati, 1990, Alessandro Mendini Archive;
P. 78 (image 49): Casa di Ambrogio Milan, 1983, drawing, felt-tip pen and coloured pencils on paper, 21×29.7cm, courtesy: FFMAAM | Collezione Francesco Moschini e Gabriel Vaduva A.A.M. Architettura Arte Moderna © Eredi Alessandro Mendini | ph Gabriel Vaduva;
P. 79 (image 50): *Kandissone* tapestry, 1978, drawing, felt-tip pen and coloured pencils on paper 21×29.7cm, Alessandro Mendini Archive;

CHAPTER 4

P. 80: *Move every thing a little* for the modular elements (Abaco) of *Tea & Coffe Piazza*, Alessi, 1983, drawing, felt-tip pen on paper, 21×29.7cm, Alessandro Mendini Archive;
P. 86 (top): Tiger Tateishi, portrait of Alessandro Mendini for *Domus* magazine, 1979, Alessandro Mendini Archive;
P. 86 (middle): Mendini and Gio Ponti, Triennale di Milano, 1979, Alessandro Mendini Archive;
P. 86 (bottom): *Domus* cover, Aldo Rossi, N.602/ 1980, photography by Occhiomagico, processing by Emilie van Hees, graphic design by Ettore Sottsass, courtesy Domus Archive;
P. 86 (bottom): *Domus* cover, Meret Oppenheim, N.605/1980, photography by Maria Mulas, processing by Emilie van Hees, graphic design by Ettore Sottsass, courtesy Domus Archive;
P. 86 (bottom): *Domus* cover, Morris Lapidus, N.610/1980, photography by Maria Mulas, processing by Emilie van Hees, graphic design by Ettore Sottsass, courtesy Domus Archive;
P. 86 (bottom): *Domus* cover, Enzo Mari, N.607/1980, photography by Maria Mulas, processing by Emilie van Hees, graphic design by Ettore Sottsass, courtesy Domus Archive;
P. 89 (top left): *Domus* Cover, Michele De Lucchi, Ettore Sottsass and Gio Ponti, N.617/1981, photography by Maria Mulas, processing by Emilie van Hees with Alchimia, graphic design by Ettore Sottsass, courtesy Domus Archive;
P. 89 (top right): *Domus* cover, *Arredare come Esistere*, N.624/1982, installation with walls of Hermaphrodite Architecture (PAC Milan), Alchimia and Occhiomagico project, Phoenix Color processing, graphic design by Ettore Sottsass, courtesy Domus Archive;
P. 89 (bottom): *Domus* cover, Emilio Ambasz, N.639/1983, Occhiomagico and Alchimia project, graphic design by Ettore Sottsass, courtesy Domus Archive;
P. 89 (bottom): *Domus* cover, Piero Busnelli, N.642/1983, Occhiomagico and Alchimia project, graphic design by Ettore Sottsass courtesy Domus Archive;
P. 89 (bottom): *Centrodomus: For a map of decoration*, 1981, research on decoration conducted with Stefano Casciani, Carla Ceccariglia, Guido Jannon, Paola Navone, Rosa Maria Rinaldi, promoted by Abet Laminati, Alessi, Editoriale Domus, Fiat, Zanotta, graphic design by Studio Alchimia, 1981, Alessandro Mendini Archive;
P. 89 (bottom): *Centrodomus: For a manual of decoration*, 1981, Research on decoration conducted with Stefano Casciani, Carla Ceccariglia, Guido Jannon, Paola Navone, Rosa Maria Rinaldi. Promoted by Abet Laminati, Alessi, Editoriale Domus, Fiat, Zanotta, graphic design by Studio Alchimia, Alessandro Mendini Archive;
P. 90 (top): Mendini in the *Stanza Banale*, First Architecture Biennale, Project with Alchimia, Franco Raggi, Paola Navone, Daniela Puppa, Corderie dell'Arsenale, Venice, 1980, International Architecture Exhibition *The Presence of the Past* curated by Paolo Portoghesi, Ph Santi Caleca;
P. 90 (bottom left): Mendini with Richard Meier working on the *Tea & Coffee Piazza* project, New York, 1983, Alessandro Mendini Archive;
P. 90 (bottom right): Mendini, Milan, 1980s, Alessandro Mendini Archive;
P. 93 (top left): Cover of the *Forum Design* exhibition guide, Linz, Austria, 1980, Stefano Casciani Archive;
P. 93 (top right): Michele De Lucchi, Martine Bedin, Casciani, Mendini, Achille Castiglioni, Ettore Sottsass, *Forum Design*, Linz, 1980, Stefano Casciani Archive;
P. 93 (middle): Mendini with Casciani, *Forum Design*, Linz, 1980, Stefano Casciani Archive;
P. 93 (bottom): *Forum Design* exhibition guide with contributors to the Thematic Sections, curated by Mendini, Linz, Austria, 1980, Stefano Casciani Archive;
P. 97 (top left): Theoretical drawing for Centro Studi Alessi, 1991, drawing, felt-tip pen on paper, 21×29.7cm, Fondo Alessandro Mendini – Triennale Milano;
P. 97 (top right): *Paesaggio Casalingo*, catalogue of the exhibition at Triennale di Milano, Alessi, 1980;
P. 97 (bottom left): Hans Hollein and Alberto Alessi at the *Paesaggio Casalingo* exhibition, Triennale di Milano, extract from *Paesaggio Casalingo* book, 1980;
P. 97 (bottom right): *Tea & Coffee Piazza* book, graphic design by Bruno Munari, Alessi, 1983;
P. 100 (image 51): *Forum Design*, Linz: entrance to the *Space Design* section in the exhibition *Design Phenomene*: Arte Moda Design, Linz, Austria, 1980, project with Alchimia, Bruno Gregory, Giorgio Gregori, Alessandro Guerriero, Maria Christina Hamel, Ph Santi Caleca;
P. 101 (image 52): *Forum Design*, Linz: entrance to the *Fashion Design* section in the exhibition *Design Phenomene*: Arte Moda Design, Linz, Austria, 1980, project with Alchimia, Bruno Gregory, Giorgio Gregori, Alessandro Guerriero, Maria Christina Hamel, Ph Santi Caleca;
P. 102 (image 53): *Paesaggio Banale*, Alchimia, 1980, drawing by Giorgio Gregori, felt-tip pen and coloured pencils on paper, 21×29.7cm, image courtesy FFMAAM | Collezione Francesco Moschini e Gabriel Vaduva A.A.M. Architettura Arte Moderna © Eredi Alessandro Mendini | ph Gabriel Vaduva;
P. 103 (image 54): *Untitled* (Psychological study for *Casa di Giulietta* exhibition in Verona), 1982, drawing, felt-tip pen on paper, 21×29.7cm, image courtesy: FFMAAM | Collezione Francesco Moschini e Gabriel Vaduva A.A.M. Architettura Arte Moderna © Eredi Alessandro Mendini | ph Gabriel Vaduva;
P. 104 (image 55): *Untitled* (first drawing for *Mobile Infinito*), 1980-1981, drawing, felt-tip pen and coloured pencils on paper, 21×29.7cm, image courtesy: FFMAAM | Collezione Francesco Moschini e Gabriel Vaduva A.A.M. Architettura Arte Moderna © Eredi Alessandro Mendini | ph Gabriel Vaduva;
P. 105 (image 56): *Redesign of objects: Lamp*, for the *L'Oggetto Banale* exhibition, First Biennale of Architecture, Venice, 1980, project with Alchimia, Paola Navone,

EXTENDED PICTURE CAPTIONS AND CREDITS 293

Franco Raggi, Daniela Puppa, photo retouched with airbrush 50×70cm, Collezione Groninger Museum;
P. 105 (image 57): *Redesign of objects: Vaporizer*, for the *L'Oggetto Banale* exhibition, First Biennale of Architecture, Venice, 1980, project with Alchimia, Paola Navone, Franco Raggi, Daniela Puppa, photo retouched with airbrush 50×70cm, Collezione Groninger Museum;
P. 106 (image 58): Alessi *Programma 6: Tea & Coffee Piazza*, tea and coffee set for Alessi, screen print, drawing by Maria Christina Hamel, 1983, Alessandro Mendini Archive;
P. 106 (image 59): Alessi *Programma 6: Tea & Coffee Piazza*, tea and coffee silver set, Alessi, 1983, Alessi Archive;
P. 107 (image 60): *Redesign of objects: coffee maker* in painted aluminium, for the *L'Oggetto Banale* Exhibition, First Biennale of Architecture, Venice, 1980, project with Alchimia, Paola Navone, Franco Raggi, Daniela Puppa (Limited edition 1994), Alessandro Mendini Archive;
P. 108 (image 61): Alessi *Programma 3*, steel tray, technical drawing, Alessi, 1978, Museo Alessi Collection;
P. 108 (image 62): Alessi *Programma 3*, steel tray, illustration by Tiger Tateishi for *Paesaggio Casalingo* book, Alessi, 1978, Alessandro Mendini Archive;
P. 109 (image 63): *Alessofono*, redesign of the Saxophone made by Alessi, black chromed brass with gilded decorations, coral and gold, project with Maria Christina Hamel, 1994;

CHAPTER 5

P. 110: *Arredi Vestitivi*, 1982, drawing, felt-tip pen on paper, 21×29.7cm, Fondo Alessandro Mendini – Triennale Milano;
P. 115 (top left): *Domus Moda* 1, N.617 supplement/1981, cover: Decorated Face, make-up by Keiko, Alchimia project, Ph George Holz, courtesy Domus Archive;
P. 115 (top right): *Domus Moda* 2, N.621 supplement/1981, cover: Tutankhamun, project by Occhiomagico – System video processing Tasco, courtesy Domus Archive;
P. 115 (middle): Alessandro Mendini, *Progetto Infelice*, edited by Rosa Maria Rinaldi, RDE (Ricerche Design Editrice), 1983, graphic design: Paola Bianchi, Michele De Lucchi, Mauro Panzeri, editorial coordination: Alchimia, image of the men's set over-blanket: Elmo, Pistol, Hat, drawing by Bruno Gregory, 1983;
P. 115 (bottom): Invitation card for *Arredo Vestitivo*, performance project with Alchimia at Fiorucci Shop for the new furniture column in *Domus* magazine, Milan, 1982, Alessandro Mendini Archive;
P. 117 (top left): Anna Gili, *Abito Monumentale* for *Black Out* Installation, *Affinità Elettive* exhibition, XVII Triennale di Milano, 1985: The *Black Out* installation was composed of two parts, BLACK (above) by Alessandro Mendini and OUT (below) by Anna Gili. Anna Gili's OUT installation was closed inside a black marble cube, the *Abito Monumentale* in the centre of the space lined with mirrored walls was visible through a crack. The presence of the mirrored walls multiplied the *Abito Monumentale* infinitely. Image courtesy Archivio Anna Gili;
P. 117 (top right): *Nulla, Idea per un ambiente*, performance with *Abito Sonoro* by Anna Gili. Detail of the wall design by Mendini and Gili, Memorie e Luoghi del XX secolo gallery, Florence, 1984, image courtesy Archivio Anna Gili;
P. 117 (middle): Mendini and his double, sculpture for *Black Out* installation, Triennale Milano, 1985, Ph Ambrogio Beretta, Alessandro Mendini Archive;
P. 117 (bottom): *Black Out* installation, *Affinità Elettive* exhibition, XVII Triennale di Milano, 1985, project with Alchimia. Black: Giorgio Gregori, Maria Christina Hamel, Reiner Haegele, Jeremy King, Giorgio Gregori, Occhiomagico. Out: Anna Gili. Lighting consultancy: Piero Castiglioni. Collage on cardboard, 70×100cm, 1985, Alessandro Mendini Archive;
P. 120 (image 64): *Rampichino*, Cinelli bike screen-printed for Alchimia Fast Design, Museo Alchimia, 1985, project with Bruno Gregory, Alessandro Mendini Archive;
P. 120 (image 65): *Vasi di manici* ceramic for Alchimia Fast Design, 1985, Collection Pannocchia Campatelli, Alessandro Mendini Archive;
P. 121 (image 66): Cover of the *Mobile Infinito* catalogue, drawing by Mimmo Paladino, Alchimia Editore, 1981, graphic design by Mauro Panzeri, Alessandro Mendini Archive;
P. 122 (image 67): *Mobile Infinito: Bedside Table*, 1981-1994, project with Alchimia. Abet laminate covering; magnetic decorations by Mimmo Paladino; feet by Denis Santachiara, ph Weshoot, Collection Design Museum, Triennale Milano;
P. 123 (image 68): *Mobile Infinito Japan: Bedside Table*, project with Alchimia and Sinya Okayama, pink version, 1985. Magnetic decorations by Clelia Ravone; feet by Denis Santachiara, Collection Museum of Contemporary Art of Osaka, Japan;
P. 123 (image 69): *Mobile Infinito: Table*, 1981-1994, project with Alchimia. Abet laminate covering; on the medallion surface *La morte che mangia l'uva* by Francesco Clemente, photographic reproduction; magnetic decorations by Mimmo Paladino; internal decorations on the legs by Gio Ponti, Bruno Munari and Alessandro Mendini; feet by Denis Santachiara, ph Carlo Lavatori;
P. 123 (image 70): *Mobile Infinito: Bookcase*, back laminate panel by Gio Ponti (Abet Laminati), project with Alchimia, 1981, Installation in the Gio Ponti pavilion library at Milan Polytechnic, 1981, Ph Franco Raggi;
P. 124 (image 71): *Black Out*, bar cabinet for the installation *Black Out, Affinità Elettive* exhibition, XVII Triennale di Milano, 1985, lacquered wood and painted metal, 200×40×170cm, 1985, Antonello collection, Alessandro Mendini Archive;
P. 125 (image 72): *Tender Architecture* for the *Alcantara* installation, *Materiali Idea* exhibition, PAC Milano,1982, drawing, felt-tip pen on paper, 21×29.7cm, courtesy: FFMAAM | Collezione Francesco Moschini e Gabriel Vaduva A.A.M. Architettura Arte Moderna © Eredi Alessandro Mendini | ph Gabriel Vaduva;
P. 126 (image 73): *Nulla, Idea per un ambiente* performance with *Abito Sonoro* by Anna Gili, installation on the wall by Mendini with Gili, musical consultancy by Davide Mosconi and Giuseppe Chiari, Memorie e luoghi del XX° Secolo gallery, Florence, 1984, courtesy Archivio Anna Gili;
P. 126 (image 74): *Abito Sonoro* performance by Anna Gili, PAC Milano, 1984, courtesy Archivio Anna Gili;
P. 127 (image 75): *Arredo Vestitivo*, performance for Fiorucci, Milan, 1982, project with Alchimia, Alessandro Mendini Archive;
P. 127 (image 76): *Ambienti di Transito* performance, Alchimia, Stefano Casciani and Carla Ceccariglia, Naples, 1983;

CHAPTER 6

P. 128: *Zabro* chair/table, *Nuova Alchimia* collection for Zabro (Zanotta), 1984, drawing, felt-tip pen on paper, 21×29.7cm, Fondo Alessandro Mendini – Triennale Milano;
P. 132 (top left): Mendini and Toshiyuki Kita, Los Angeles, 1985, Stefano Casciani Archive;
P. 132 (top right): Aurelio Zanotta and the *Zabro* chair/table, 1984, ph Susana Bruell, Stefano Casciani Archive;
P. 132 (middle): *Zabro Nuova Alchimia* collection catalogue, 1984, Stefano Casciani Archive;
P. 132 (bottom left): Invitation to the *Ambiente di Piante Mobili* exhibition, Milan, 1981, Stefano Casciani Archive;
P. 132 (bottom right): At the Temporary Contemporary conference, Los Angeles, 1985, Stefano Casciani Archive;
P. 137 (top left): Andrea Branzi, Invitation card for *Mussolini's Bathroom* exhibition at Centrodomus, Milan, 1982, Stefano Casciani Archive;
P. 137 (top right): *Domus* N.627, featuring *Mussolini's Bathroom* exhibition by Andrea Branzi and Alchimia, 1982, project with Occhiomagico, graphic design by Ettore Sottsass, courtesy Domus Archive;
P. 137 (bottom left): Andrea Branzi, *Mussolini's Bathroom* exhibition at Centrodomus, Milan, 1982, project with Alchimia, Stefano Casciani Archive;
P. 137 (bottom right): *Ollo: Magazine Without a Message*, issue 2, 1990, art direction by Alessandro Mendini with Alessandro Guerriero, Oliviero Toscani, Wist Thrope, Stefano Casciani, Giacinto Di Pietrantonio, Walter Garro, Anna Gili, Cinzia Ruggeri, Silvio San Pietro. On the cover, drawing by Alessandro Mendini, Edizioni L'Archivolto – Alchimia, Milan, Alessandro Mendini Archive;
P. 140 (image 77): *Gioiello*, pendant for Cleto Munari, 1983, drawing, felt-tip pen on paper, 21×29.7cm, Fondo Alessandro Mendini – Triennale Milano;
P. 140 (image 78): *Gioiello*, 24kt gold pendant for Cleto Munari, 1983, Alessandro Mendini Archive;
P. 141 (image 79): *Untitled*, nitro painting on wood, 90×75cm, 1986, Alessandro Mendini Archive;
P. 142 (image 80): *Untitled*, nitro painting on wood, 150×180cm, 1986, Alessandro Mendini Archive;
P. 143 (image 81): *Untitled*, nitro painting on wood, 150×180cm, 1986, Alessandro Mendini Archive;
P. 143 (image 82): *Untitled*, nitro painting on canvas, 150×180cm, 1986, Frédéric Le Gorrec collection, Grenoble, France, Alessandro Mendini Archive;
P. 144 (image 83): *Sabrina* armchair, Driade, 1982, drawing, felt-tip pen and coloured pencils on paper, 21×29.7cm, Fondo Alessandro Mendini – Triennale Milano;
P. 144 (image 84): *Sabrina* armchair covered in Bauhaus fabric, 76×80×115cm, Driade, 1983, Ph Ugo Pons Salabelle;
P. 145 (image 85): *Omaggio a Gropius* steel handles for FSB Brakel, Germany, 1986, Alessandro Mendini Archive;
P. 146 (image 86): *Nuova Alchimia* Collection for Zabro (Zanotta), poster, 1984, project with Alessandro Guerriero, Alchimia, Alessandro Mendini Archive;
P. 147 (image 87): *Agrilo* console, lacquered and silk-screened wood, 80×40×90cm, *Nuova Alchimia* collection for Zabro (Zanotta), 1984, project with Alchimia, Bruno Gregory and Giorgio Gregori, Alessandro Mendini Archive;
P. 149 (image 88): *Atomaria* floor lamp, lacquered wood and metal, 50×18×186cm, *Nuova Alchimia* collection for Zabro (Zanotta), 1984, project with Alchimia, Bruno Gregory and Giorgio Gregori, Alessandro Mendini Archive;
P. 147 (image 89): *Zabro* chair/table, lacquered and silk-screened wood, 93×50×137cm, *Nuova Alchimia* collection for Zabro (Zanotta), 1984, project with Alchimia, Bruno Gregory and Giorgio Gregori, Alessandro Mendini Archive;
P. 148 (image 90): *Cipriani* bar/cabinet, black painted wood covered in mirror, legs and decorations in metal, 85×50×223cm, Memphis, 1981, edition of 20 copies, Victoria & Albert Museum Collection London, Alessandro Mendini Archive;
P. 149 (image 91): Gold and hematite watch and jewellery for Türler, 1988, project with Maria Christina Hamel, courtesy Türler Schmuck & Uhren;
P. 149 (image 92): Gold and hematite watches for Türler, 1988, drawing, felt-tip pen and coloured pencils on paper, 21×29.7cm, Fondo Alessandro Mendini – Triennale di Milano;
P. 150 (image 93): *Stelline* chair for Elam Uno, 1987, drawing, felt-tip pen and coloured pencils on paper, 21×29.7cm, Fondo Alessandro Mendini – Triennale di Milano;
P. 151 (image 94): *Stelline* series, chair with armrests, metal and polyurethane, 41×41×83cm for Elam Uno, 1987, Alessandro Mendini Archive;
P. 152 (image 95): *Stella*, 1990, drawing, felt-tip pen and coloured pencils on cardboard, 100×70cm, Alessandro Mendini Archive;
P. 153 (image 96): *Gallinella*, 1990, drawing, felt-tip pen and coloured pencils on cardboard, 100×70cm, Frédéric Le Gorrec Collection, Grenoble, France, Alessandro Mendini Archive;
P. 153 (image 97): *Gallinella*, painted wooden sculpture, 7.5×25×32cm, Spiritelli Alchimia, 1990, Giuliano Gori collection – Fattorie di Celle, Alessandro Mendini Archive;
P. 154 (image 98): Decoration for the Renault *Super 5* car, 1985, project with Alchimia, Alessandro Mendini Archive;
P. 154 (image 99): *Design Pittorico*, drawing for the Zabro (Zanotta) sideboard, 1986, project with Alchimia, Alessandro Mendini Archive;
P. 155 (image 100): *Lampada di Milo* floor lamp in lacquered steel, 33×170cm, Segno, 1988, re-edition Codice Icona, 2020, Alessandro Mendini Archive;

CHAPTER 7

P. 156: Groninger Museum, study for the Ancient, Contemporary, Decorative, Regional Art pavilions, Groningen, Netherlands, 1990, drawing, felt-tip pen and coloured pencils on paper, 21×29.7cm, Fondo Alessandro Mendini – Triennale Milano;
P. 160 (top left): Alberto Alessi, Achille Castiglioni, Enzo Mari, Aldo Rossi, Alessandro Mendini, Officine Alessi, Crusinallo, 1989, Ph Gianni Berengo Gardin, courtesy Gianni Berengo Gardin;
P. 160 (top right): Robert Venturi, Denise Scott Brown, Steven Izenour, *Imparando da Las Vegas* (Learning from Las Vegas), introduction by Alessandro Mendini and Stefano Casciani, edited by Margherita Rossi Paulis, CLUVA, Venezia, 1985;
P. 160 (middle): Mendini with Robert Venturi working on the *Tea & Coffee Piazza* project, Philadephia, 1983, Alessandro Mendini Archive;
P. 160 (bottom): Mendini and the *Peyrano* box for Alessi, 1990, Ph Paola Mattioli;
P. 164 (top): Alessandro and Francesco Mendini, *Casa della Felicità*, library, project by Robert Venturi in the house on Orta lake, Omegna, 1983-1988, project with Alchimia – Giorgio Gregori, Bruno Gregory, Alessandro Guerriero. Guest architects: Andrea Branzi, Achille Castiglioni, Riccardo Dalisi, Frank Gehry, Milton Glaser, Aldo Rossi, Ettore Sottsass, Robert Venturi. Ph Aldo Ballo, courtesy Archivio Ballo + Ballo, Maria Rosa Toscani Ballo: Comune di Milano Archivio fotografico;
P. 164 (bottom): Alessandro and Francesco Mendini, *Casa della Felicità*, living room with central fireplace designed by Ettore Sottsass in the house on Orta lake, Omegna, 1983-1988, project with Alchimia – Giorgio Gregori, Bruno Gregory, Alessandro Guerriero. Guest architects: Andrea Branzi, Achille Castiglioni, Riccardo Dalisi, Frank Gehry, Milton Glaser, Aldo Rossi, Ettore Sottsass, Robert Venturi. Ph Aldo Ballo, courtesy Archivio Ballo + Ballo, Maria Rosa Toscani Ballo: Comune di Milano Archivio fotografico;
P. 166 (top left): Atelier Mendini, studio of Alessandro and Francesco Mendini on Via Sannio, Milan, 1989, project with Piero Gaeta and Emanuela Morra. On the wall paintings by Alessandro Mendini, Ph Emilio Neri Tremolada;
P. 166 (top right): Atelier Mendini, 1994, from top left: Rudi Von Wedel, Cristina Marino, Ronen Joseph, Emanuela Morra, Jacopo Ninni, Giuliana Gaeta, Matteo Tresoldi, Francesco Mendini, Marco Poma; Stefano Casciani, Beatrice Felis, Mattias Reuter, Elisa Mendini, Davide Sgalippa; Carla Ceccariglia, Maria Christina Hamel, Massimo Caiazzo, Dagmar Trinks, Momi Modenato; Pietro Gaeta, Costantino Lanteri, Gaia Longhi, Sergio Fabio Rotella, Sandrely Cunha Silva, Bruno Gregory, Alessandro Mendini, Maki Kasano, Mariapia Bobbioni; Anna Gili, Cristiana Vannini, Ezio Manciuca, Andrea Balzari, Francesco Castiglioni Morelli, Annalisa Margarini, Tina Corti; Luca Panaro, Alex Mocika, Raffaella Poletti, Silvia Giuli, Fulvia Mendini, Jesus Montezuma, Giorgio Gregori, Ph Sergio Efrem Raimondi;
P. 166 (bottom): Atelier Mendini, studio of Alessandro Mendini and Francesco Mendini on Via Sannio, Milan, 1989, project with Pietro Gaeta, Emanuela Morra, Ph Emilio Neri Tremolada;
P. 169 (top): Alessandro and Francesco Mendini with Alchimia, Michele De Lucchi, Philippe Starck, Groninger Museum, with the unbuilt project of the Ancient Art pavilion 1500-1950 by Frank Stella, 1988-1990, model in methacrylate and painted wood, 110×41×25cm, Ph Roberto Gennari Feslikenian, Alessandro Mendini Archive;
P. 169 (bottom): Alessandro and Francesco Mendini, Groninger Museum, gilded storage tower and entrance to the museum, restaurant and technical spaces on the sides, 1988-1994, drawing, ink on gloss, 70×80cm, Alessandro Mendini Archive;
P. 170 (image 101): Design for the new Ponte dell'Accademia for the Architecture Biennale Venice, 1985, project with Alchimia, Alessandro Guerriero, Pier Carlo Bontempi, Bruno Gregory, Giorgio Gregori, tempera on cardboard, 105×75cm, Alessandro Mendini Archive;
P. 171 (image 102): *Casa della Felicità*, garden plan, painting, nitro on canvas, 80×50cm, 1988, Alessi Collection;
P. 171 (image 103): *Casa della Felicità*, garden plan, study for painting, 1983-1988, drawing, felt-tip pen and coloured pencils on paper, 21×29.7cm, Fondo Alessandro Mendini – Triennale Milano;
P. 172 (image 104): Groninger Museum, study for the island museum with Ancient, Contemporary, Decorative, Regional Art pavilions and connecting bridges, Groningen, Netherlands, 1989, drawing, felt-tip pen and coloured pencils on paper, 29.7×21cm, Fondo Alessandro Mendini – Triennale Milano;

P. 173 (image 105): Alessandro and Francesco Mendini with Alchimia, Groninger Museum, East Pavillion with the lower section designed by Mendini clad in the *Proust* motif and the upper section designed by Coop himmel(b)lau, Groninger, Netherlands, 1988-1994 (restoration 2010), Ph Ralph Richter © Groninger Museum;
P. 174 (image 106): Groninger Museum, study for the island museum, Groningen, Netherlands, 1990, drawing, felt-tip pen and coloured pencils on paper, 21× 29.7cm, Fondo Alessandro Mendini – Triennale Milano;
P. 175 (image 107): Alessandro and Francesco Mendini, Groninger Museum, Ancient, Contemporary, Decorative, Regional Art pavilions, Groningen, Netherlands, 1989-1994 (renovation 2010), project with Alchimia, Alessandro Guerriero, Giorgio Gregori, Bruno Gregory, Alex Mocika, Gerda Vossaert and Pietro Gaeta for the interiors. Guest architects: Michele De Lucchi, with G. Koster, F. Laviani (interior of Archeology and History Pavilion), Philippe Starck with A. Geertjes (interior of Decorative Arts pavilion), Frank Stella (Pavilion of Ancient Art 1500-1950, unbuilt), Coop Himmelb(l)au (Pavilion of Ancient Art 1500-1950); lighting design Piero Castiglioni; colour design Peter Struychen; works management Team 4; static project Otto Wassenaar-Ingenieursbureau Wassenaar, Haarlem. Museum Director: Frans Haks (1978-1995), Ph Ralph Richter © Groninger Museum
P. 174 (image 108): Alessandro and Francesco Mendini with Alchimia, Groninger Museum, Decorative Arts department, interior design by Philippe Starck, Groningen, Netherlands, 1988-1994, Ph Beba Stoppani © Groninger Museum;
P. 176 (image 109): Groninger Museum, *Tutto d'oro?*, Groningen, Netherlands, 1990, drawing, felt-tip pen and coloured pencils on paper, 21× 29.7cm, Fondo Alessandro Mendini – Triennale Milano;
P. 177 (image 110): Alessandro and Francesco Mendini with Alchimia, Groninger Museum, connecting square with the East pavilion, Ancient Art 1500-1950 and Contemporary Art sector, Groningen, Netherlands, 1994, facade cladding in *Proust* laminate (Abet laminati), Ph Beba Stoppani © Groninger Museum;
P. 177 (image 111): Alessandro and Francesco Mendini, Groninger Museum, gilded storage tower and entrance to the museum, on the sides the restaurant buildings and technical spaces, Groningen, Netherlands, 1994, facade clad in Gold laminate (Abet Laminati), Ph Beba Stoppani © Groninger Museum;
P. 178 (image 112): Groninger Museum, study for sculpture in the entrance square to the museum, Groningen, Netherlands, 1994, drawing, felt-tip pen and coloured pencils on paper, 29.7×21cm, Fondo Alessandro Mendini – Triennale Milano;
P. 178 (image 113): Alessandro and Francesco Mendini, Groninger Museum, sculpture in the entrance square to the museum, Groningen, Netherlands, 1994, Ph Ralph Richter © Groninger Museum;
P. 179 (image 114): Coop-Himmel(b)lau, Groninger Museum, drawing for the Pavilion of Ancient Art 1500-1950, Groningen, Netherlands, 1990, Collection Groninger Museum;
P. 179 (image 115): Alessandro and Francesco Mendini with Alchimia, Groninger Museum, central staircase connecting the pavilions of contemporary art and ancient art 1500-1950, Groningen, Netherlands, restyling 2010, Ph Peter Tahl © Groninger Museum;
P. 180 (image 116): Alessandro and Francesco Mendini with Alchimia, Groninger Museum, entrance hall to the museum with Bisazza mosaic staircase, light installation on the ceiling by François Morellet, Groningen, Netherlands, restyling 2010, Ph Marten de Leeuw © Groninger Museum;
P. 181 (image 117): Alessandro and Francesco Mendini with Alchimia, Groninger Museum, central staircase in Bisazza mosaic, Groningen, Netherlands, 1994, Ph Gerhard Taatgen © Groninger Museum;

CHAPTER 8

P. 182: *Lot of Dots*, wristwatch with *Proust* pattern for Swatch,1990, drawing, felt-tip pen and coloured pencils on paper, 29,7×21cm, Fondo Alessandro Mendini – Triennale Milano;
P. 187 (top left): Alessandro and Francesco Mendini, Casa Bisazza, showroom, Milan, 1994, project with Silvia Giuli, Giorgio Gregori, Bruno Gregory, Emanuela Morra, Fabio Rotella, environment in Bisazza mosaic, mosaic coffee tables by Ugo Marano, glass works by Riccardo Dalisi and Ugo Marano, © Archivio Bisazza;
P. 187 (top right): Casciani, Mendini and Italo Lupi, presentation of the book *L'architettura presa per mano*, Olivari, Idea Books, Milan, 1992, Stefano Casciani Archive;
P. 187 (middle left): Opening of the Bisazza Foundation, Vicenza, 2012, Mendini and Casciani with (behind) Piero and Rossella Bisazza, John Pawson and front from left: Carlo Dal Bianco, Hervé Chandes, Guta Moura Guedes, Maria Cristina Didero, Fabio Novembre, Aldo Cibic, Anna Gili, Alexander von Vegesach, Arik Levy;
P. 187 (middle right): Mendini and Casciani with (among others) Giusi Laurino (right) and Ugo Marano (back right) at the inauguration of the Salvator Rosa Metro Station, Naples, 2001, ph Pino Guidolotti;
P. 187 (bottom): Alessandro and Francesco Mendini, Salvator Rosa Metro Station, Line 1, Naples, 2001. From left: works by Ernesto Tatafiore, *Diderot Filosofia* (Bisazza mosaic), 2001; Mimmo Rotella, *The Flight of Icarus* (Bisazza mosaic), 2001; Salvatore Paladino, *Playful Sculptures*, 2001; Mimmo Paladino, *Untitled*, 2001; Gianni Pisani, *The train that leaves the island* (Bisazza mosaic) 2001, project with Andrea Balzari, Filippo Ferrari, Bruno Gregory, Alex Mocika, Sergio Sinopoli, Sam Stone, Lorena Vieyra, Marisa A Vihna, Barbara Zanotta, Ph Peppe Avallone © MN Naples Metro;
P. 191 (top left): Young design team of Swatch Lab, art director Mendini, Milan, 1994, among others: Adelina Bissolo, Walter Garro, Cristina Marino, Judith Mc Kimm, Nadia Morelli, Jesus Montezuma, James Smith, Alessandro Mendini Archive;
P. 191 (top right): Mendini with the collection of Swatch watches designed by him, Seoul, 2016, © Swatch;
P. 191 (bottom left): Mendini and Ettore Sottsass photographed by Johanna Grawunder, Venice, 1993, Alessandro Mendini Archive;
P. 191 (bottom right): Alessandro and Francesco Mendini, Swatch Corner Fiorucci, Milan, 1994, project with Dagmar Trinks, Ph Santi Caleca;
P. 192 (image 118): Torre Paradiso, steel tower, realized for Expo Hiroshima, Hatoba Park, Hiroshima, Japan, 1989, methacrylate model and applied decoration, 60×60×52cm, project with Yumiko Kobayashi, Ph Roberto Gennari Feslikenian;
P. 192 (image 119): Torre Paradiso, steel tower, realized for Expo Hiroshima, Hatoba Park, Hiroshima, Japan, 1989, drawing, felt-tip pen and coloured pencils on paper, 21×29.7cm, Fondo Alessandro Mendini – Triennale Milano;
P. 193 (image 120): Torre Paradiso, steel tower, realized for Expo Hiroshima, Hatoba Park, Hiroshima, Japan, 1989, project with Yumiko Kobayashi, music by Davide Mosconi, Alessandro Mendini Archive;
P. 194 (image 121): Alessandro and Francesco Mendini, *Swatch Emotion* exhibition at the World Trade Center Singapore, 1994, drawing by Bruno Gregory, project with Bruno Gregory, Giorgio Gregori, Silvia Giuli, Jacopo Ninni, Alessandro Mendini Archive;
P. 195 (image 122): Alessandro Mendini and Francesco Mendini, *Swatch Emotion* exhibition at the World Trade Center Singapore, 1994, project with Bruno Gregory, Giorgio Gregori, Silvia Giuli, Jacopo Ninni, Ph Francesco Mendini, Alessandro Mendini Archive;
P. 195 (image 123): Alessandro Mendini and Francesco Mendini, Swatch Shop, Via Montenapoleone, Milan, Italy, 1994, project with Andrea Balzari, wall decor by Massimo Iosaghini, Alessandro Mendini Archive;
P. 196 (image 124): *Little Monument to the Swatch*, table clock, Swatch, 1990-1991, drawing, felt-tip pen and coloured pencils on paper, 21×29.7cm, Fondo Alessandro Mendini – Triennale Milano;
P. 197 (image 125): Alessandro and Francesco Mendini, display piece for Swatch installation, drawing by Massimo Caiazzo, Bruno Gregory, Annalisa Margarini, 1994, Alessandro Mendini Archive;
P. 197 (image 126): Alessandro and Francesco Mendini, display piece for Swatch installation, drawing by Massimo Caiazzo, Bruno Gregory, Annalisa Margarini, 1994, Alessandro Mendini Archive;
P. 198 (image 127): *Spot the Dot*, wristwatch with *Proust* decoration, Swatch Switzerland, 2015-2016, drawing, felt-tip pen and coloured pencils on paper, 21×29.7cm, Alessandro Mendini Archive;
P. 199 (image 128): *Spot of Dot*, wristwatch, Swatch, 2016, © Swatch;
P. 199 (image 129): Swatch Lab S/S and A/W 1994-1995: Swatch wristwatches by W Garro: *Sizung*; C Marino: *Poncho*; N Morelli: *Azimut*; A Bissolo: *Avenida*; J McKimm: *Anguria*; I Garòati: *Lemon breeze*; J Moctezuma: *Echodeco*; A Arrigoni: *Quasimodo*; © Swatch;
P. 200 (image 130): *Venere*, steel and coloured glass handle, Olivari, 2001, drawing, felt-tip pen and coloured pencils on paper, 21×29.7cm, Fondo Alessandro Mendini – Triennale di Milano;
P. 201 (image 131): *Aurora*, steel and coloured glass handles, Olivari, 1994, Alessandro Mendini Archive;
P. 201 (image 132): Alessandro and Francesco Mendini, Chiesa del Vasaio, entrance of the small building in Bisazza mosaic for *Artinmosaico: The Bisazza collection*, Scuderie di Palazzo Reale, Naples, 1996, project with Giorgio Gregori, Silvia Giuli, © Archivio Bisazza;
P. 202 (image 133): *Mobili per Uomo: Stella*, metal storage unit and gold leaf mosaic sculpture, 129×80×270cm, Bisazza, 2002, Project with Bruno Gregory, Ph Lorenzo Ceretta, © Archivio Bisazza;
P. 202 (image 134): *Mobili per Uomo: Guanto*, metal storage unit and gold leaf mosaic sculpture, 91×70×236cm, Bisazza, 1997, Ph Lorenzo Ceretta, © Archivio Bisazza;
P. 203 (image 135): *Mobili per Uomo: Testa*, metal storage unit and gold leaf mosaic sculpture, 72×72×238cm, Bisazza, 1997, Ph Lorenzo Ceretta, © Archivio Bisazza;
P. 204 (image 136): Alessandro Mendini and Francesco Mendini, Stuttgarter Bank, mural in Bisazza mosaic in the entrance hall, Stuttgart, Germany, 1996, project with Bruno Gregory, Ph Alberto Ferrero, © Archivio Bisazza;
P. 205 (image 137): *Mobili per Uomo: Stella*, another furniture piece for Bisazza, 2003, drawing, felt-tip pen and coloured pencils on paper, 21×29.7cm, Fondo Alessandro Mendini – Triennale di Milano;
P. 205 (image 138): *Stella*, sculpture, lacquered metal and Bisazza mosaic, H260cm, in the park of the Sieger family castle, Schloss Harkotten, Germany, 1999, project with Massimo Caiazzo, Bruno Gregory, Alessandro Mendini Archive;
P. 206 (image 139): Alessandro and Francesco Mendini, Maghetti District, redevelopment of the district using Bisazza mosaic, Lugano Switzerland, 1998-1999, project with Bruno Gregory, Dorota Koziara, Alex Mocika, Giovanna Molteni, Michela Pagani, Tommaso Teodonio, Matteo Tresoldi, Alessandro Mendini Archive;
P. 206 (image 140): Alessandro and Francesco Mendini, Maghetti District, redevelopment of the district using Bisazza mosaic, Lugano Switzerland, 1998-1999, project with Bruno Gregory, Dorota Koziara, Alex Mocika, Giovanna Molteni, Michela Pagani, Tommaso Teodonio, Matteo Tresoldi, Alessandro Mendini Archive;
P. 207 (image 141): Alessandro and Francesco Mendini, Salvator Rosa metro station, Naples Metro Line 1, exit 2, with ceramic piece *Napoli città madre* by Ugo Marano, 2003, project with Andrea Balzari, Alex Mocika, Sergio Sinopoli, Ph Peppe Avallone, © MN Metropolitana di Napoli;
P. 207 (image 142): Alessandro and Francesco Mendini, Salvator Rosa metro station, Naples Metro Line 1, exit 2, with ceramic piece by Enzo Cucchi and facade by Mimmo Paladino, 2003, project with Andrea Balzari, Alex Mocika, Sergio Sinopoli, Ph Peppe Avallone, © MN Metropolitana di Napoli;
P. 208 (image 143): Salvator Rosa and Materdei metro stations, Naples, 1999, drawing, felt-tip pen and coloured pencils on paper, 21×29.7cm, Fondo Alessandro Mendini – Triennale di Milano;
P. 209 (image 144): Karim Rashid, Alessandro and Francesco Mendini, Università metro station, Naples Metro Line 1, Naples, 2010, project with Andrea Balzari, Ph Iwan Baan, © MN Metropolitana di Napoli;
P. 209 (image 145): Alessandro and Francesco Mendini, Materdei metro station, Naples Metro Line 1, lift entrance with ceramic piece by Lucio Del Pezzo, 2003, project with Andrea Balzari, Alessandro Busci, Filippo Ferrari, Bruno Gregory, Alex Mocika, Debora Passaleva, Sergio Sinopoli, © MN Metropolitana di Napoli;
P. 210 (image 146): *Cavaliere di Dürer* with *Proust* decoration, Bisazza, 2010, drawing, felt-tip pen and coloured pencils on paper, 21×29.7cm, Alessandro Mendini Archive;
P. 210 (image 147): *Cavaliere di Dürer*, equestrian sculpture in Bisazza mosaic with Delft colours, Collection Fondazione Bisazza, Vicenza, 2010, project with Bruno Gregory, Giovanna Molteni, Ph Lorenzo Ceretta, © Archivio Bisazza;
P. 211 (image 148): *Cavaliere di Dürer* with Delft colours, Bisazza, 2010, drawing, felt-tip pen and coloured pencils on paper, 21×29.7cm, Alessandro Mendini Archive;

CHAPTER 9

P. 212: *I am Mr Ciao*, fibreglass sculpture, H470cm, SPC Group, South Korea, 2015, drawing, felt-tip pen and coloured pencils on paper, 21×29.7cm, Alessandro Mendini Archive;
P. 217 (top left): Alberto Alessi pushes the *Standard* trolley by Enzo Mari with *100% Make-Up* vases – *100% Make-Up*: Ellinor Flor, Peter Struychen, Mara Voce, Giusi Mastro, YAYA Young Aspirations/Young Artists, Brian Eno, Alex Mocika, Raja Babu Sharma, Lapo Binazzi, Ettore Sottsass, 1992, Ph Giuseppe Pino, Archivio fotografico Alessi;
P. 217 (top right): Ettore Sottsass, Enzo Mari, Andrea Branzi, Alessandro Mendini, Vico Magistretti, *Domus* cover, April 2004, © Domus 869, Ph Ramak Fazel;
P. 217 (bottom left): Alessandro and Francesco Mendini, 1999, Ph Ambrogio Beretta, Alessandro Mendini Archive;
P. 217 (bottom right): *100% Make-Up*, display of the 100 vases, 27th Florence Gift Mart Fair, Florence, 1992, project with Massimo Caiazzo, Pietro Gaeta, Maria Christina Hamel, Dagmar Trinks, Alessandro Mendini Archive;
P. 221 (top left and top right): Alessandro and Francesco Mendini, *Tea & Coffee Towers Alessi*, exhibition, Triennale di Milano, 2003, Tea & Coffee sets by: Vito Acconci, Will Alsop, Weil Arets, Shigeru Ban, Gary Chang, David Chipperfield, Denton Corker Marshall, Dezső Ekler, Massimiliano Fuksas Doriana O Mandrelli, Future Systems, Zaha Hadid, Toyo Ito, Tom Kovac, Grey Lynn, FORM, Alessandro Mendini, Morphosis, MVRDV, Juan Navarro Baldeweg, Jean Nouvel, Dominique Perrault, Kazuyo Sejima Ryue Nishizawa SANAA, UN Studio. Eight Models of Utopian Towers (one hundred floors high and one hundred in scale) by David Chipperfield, Future Systems, Zaha Hadid, Denton-Corker-Marshall, Toyo Ito, Thom Mayne-Morphosis, MVRDV, Jean Nouvel, exhibition design with Andrea Balzari, Ph Carlo Lavatori;
P. 221 (middle): Alessandro and Francesco Mendini, La Punta, pavilion for the Seoul Design Fair, Olympic Stadium, Seoul, South Korea, 2010, project with Young hee Cha, Bruno Gregory, Giovanna Molteni, Alessandro Mendini Archive;
P. 221 (bottom): Alessandro and Francesco Mendini, render of La Punta pavilion, Olympic Stadium Seoul, South Korea, 2010, project with Young Hee Cha, Bruno Gregory, Giovanna Molteni, Alessandro Mendini Archive;
P. 224 (image 149): *100% Make-Up*, vase for Alessi Tendentse, decoration by Mendini, 1992, porcelain vase, H27cm, project for the 100 vases collection with Stefania Campatelli, Flavio Pannocchia, Maria Christina Hamel, Dagmar Trinks, Danilo Aliata, Ph Occhiomagico;
P. 225 (image 150): *100% Make-Up*, vase for Alessi Tendentse, decoration by Mark Kostabi, 1992, porcelain vase, H27cm, Ph Salvatore Licitra;
P. 225 (image 151): *100% Make-Up*, vase for Alessi Tendentse, decoration by Robert Venturi, 1992, porcelain vase, H27cm, Ph Salvatore Licitra;
P. 226 (images 152 and 154): Icheon vase, Celadon ceramic vase, Interart Gallery Seoul, South Korea, 2009, edition of 9, project with Young hee Cha, Alessandro Mendini Archive;
P. 226 (image 153): *Icheon* vase, Celadon ceramic vase, Interart Gallery Seoul, South Korea, 2009, drawing, felt-tip pen and coloured pencils on paper, 21×29.7cm, Alessandro Mendini Archive;
P. 227 (image 155): *Vaso Utopico*, white ceramic vase with pure gold decorations (different for each piece), 35×50cm, Produzione Storica collection, self-production, 1994, edition of 12 copies, project with Bruno Gregory, Alessandro Mendini Archive;
P. 228 (image 156): Headquarters of the Triennale di Milano, now offices and headquarters of a Korean television broadcaster, Incheon, South Korea, 2009,

EXTENDED PICTURE CAPTIONS AND CREDITS 295

drawing, felt-tip pen and coloured pencils on paper, 21×29.7cm, Alessandro Mendini Archive;
P. 229 (image 157): Alessandro and Francesco Mendini, Cha Bio Complex: entrance to the Cha Health Sistems Hospital, Seoul, South Korea, 2015, project with Young hee Cha, Alex Mocika, Giovanna Molteni, Alessandro Mendini Archive;
P. 230 (image 158): Alessandro and Francesco Mendini, La Punta, pavilion for the Seoul Design Fair, Olympic Stadium, Seoul South, Korea, model in methacrylate and applied decoration, 50×40×25cm, 2010, Abet laminati Archive, project with Young Hee Cha, Bruno Gregory, Giovanna Molteni, Ph Roberto Gennari Feslikenian;
P. 231 (image 159): La Punta pavilion for the Seoul Design Fair, Olympic Stadium Seoul, South Korea, 2010, drawing, felt-tip pen and coloured pencils on paper, 21×29.7cm, Alessandro Mendini Archive;
P. 232 (image 160): Outfits for *Alessandro M* corkscrew for Alessi, drawing by Giovanna Molteni, 2009, Alessandro Mendini Archive;
P. 233 (image 161): *Alessandro M and Anna G Orchestra*, musical carillon for Alessi, 2003, Collection Museo Alessi, Archivio fotofrafico Alessi;
P. 233 (image 162): *Alessandro M* and *Anna G* corkscrews for Alessi, new colourways, 2021, ph Matteo Imbriani, styling by Irene Baratto;
P. 234 (image 163): *Anna G: Arborea*, corkscrew in Alkipaper and zamac chromed, by Mendini (2014), decorated by Fulvia Mendini for Alessi, 2024;
P. 234 (image 164): *Anna G: Parade*, corkscrew in Alkipaper and zamac chromed, by Mendini (2014), decorated by Arthur Arbesser for Alessi, 2024;
P. 234 (image 165): *Anna G: Liquid*, corkscrew in Alkipaper and zamac chromed, by Mendini (2014), decorated by Studio Temp for Alessi, 2024;
P. 235 (image 166): *Alessandro M: Arborea*, corkscrew in Alkipaper and zamac chromed, by Mendini (2014), decorated by Fulvia Mendini for Alessi, 2024;
P. 235 (image 167): *Alessandro M: Parade*, corkscrew in Alkipaper and zamac chromed, by Mendini (2014), decorated by Arthur Arbesser for Alessi, 2024;
P. 235 (image 168): *Alessandro M: Liquid*, corkscrew in Alkipaper and zamac chromed, by Mendini (2014), decorated by Studio Temp for Alessi, 2024;
P. 236 (image 169): *Tea & Coffee Towers*, tea and coffee set for Alessi, 2002, drawing, felt-tip pen and coloured pencils on paper, 21×29.7cm, Alessandro Mendini Archive;
P. 237 (image 170): *Tea & Coffee Towers*, tea and coffee set for Alessi, 2002, drawing, felt-tip pen and coloured pencils on paper, 21× 29.7cm, Alessandro Mendini Archive;
P. 237 (image 171): *Tutta*, office chair for Iloom, South Korea, 2015-2016, drawing, felt-tip pen and coloured pencils on paper, 21×29.7cm, Alessandro Mendini Archive;
P. 238 (image 172): *Linea*, cabinet in rigid cellulose acetate, 110×40×83cm and 90×30×135, Porro, designed 2015, released 2023, project with Young hee Cha, Giovanna Molteni;
P. 238 (image 173): Alessandro and Francesco Mendini, dormitory building for the furniture company Iloom-Fursys, Chung Ju, South Korea, 2018, model in methacrylate alluminium and applied decoration, 29×20×24cm, Chung Ju, South Korea, 2018, project with Andrea Balzari, Young hee Cha, Bruno Gregory, Abet Laminati Archive, Ph Roberto Gennari Feslikenian;
P. 239 (image 174): Alessandro and Francesco Mendini, office building for the furniture company Iloom-Fursys, Chung Ju, South Korea, 2018, model in methacrylate alluminium and applied decoration, 29×20×24cm, Chung Ju, South Korea, 2018, project with Andrea Balzari, Young hee Cha, Bruno Gregory, Abet Laminati Archive, Ph Roberto Gennari Feslikenian;
P. 239 (image 175): Alessandro and Francesco Mendini, render of the decoration for the facade of the headquarters of furniture company Iloom-Fursys, Chung Ju, South Korea, 2018, project with Andrea Balzari, Young hee Cha, Bruno Gregory, Alessandro Mendini Archive;
P. 240 (image 176): *The Bird of Flower*, sculpture for Suncheon Bay National Garden, South Korea, 2016, drawing, felt-tip pen and coloured pencils on paper, 21×29.7cm, Alessandro Mendini Archive;
P. 241 (image 177): Alessandro and Francesco Mendini, Torre Panoramica, belvedere, exhibition, commercial spaces, for Suncheon Bay National Garden, South Korea, 2018, model in methacrylate and applied decoration, 50×80cm, project with Andrea Balzari, Young hee Cha, Bruno Gregory, Abet Laminati Archive, Ph Roberto Gennari Feslikenian;

CHAPTER 10

P. 242: *Margaret and Thomas More: Utopia Island*, 2015, drawing, felt-tip pen and coloured pencils on paper, 21×29.7cm, Alessandro Mendini Archive;
P. 247 (middle): Mendini and Enzo Mari, presentation of the first issue of *Domus Nuova Utopia*, Milan, 2010;
P. 247 (top left): Mendini and Morris Lapidus at the Futurists of Today conference, Wolfsonian Museum, Miami, 1999, Stefano Casciani Archive;
P. 247 (bottom): Lorenzo Mattotti, portrait of Alessandro Mendini, coloured pencils on cardboard, 37.8×49.9cm, 2011, gift from the *Domus* Staff – the idea of Giuseppe Basile, *Domus* art director, Alessandro Mendini Archive;
P. 247 (top right): Mendini sketching with *Campanello Ramun* light and sound object on the table, Milan, 2015, Ph Roberto Gennari Feslikenian;
P. 250 (top right): Kazuyo Sejima portrait by Lorenzo Mattotti on *Domus* cover, issue 939, 2010, courtesy Domus Archive;
P. 250 (top left): Plan for *Domus* issue 935, 2010, drawing, felt-tip pen and coloured pencils on paper, 21×29.7cm, Alessandro Mendini Archive;
P. 250 (bottom): Wim Wenders portrait by Lorenzo Mattotti on *Domus* cover, issue 943, 2011, courtesy Domus Archive;
P. 253 (bottom left): The Futurists of Today conference, Wolfsonian Museum, Miami, 1999, Mendini and Casciani with (among others) Gaetano Pesce, Ennio Capasa, Denis Santachiara, Alberto Meda, Stefano Casciani Archive;
P. 253 (top): *Wunderkammer Design*, exhibition curated by Peter Weiss, Neues Museum Nürnberg, Nuremberg, Germany, 2011, project with Alex Mocika, Giovanna Molteni, Beatrice Felis, Ph Peter Weiss;
P. 253 (bottom right): Mendini with his grandsons Tommaso and Michele at the awarding of the Laurea Honoris Causa, Eugeniusz Geppert Academy of Art and Design Wroclaw, Poland, 2014, ph Alex Figura, Alessandro Mendini Archive;
P. 256 (image 179): *Oggetto Meditativo*, crystal monstrance for Swarovski, 1999, project with Michela Pagani, Alessandro Mendini Archive;
P. 256 (image 178): Stopper for *Tonda* bottle, Venini, 1988, drawing, felt-tip pen on paper, 21×29.7cm, Fondo Alessandro Mendini – Triennale Milano;
P. 257 (image 180): *Dor*, Murano glass vase for Venini, 1988, courtesy Venini Archive;
P. 257 (image 181): *Amboise*, Murano glass bottle for Venini, 1990, courtesy Venini Archive;
P. 258 (image 182): Casa Mendini: *Achernar* Murano glass pendant for Venini and *100% Make-Up* Alessi Tendentse vases, Milan, 1993. The 100 authors of the *100% Make-Up* vases: 1.Antonio Abate, 2.Carla Accardi, 3.Sanchita Ajjampur, 4.Yael Applefeld, 5.Qinuajuaq Ashevak, 6.Paolo Bertozzi-Stefano Del Monte Casoni, 7.Gabriel Bien-Aimé, 8.Lapo Binazzi, 9.Alighiero Boetti, 10.Andreas Brandolini, 11.Frédéric Bruly Bouabré, 12.Sergio Calatroni, 13.Juli Capella, 14.Sergio Cappelli-Patrizia Ranzo, 15.Nigel Coates, 16.Cocktail, 17.Gianni Colombo, 18.Riccardo Dalisi, 19.Nicola De Maria, 20.Jan Diggerud, 21.Emmanuel Ekefrey, 22.Brian Eno, 23.Ellinor Flor, 24.Dan Friedman, 25.Elizabeth Fritsch, 26.Piero Gaeta, 27.Giorgio Galli-Beatrice Santiccioli, 28.Louise Gibb, 29.Piero Gilardi, 30.Anna Gili, 31.Milton Glaser, 32.Michael Graves, 33.Maria Christina Hamel, 34.Jan Mohamed Hanif, 35.Pitt Heinke, 36.Yoshiki Hishinuma, 37.Susan Holm, 38.Yong Ping Huang, 39.Aussi Jaffari, 40.Christer Jonson, 41.Bodys Isek Kingelez, 42.Inka Kivalo, 43.Mark Kostabi, 44.Randi Kristensen, 45.Milan Kunc, 46.Kunstflug, 47.Shiro Kuramata, 48.Quim Larrea, 49.Cheikh Ledy, 50.Stefan Lindfors, 51.Kamba Luesa, 52.Ester Mahlangu, 53.Valente Malangatana, 54.Karel Malich, 55.Massimo Mariani, 56.Giusi Mastro, 57.Kivuthi Mbuno, 58.Alessandro Mendini, 59.Antonio Miralda, 60.Sergei Vladimir Mironenko, 61.Alex Mocika, 62.Paola Navone, 63.Sinya Okayama, 64.Luigi Ontani, 65.Heikki Orvola, 66.Salcido Javier Perez-Gil, 67.Edoardo Pla, 68.Plumcake, 69.Giorgio Rava, 70.Ravage, 71.Rolando Pereira Rego, 72.Roberto Remi, 73.Cheri Samba, 74.Andreas Schulze, 75.Suresh Sethi, 76.Raja Babu Sharma, 77.Jari Silvennoinen, 78.Ettore Sottsass, 79.Gregorio Spini, 80.Philippe Starck, 81.Peter Struycken, 82.Sybilla, 83.Guillermo Tejeda, 84.Cyprien Tokoudagba, 85.Dagmar Trinks, 86.Maurizio Turchet, 87.Twins Seven Seven, 88.Masanori Umeda, 89.Hilde Vemren, 90.Robert Venturi, 91.Guido Venturini, 92.Nanda Vigo, 93.Mara Voce, 94.Acharya Vyakul, 95.Brigitta Watz, 96.Gisbert Weiss, 97.Hannes Wettstein, 98.Y.A.Y.A., 99.Leonid Yentus, 100.Rhonda Zwillinger;
P. 259 (image 184): Decorations for plates for Venini, 1988, drawing, felt-tip pen and coloured pencils on paper, 21×29.7cm, Fondo Alessandro Mendini – Triennale Milano;
P. 259 (image 183): Decorations for plates for Venini, 1988, drawing, felt-tip pen and coloured pencils on paper, 21×29.7cm, Fondo Alessandro Mendini – Triennale Milano;
P. 260 (image 185): *Cavallino*, sculpture for Venini, 2008, drawing, felt-tip pen and coloured pencils on paper, 21×29.7cm, Fondo Alessandro Mendini – Triennale Milano;
P. 260 (image 186): *Cavallino*, sculpture in blown glass for Venini, 2008, 44×12×49cm, courtesy Venini Archive;
P. 261 (image 187): *Fragilisme*, Fondation Cartier pour l'Art contemporain Paris: *Tête Géant* and *Visage Archaïque*, sculptures, 2002, drawing, felt-tip pen and coloured pencils on paper, 21×29.7cm, Fondo Alessandro Mendini – Triennale Milano;
P. 261 (image 188): *Guerrier de Verre*, red incalmo glass sculpture with gold earrings, 28×49cm, Venini, 2002, project with Dorota Koziara, edition of 36 copies for the exhibition *Fragilisme*, Fondation Cartier pour l'art contemporain Paris, Ph Archivio Anna Gili Design Studio – Sofia Masina;
P. 262 (image 189): Alessandro and Francesco Mendini, *Le Salon Précieux Cartier*, installation for Fondation Cartier pour l'art contemporain, Art 40 Basel, 2009, *Colonna di Cartier* in gold, precious stones, crystal, granite; sofa *Settecento* for Meritalia, project with Bruno Gregori, Alex Mocika, Giovanna Molteni, Emanuela Morra, Ph Philippe Contier;
P. 262 (image 190): *Colonna di Cartier*, detail of the gold column with gems, crystal, granite, 45×233cm, 720kg, Cartier, Paris, 2009. Exterior surface: 23.6kg of 18 carat gold-colours 4 N pink gold, 140 flutes, thickness: 5 tenths, 30×7cm, average weight per flute: 165g, base: black granite, cover (upper part): bronze covered with 5 microns of gold, 329 tubes: 255 measuring 10cm, 57 measuring 20cm, 17 measuring 30 cm. Total weight of stones and pearls: 17,763.079 carats. Diamonds: 61 carats; emeralds: 920 carats; sapphires: 3,067 carats; rubies: 1,293 carats; pearls: 9,865 carats; tourmaline: 695 carats; aquamarine: 75 carats; chalcedony: 831 carats; amethysts: 336 carats; garnets: 295 carats; moonstone: 307 carats; cordierite: 17 carats, Ph Philippe Contier;
P. 263 (image 192): Skateboard for Supreme, 2016, project with Elisa and Fulvia Mendini;
P. 263 (image 191): *Fragilisme*, exhibition with Vincent Beaurin and Fabrice Domercq, Fondation Cartier pour l'Art contemporain, Paris, France, 2002, project with Beatrice Felis, Silvia Giuli, Bruno Gregory, Dorota Koziara, Alex Mocika, Giovanna Molteni. In the photo: *Tête Géante*, fibreglass sculpture, 210×130×390cm, 2002, Collection Groninger Museum; *Pétite Cathedrale*, small building in Bisazza mosaic 300×250×500cm, 2002, Collection Fondation Cartier pour l'art contemporain;
P. 264 (image 193): *Alessandro Mendini and his Artisans: Three*, ceramic sculpture for Superego Design, Vacheron Constantin, Fondation Cartier pour l'art contemporain, Fondazione Cologni, 2013, project with Bruno Gregory, Ph Emanuele Zamponi;
P. 265 (image 194): *Alessandro Mendini and his Artisans: Four*, sculpture in polyuretane, 40×100cm, for Slide, Vacheron Constantin, Fondation Cartier pour l'art contemporain, Fondazione Cologni, 2013, project with Bruno Gregory, Ph Emanuele Zamponi;
P. 265 (image 195): *Alessandro Mendini and his Artisans: Nine*, gold-plated brass vase 35×55cm for Cleto Munari, Vacheron Constantin, Fondation Cartier pour l'art contemporain, Fondazione Cologni, 2013, project with Bruno Gregory, Ph Emanuele Zamponi;
P. 266 (image 196): *Alessandro Mendini and his Artisans: Seven*, sculpture for Gori Lab, Vacheron Constantin, Fondation Cartier pour l'art contemporain, Fondazione Cologni, 2013, drawing, felt-tip pen and coloured pencils on paper, 21×29.7cm, Alessandro Mendini Archive;
P. 267 (image 197): *Tre Primitivi: Luna & Sole*, storage unit covered in Alpi Wood Pointilisme COL, 115×45×210cm, Alpi, 2018, edition of 3 copies, project with Bruno Gregory, Alex Mocika, Ph Federico Cedrone;
P. 267 (image 198): *Tre Primitivi: QFWFQ*, storage unit covered in Alpi Wood Pointilisme COL, 98×45×220cm, Alpi, 2018, edition of 3 copies, project with Bruno Gregory, Alex Mocika, Ph Federico Cedrone;
P. 268 (image 199): *Amuleto*, table lamp, Ramun, 2010, drawing, felt-tip pen and coloured pencils on paper, 21× 29.7cm, Alessandro Mendini Archive;
P. 269 (image 200): *Amuleto*, table lamp, aluminium, steel, LED light crown, 51×20×51cm, Ramun, 2012, project with Young hee Cha;
P. 270 (image 201): Galleria Mendini, multi-functional building for housing, commercial and recreational spaces in Lörrach, Germany, 2000-2004, drawing, felt-tip pen and coloured pencils on paper, 21× 29.7cm, Alessandro Mendini Archive;
P. 271 (image 203): Alessandro and Francesco Mendini, busstop, Steintor stop, Hannover, Germany, 1992, project with Giorgio Gregori, Ph Thomas Deutschmann;
P. 271 (image 202): Alessandro and Francesco Mendini, Galleria Mendini, multifunctional building for homes, commercial and recreational spaces, Lörrach, Germany, 2000-2004, model in methacrylate and applied decoration, 52×44×22cm, project with Claudio Guida, Bruno Gregory, Michela Pagani, Ph Roberto Gennari Feliskenian;
P. 272 (image 204): *Piccole fantasie quotidiane*, exhibition curated by Arianna Rosica and Gianluca Riccio, *Poltrona di Paglia* in the Francesco Clemente painted room, Madre Museum, Naples, 2020, project by Elisa and Fulvia Mendini, Alex Mocika, Beatrice Felis, Ph Amedeo Benestante, Alessandro Mendini Archive;
P. 273 (image 205): *Piccole fantasie quotidiane*, *Proust* armchair and *Proust* objects, Madre Museum, Naples, 2020, project by Elisa and Fulvia Mendini, Alex Mocika, Beatrice Felis, Ph Amedeo Benestante, Alessandro Mendini Archive;
P. 273 (image 206): *Piccole fantasie quotidiane*, *Zabro* chair/table, *Kandissi* sofa and *Depero* tapestries, Madre Museum, Naples, 2020, project by Elisa and Fulvia Mendini, Alex Mocika, Beatrice Felis, Ph Amedeo Benestante, Alessandro Mendini Archive;

EPILOGUE AND SKETCHBOOK

P. 275: Alessandro Mendini, portrait by Mario Ermoli, 1994;
P. 277: *Art of Italian Design*, theoretical diagram, 2008, drawing, felt-tip pen and coloured pencils on paper, 21× 29.7cm, Fondo Alessandro Mendini – Triennale di Milano;
P. 278: *La cucina Alessi: Agreste*, Alessi with Oras, Fores and Valcucine, 2005, drawing, felt-tip pen and coloured pencils on paper, 21×29.7cm, Fondo Alessandro Mendini – Triennale di Milano;
P. 279: *MicroMacro*, Murano glass vases blown and caged in metal grids, Cleto Munari, 2003, drawing, felt-tip pen and coloured pencils on paper, 21×29.7cm, Fondo Alessandro Mendini – Triennale Milano;
P. 280: *Craquelé*, installation, *Abitare il tempo*, Verona, 2006, drawing, felt-tip pen and coloured pencils on paper, 21×29.7cm, Alessandro Mendini Archive;
P. 281: *DiADaInConSuPerTraFra*, decorations for cabinet, Zerodisegno, Carlo Poggio, 2007, drawing, felt-tip pen and coloured pencils on paper, 21×29.7cm, Fondo Alessandro Mendini – Triennale Milano
P. 282: *Mendinismi*, fibreglass vases and plates, Corsi Design, 2008, drawing, felt-tip pen and coloured pencils on paper, 21×29.7cm, Fondo Alessandro Mendini – Triennale Milano;
P. 283: *La cucina Alessi: Sinuosa*, Alessi by Valcucine Italia, 2005, drawing, felt-tip pen and coloured pencils on paper, 21×29.7cm, Fondo Alessandro Mendini – Triennale Milano;
P. 284: *Omaggio a Palladio*, sculptures in mosaic, Bisazza, 2000, drawing, felt-tip pen and coloured pencils on paper, 21×29.7cm, Alessandro Mendini Archive;
P. 285: *Ebdomero*, bench for Abet Laminati in the garden of the Triennale di Milano, drawing, felt-tip pen and coloured pencils

on paper, 21×29.7cm, Fondo Alessandro Mendini – Triennale Milano;
P. 286: *Normali Meraviglie: A map of small fantasies* for Genoa, the capital of European culture, 2004, drawing, felt-tip pen and coloured pencils on paper, 21×29.7cm, private collection;
P. 287: *Torre dell'Orologio*, Gibellina, Sicily, 1987, drawing, felt-tip pen and coloured pencils on paper, 21×29.7cm, Alessandro Mendini Archive;
P. 288: *Casa a Olda*, drawing of the house dedicated to Mendini's daughter Fulvia, Olda Val Taleggio, 2006, drawing, felt-tip pen and coloured pencils on paper, 21×29.7cm, Alessandro Mendini Archive;
P. 289: *Alessandro M Ciao!* for Alessi, 2003, drawing, felt-tip pen and coloured pencils on paper, 21×29.7cm, Fondo Alessandro Mendini – Triennale Milano;

INDEX

References in *italics* indicate images.

70 Angels on the Façade theatre project 8
100% Make-Up vase series 215–18, *217*, *224–25*
1928/73 Domus: 45 ans d'architecture, design, art (exh., 1973) 83

A

Abet Laminati 94, 162, 220
  Proust laminate 77, 162, 168, *173*, *182*
Abito Sonoro (Sound Dress) performance *117*, 119, *126*
abstraction 66, 133, 138
Acerbi, Adelaide 131
Achernar Murano glass pendant *258*
AD magazine 39, 83
Affinità Elettive (Elective Affinities, exh., 1985) 119
Agrilo console *147*
AkzoNobel, *Alessandro Mendini: 30 Colours* 245–46
Albini, Franco 19, 21, 35
Alcantara 118
Alessandro M corkscrew 219–20, *232–33*, *235*
Alessi, Alberto 91, 94–95, 98, 131, *160*, 185, 215, 216, *217*, 220, *253*
  Casa della Felicità (Happiness House) project 162, 163–65, *164*, *170*
Alessi Anghini, Carlo 94
Alessi Anghini, Giovanni 94
Alessi 14, 39, 44, 88, 94–99, 119, 131, 215
  100% Make-Up vase series 215–18, *217*, *224–25*
  Alessandro M corkscrew 219–20, *232–33*, *235*
  Alessofono saxophone *109*
  Anna G corkscrew 219, *233–34*
  factory *160*, 219
  Peyrano box *160*
  Tea & Coffee Towers (exh., 2002) 218–19, *221*, *236–37*
  Tea & Coffee Piazza programme 94, *97*, 98–99, *106*, 113, 159
  tray 99, *108*
Alessofono saxophone *109*
Alpi *267*
Altan, Francesco Tullio 46–47
Ambasz, Emilio 38, 87, *89*, 91, 96, 131, 251
Ambiente di Piante Mobili (Furniture Plant Landscape, exh., 1981) *132*, 133
Amboise glass bottle *257*
American design 98, 135
Amuleto (Amulet) table lamp 255, *268–69*
Anna G corkscrew 219, *233–34*
Anni Trenta Arte e Cultura in Italia (1930s Art and Culture in Italy, exh., 1982) 133
Annicchiarico, Silvana 252
anti-design 66, 83, 99, 113
Arbersec, Arthur 234–235
Architectural Review, ITALY special issue (1982) *68*
Architettura addio (Farewell to Architecture) book 116–18
L'architettura. Cronache e storia magazine 136
Architettura Sussurrante (Whispering Architecture) record project 135
Archizoom 36, 38, 40, 43, 116
Argan, Giulio Carlo 83
Arredo Vestitivo (Wearable Furniture, exh., 1982) *110*, 114, *115*, *127*
Art Basel 248
Arte come forza-lavoro (Art as Workforce) 38
Arte Povera 138
Asea Brown Boveri (ABB) 165

Astori, Enrico 131
Atelier Mendini 165, *166*, 186, 189, 218, 219, 245, 248, 254, 255, 274
Atomaria floor lamp 133, *147*
Aulenti, Gae 35, 38, 47, 131, 186
Aurora door handles 185, *201*
Automobile (Car) *28*
Autoritratto (Self-portrait) *24*
avant-garde 13, 14, 19, 36, 38, 39, 40, 43, 69, 83, 88, 131, 133, 138, 162–65, 185; *see also* neo-avant-garde; post-avant-garde

B

Baleri Italia 134
Balla, Giacomo 133
Balzari, Andrea 165
banal design 69, 88, *90*, 91–94, *102*, 134, 185, 222
  L'oggetto banale (The Banal Object, exh., 1980) 88, 91–94, *105*, *107*
Banfi, Gianluigi 19
Barbiano di Belgiojoso, Lodovico 19
Barisani, Renato 186
Baroque 161
Barthes, Roland 167
Bartolini, Dario 36, 116
Basile, Giuseppe 7, 251
Basilico, Gabriele 116
Bauhaus 38, 66, 83, 131
Bau-Haus I collection 66, *68*, 69, 114
Bayer, Herbert 38
BBPR group 18–19, 21
Beat Generation 43
Il Becco Giallo magazine 13
Beckmann, Liisi 65
Benjamin, Walter 113
Beretta, Ambrogio 85, *117*
Bernasconi, Gian Antonio 35, 36
Bertolini, Lucia 40
Betsky, Aaron 162
Bettini, Paolo 119
Bialetti, Alfonso 94
Bien-Aimé, Gabriel 216
Binazzi, Lapo 36, 65
Binfaré, Francesco 65, 131
The Bird of Flower sculpture *240*
Bisazza family 185–86
Bisazza mosaics 185–88, *187*, 246, 248
  Il Cavaliere di Dürer (Dürer's Knight) sculpture 188, *210–11*
  Chiesa del Vasaio (Church of the Potter) entrance *201*
  Maghetti District redevelopment, Lugano 206
  Mobili per uomo (Furniture for Man) series *202–3*
  Stella (Star) sculpture *205*
  Stuttgarter Bank mural, Stuttgart *204*
Black Out installation *117*, 119, *124*
Boccioni, Umberto 17
Boeri, Cini 47
Boetti, Alighiero 216
Bonetto, Rodolfo 47, 85
Bonito Oliva, Achille 186
Boschi, Antonio (uncle) 17, 18
Boschi Di Stefano, Marieda (aunt) 17, *22*
Bosisio, Franco 189
Bottoni, Piero 19
bourgeoisie 13, 14, 39, 43, 44, 66, 69, 84
Bracciodiferro 41, 57, 65
  Valigia per ultimo viaggio (Suitcase for the last journey) 39, 40, *61*
Branzi, Andrea 36, 39, 40, 43, 65, 66, 69, 88, 92–94, 133, 134, *217*
Bratislava expansion plan 35
Breuer, Marcel *75*
Brion, Rina 85
Brunati, Mario 13, *22*, 35
Burdick, Bruce 135
Burkhardt, François 91
Busnelli, Piero *89*

C

Cacciari, Massimo 8
Caiazzo, Massimo 165, 189
Calò, Aldo 47
Cantafora, Arduino, *La Città Banale* (The Banal City) 91
capitalism 8, 19, 83, 85, 98, 113, 216
Cappella Cantone, Cremona *49*
Cappellini 17
Cartier 248, *262*
Casa della Felicità (Happiness House) project 162, 163–65, *164*, *170*
Casabella magazine 19, 21, 35–44, 83, 84, 87, 88, 96, 118, 163, 215, 220
  Architettura per l'Uomo Dimenticato (Architecture for the Forgotten Man) article 38
  covers *37*, 40, *50*
  Documenti (Documents) series 44
  Il Pianeta come festival (The Planet as a Festival) series 43–44
  masthead font 38
  'Metaprogetto si e no' (Metadesign: yes and no) essay 35–36

Note Radicali (Radical Notes) column 40
Per ritardato arrivo dell'aeromobile (Because of the Late Arrival of the Airplane) column 43–44
Cascella, Andrea 95
Casciani, Stefano 9, 87, 91, *93*, 94, 135, 138, 139, 159–61, 162, 185, *187*, 188, 218, 245, 249
  letter to Mendini 7–8
Casino, Arosa 219
Cassina 39, 40, *61*, 65, 131
Castelli, Franco 43
Castelli, Giulio 44
Castelli, Valerio 46
Castelli Ferrieri, Anna 44
Castiglioni, Achille 47, 88, 91, 131, 135, *160*, 220
Castiglioni brothers 47
Castro, Federica di 44
Il Cavaliere di Dürer (Dürer's Knight) sculpture 188, *210–11*
Cavallino sculpture *260*
Cavart group 39
Ceccariglia, Carla 94, 165
Celant, Germano 23, 36, 38
Centrodomus 87, 88, *89*, 94, 133, *137*
CentroKappa 44, 87, 215
Cha, Young hee 254
Cha Bio Complex, Cha Health Systems Hospital, Seoul *229*
Chandès, Hervé 248
Charpin, Pierre 252
Cheti, Fede 21
Chia, Sandro 138, 186, 188
Chiesa del Vasaio (Church of the Potter) entrance *201*, 248
Ciardi, Nives 46, 87
Cinelli bike *120*
Cipriani bar/cabinet *148*
Clemente, Francesco 118, 255
Cleto Munari 135, *140*, *265*
Clotet, Lluís 88
CLUVA 159
Codice Icona *155*
collaboration 163–67, 185–88, 245, 274
collage 162, 165
collecting, low-cost 188–90, 219
Colombo, Gianni 21
Colombo, Joe 18, 21, *72*
Colonetti, Aldo 220
Colonizing the American Marketplace: Contemporary Italian Industrial Design (conference, 1985) 135
colour 17, 66, 69, 99, 163, 185–86, 188, 189, 222, 245–48
communism 216
Consagra, Pietro 95
conservatism 39–40
consumerism 188, 190
contemporary art 17, 88, 186
Cook, Peter 83
Coop Himmelb(l)au 162, 167, 168, *173*, *179*
Corrado, Maurizio 251
Corso, Gregory 43
Crippa, Roberto 21
Cubism 246
Cucchi, Enzo 138, 186, 188

D

Dalí, Salvador 95
Dalisi, Riccardo 43, 96, 216, 255
Danese, Bruno 188
DATA magazine 46, 83
De Chirico, Giorgio 17
De Lucchi, Michele 39, 66, *89*, 167, 168, 255
deconstructivism 168
Deganello, Paolo 36
Del Pezzo, Lucio 186
democracy *see* social-democratic ideals
Derossi, Pietro 36
design exhibitions 88–91
Design Gallery 114
design schools 47
Il design e le sue prospettive disciplinari (Design and its disciplinary perspectives, talk, 1977) 215
Il design Italiano degli anni Cinquanta (Italian Design in the 1950s, book/exh., 1980) 44, 87
Di Stefano, Francesco (Chichì, grandfather) 14, 17
Diagramma teorico (Theoretical diagram) *70*
Diedron Disco Complex plan, Cappella Cantone, Cremona *49*
Dipinti (Paintings, exh., 1986) 138
Divisionism 66, 246
Documenta 8 (1987) 139
Domercq, Fabrice 248
Domus magazine 7–8, 19, 36, 39, 43, 46, 47, 83–91, 96, 98, 114, 133, 135, 159, 162, *217*, 218
  1928/73 Domus: 45 ans d'architecture, design, art (exh., 1973) 83
  covers 85, *86*, 87, *89*, *137*, 161, *250*
  Diario (Diary) editor's letters 252, 254
  Mendini's return 138, 215, 248–54, *250*
  Domus Moda magazine 40, 114, *115*
  Cosmesi Universale (Universal Cosmetics)

editor's letter 114–16
Donà, Claudia 46, 87
Donna mappamondo (World map woman) *26*
Una donna (A woman) *25*
Dor Murano glass vase *257*
Dorfles, Gillo 19
Dova, Gianni 21
Dov'è l'artigiano? (Where is the artisan?, exh., 1981) 134
Dressing Design 40
Driade 131, *144*
Droog 163
dystopianism 38

E

Eisenman, Peter 85
Elam UNO 134, *150–51*
Electa 44
Eleusi 135
Elogio del Banale (Ode to the Banal) book 91–92
expressionism 13
exquisite corpse 162

F

Faculty of Architecture, Florence 36
Fagone, Vittorio 139
Fascism 18, 19, 36, 43, 133
fashion design 21, 40, 69, 88, 113–16
Feininger, Lyonel 14
Fellini, Federico 13–14
Fernandes Iglesias, Maria 119
Fiat 85, 94
Figura (Figure) *27*
Fiorucci, Elio 114
Flaiano, Ennio, *Diario degli Errori* 131
Florence Gift Mart Fair (1992) *217*
Flos 44
Fondation Cartier pour l'Art Contemporain, Paris 248, *262*
Fontana, Lucio 21
Formalism 167–68
Fornasetti, Piero 21
Fortezza da Basso, Florence 216
Forum Design, Linz (exh., 1980) 7, 88–91, *93*, 100–101
Fossati, Paolo 19
Four sculpture *265*
Fragilisme (Fragility, exh., 2002) 248
Fronzoni, Angelo 23
FSB 135, *145*
Fuksas, Doriana 186
Fuksas, Massimiliano 186, 188
functionalism 47
Funi, Achille 17
Fursys buildings 223, *238*, *239*
Futurism 19, 69, 246
Futurists of Today, Miami (conference, 1999) 253

G

Gaeta, Pietro 165, 185
Galassia (Galaxy) series 248, *258*
Galla Placidia pattern 99, 188
Galleria Margine, Zurich 138
Gallinella sculpture *153*
Gandini, Marcello 47
Gardella, Ignazio 44
Gatti, Piero 131
Gaudí, Antoni 13, *15*, 21
Gehry, Frank 85, 135
Ghini, Massimo Iosa 185
Giacon, Massimo 189
Gilardi, Piero 138
Gili, Anna 7, *117*, 119, *126*, 186, 219, 255
Ginsberg, Allen 43, 47
Gioiello d'oro (Gold jewel) pendant *140*
Gioiello (Jewel) pendant *140*
Gligorov, Robert 186
Global Tools fanzine 41, *42*, 43
Global Tools seminars *32*, 39, 43, 46, 84, 99
globalization 159–62, 223
Goethe, Johann Wolfgang von 245
Goldstein, Barbara 135
Gori Lab *266*
Graves, Michael 98
Green, Christopher 133
Gregori (also: Gregory), Bruno 65, 88, 134, 165, 189, *194–95*, *197*
Gregori, Giorgio 65, 66, 88, 118, 163, 165, 189, 190
Gregotti, Vittorio 38
Groninger Museum, Groningen 66, 131, 139, 162–63, 167–68, *169*, *172–81*
  Bisazza mosaic staircase 168, *180*
  Mondo Mendini – The World of Alessandro Mendini (exh., 2019) 220, 255
Gropius, Walter 66, 131
Gruppo Strum 38
Guerrier de Verre sculpture/earrings 248, *261*
Guerriero, Adriana 65
Guerriero, Alessandro 65, 66, 69, 87, 88, 91, 94, 118, 134, 135, 162
Gufram 56

INDEX 297

H

Haks, Frans 162–63, 167
Halley, Peter 245
Hamel, Maria Christina *106*
Hannover Bus Station 254, *271*
Haus-Rucker-Co 88, 91
Haussmann, Trix and Robert 66
Hayek, Nicolas 188
Hayon, Jaime 188
Hees, Emilie Van 85
Helander, Eija 95
Hollein, Hans 96–98
Horn, Rebecca 88, 91
Hosoe, Isao 69
Huang, Yong Ping 216
Hufnagl, Florian *253*

I

I am Mr Ciao sculpture *212*
IACP housing estate, Via dei Missaglia, Milan 35
Icheon vase *226*
'ideal home' notion 113
Iloom *237, 239*
Impressionism 66
In magazine 47
Incontri ravvicinati d'architettura (Close Architectural Encounters, exh., 1978) 65, 66
industrial archaeology 165
industrial design 19, 43, 69, 85, 91, 134, 167, 185
Innocente 186
Ipotesi di lavoro per la progettazione totale (Hypothesis for Total Design) manifesto 23
Istituti Superiori per le Industrie Artistiche (ISIAs) 47, 119
Italian Communist Party 38, 85
Italsider steel plant, Taranto 35
Italy: The New Domestic Landscape (exh., 1972) 38, 91
Itten, Johannes 66
Izenour, Steven 159–62, *160*

J

Jannon, Guido 94
Japanese architecture 35
Jencks, Charles 83, 98
Johnson, Philip 85
Jsa 21
Jumbo Trams 46
Jung, Ernst 248

K

Kaess-Weiss gallery, Stuttgart 139
Kandinsky, Wassily 66, 69, 246
Kandissi sofa 65, *75*, 246
Kandissone tapestry 66, *76, 79*, 139
Kaplický, Jan 188
Kartell 44
Kerouac, Jack 43
King, Perry 135
Kita, Toshiyuki *132*, 135
kitsch 65, 66, 161, 162–65, 168, 188, 220
Kobayashi, Yumiko 185
Koenig, Giovanni Klaus 19, 36, 38, 46
Koolhaas, Rem 163, 220
Kostabi, Mark 216, *225*
Kounellis, Jannis 138
Kunstmuseum, Düsseldorf 119

L

La Pietra, Ugo 38, 43, 47
Lampada di Milo 155
Lampada letargo (Letargo lamp) *57*
Lao Tse 7
Lapidus, Morris *86*, 161, *247*
Las Vegas 159–62
Lassù (Up there) chair 39, *42, 58*, 220
Le Corbusier 83
left-wing politics 84, 220
Léger, Fernand, *Abstraction* 133–34
Levi-Montalcini, Gino 133
Lévi-Strauss, Claude 167
LeWitt, Sol 186
Linea cabinets *238*
Linus magazine 47
Little Monument to the Swatch table clock *196*
Longobardi, Nino 186
Lorenz, Marianne 85
Los Angeles conference (1985) *132*, 135
Lots of Dots wristwatch *182*, 188
Lugtenberg, Corien 163
Luna & Sole (Moon & Sun) storage unit *267*
Lupi, Italo *187*
Lyotard, Jean-François 83

M

Madre Museum, Naples 255, *272–73*
Magazzini Criminali 118
Maghetti District redevelopment, Lugano *206*
Magistretti, Vico 47, *217*
Maiocchi, Giancarlo 85
Maldonado, Tomás 44, 85, 251

Malossi, Giannino 94
Manifesto magazine 38
mannerism 161
Mara Voce (Mendini pseudonym) 216
Maraini, Fosco 36
Marano, Ugo 186
Marc'Aurelio magazine 13
Margaret and Thomas More: Utopia Island 242
Margarini, Annalisa *197*
Mari, Enzo 38, 85, *86*, 131, 134, *160, 217, 247*
Martone, Mario 69
Marucelli, Germana 21
Marxism 38, 218; *see also* neo-Marxism
Mary Boone Gallery, New York 245
materialism 69
Matia Bazar 135
Mattotti, Lorenzo 251
portrait of Mendini *247*
Mazzocchi, Gianni 8, 35, 83, 84, 87
Mazzocchi, Giovanna 83, 87, 251, 254
Mazzocchi, Maria Grazia 87
McLuhan, Marshall 83
Meier, Richard 85, *90*, 98
Melnikov, Konstantin 83
Memphis 118, *148*, 189, 223
Mendelsohn, Erich 13, *15*, 21
Mendelsohn, Luise 13
Mendini, Alessandro
designed paintings 138–39, *141–43*
early years 14–19
importance of drawing/painting for 13–14, 18, 113, 219, 245, 246, *247*
photographs of *9, 16, 20, 22, 42, 67, 86, 90, 93, 117, 132, 160, 187, 191, 217, 253, 275*
portraits of *10, 24, 86, 247*
professionalism 7, 36, 39, 96, 249
travels 38, *132*, 135
Mendini, Elisa (daughter) 17, *37*, 274
Mendini, Francesco (brother) 18, 35, 138, 162, 163, 165, 185, 186, *217*, 254, 274; *see also* Atelier Mendini
Mendini, Fulvia (daughter) 17, *37*, 186, 234–35, 274
Mendini, Mia (sister) *10, 16*, 17
Mendini, Vincenzo (father) 17
Mendini Di Stefano, Fulvia (mother) 14
Mendini family 14–17, *22*
art collection *16*, 17, 18
Via Giorgio Jan home, Milan 14, *16*, 18
Merletto pattern 220
Merz, Mario 88, 138
metadesign 35–36
Mies van der Rohe, Ludwig 66
Migliaccio, Franco *67*
Milan as design capital 13, 21, 47, 116
Mitsubishi Heavy Industry 185
Miyake, Issey 116
Mizrahil, Monique 88
Mobili da guerriglia (Guerrilla furniture) *55*
Mobile Infinito (Endless Furniture) project 118, *121–23*, 138
Mobili da meditazione (Meditation furniture) *55*
Mobili d'Artista (Artist Furniture) collection 138
Mobili per uomo (Furniture for Man) series *202–3*
Mocika, Alex 165, 186
Modernism 7, 14, 19, 35, 36–38, 40, 43, 44, 69, 83, 98, 113, 114, 118, 161, 163, 188
Modo magazine 8, 39, 44–47, *45*, 83, 87, 95, 116
cartoon strips 46–47
Design dove sei? (Design, where are you?) editor's letter 44–46
Mollino, Carlo 21
Molteni, Giovanna *232*
Mondo Mendini – The World of Alessandro Mendini (exh., 2019) 220, 256
Montenapoleone Metro Station, Milan 188
Monumentino da casa (Small monument for the house) *45, 52, 59*
Moore, Charles 98
More, Thomas *242*, 249
Morellet, François 180
Morganti, Mario *22*
Morozzi, Cristina Dosio 46
Morozzi, Massimo 36, 46
Mosaic School, Spilimbergo 219
Mosaico Mendini (Mendini Mosaic, exh., 2011) 188
Mosconi, Davide *42*, 185
Mucchi, Gabriele 133
Mulas, Maria 85
Multifunctional building, Lörrach *270–71*
Munari, Bruno 14, 19, 189
Murano glass *257*
Musée des Arts Décoratifs, Louvre, Paris 83
Museum of Modern Art (MoMA), New York 38, 91, 96, 159
Mussolini, Benito 18
Mussolini's Bathroom (exh., 1982) 133, *137*

N

Naples Metro Stations 186, *187, 207–9*, 218, 219, 254
Natalini, Adolfo 36, 43
Navone, Paola *41*, 43, 66, 91, 94
Nazism 18, 83

Neo Malevic head 248
neo-avant-garde 40, 43, 44
neocapitalism 114
neoclassicism 168
neo-expressionism 138
neo-industrialisation 85
neo-Marxism 40
neomodernism 66
neon 66, 98, 161, 220, 222
Nervi, Pier Luigi 21
Die Neue Sammlung, Munich 98
Neues Museum, Nürnberg *253*
New International Design 190
New Utopia 254
New York Times 254
New-New International Style 223
Next Cities (exh., 2002) 218, 219
Nine vase 265
Nizzoli, Marcello 35, 185
Nizzoli Associati 17, 21, 35–36, 38
Université Libre de Bruxelles project 35, *48*
non-method design 185
Novecento style 14
Nulla: Idea per un ambiente (Nothing: idea for an environment, exh., 1984) 119, *126*
Nuovo Design (New Design) essay 134
NV Nederlands GasUnie (Dutch Gas) 167

O

Occhiomagico 85, 87, 133
Oggetti ad uso spirituale (Objects for spiritual use) 39, *51*
Oggetti e Progetti (Objects and Projects, exh., 2010) 98
Oggetto Meditativo crystal monstrance 256
L'oggetto banale (The Banal Object, exh., 1980) 88, 91–94, *105, 107*
L'Oggetto Naturale (The Natural Object, exh., 1982) 119
Ogni oggetto è diverso da ogni altro (Every object is different from another) talk 135
Olivari 185, *201*
Venere door handle series 185, *200*
Oliveri, Mario 23, 35
Olivetti 21, 43, 69, 135, 218
Ollo magazine *137*, 139, 215
Omaggio a Gropius (Homage to Gropius) handles *145*
Ondoso coffee table 66, *74*
Ontani, Luigi 186
Oppenheim, Meret 85, *86*
Orlandoni, Bruno *41*, 43
Ortner, Laurids 91
Österreichisches Institut für Visuelle Gestaltung (Austrian Institute for Visual Design), Linz 88

P

Padiglione d'Arte Contemporanea (PAC), Milan 118, 119
Paesaggio banale (Banal landscape) *102*
Paesaggio Casalingo (Homely Landscape, book/exh., 1980/81) 95, 96–98
Pagano, Giuseppe 19, 35, 133
Paladino, Mimmo 138, 186, 188, 189, 255
Paladino, Salvatore 186
Palazzo dei Diamanti, Ferrara 65, 66, 222
Palazzo delle Esposizioni, Rome 87
Palazzo Reale, Milan 133
Palladio, Andrea 85
Pamuk, Orhan, *Benim adım Kırmızı* (My Name is Red) 222
Panzeri, Mauro 87, 118
Paolini, Cesare 131
Perez, Augusto 186
Perino & Vele 186
Perrault, Dominique 186
Peressutti, Enrico 19
Pedio, Renato 47
Persico, Edoardo 35
Pescatore (Fisherman) 29
Pesce, Gaetano 38, 43, 131
Pettena, Gianni 43
Peynet, Raymond 14
Peyrano box *160*
photography 43
Piacentini, Marcello 185
Piaggi, Anna 116
Pianeta Fresco magazine 47
Piccole Fantasie Quotidiane (exh., 2020) 255, *272–73*
Piccolo Teatro, Milan 8
Pidgeon, Monica 39
Pietrantoni, Marcello 83
Pirelli 14, 17, 18, 21, *29, 30–31*
Pisani, Gianni 186
Pisis, Filippo de 17
Pittura Progettata, Design Pittorico (Painting as Design, Design as Painting) essay 8, 139
Pivano, Fernanda 43, 47
Pointillism 66, 246, 255
Poli, Alessandro 36
Politecnico di Milano (Polytechnic University of Milan) 13, 18, 19, *20, 22*, 118, *263*

Politi, Giancarlo, *Alessandro Mendini* 138–39
Poltrona, tomba da soggiorno (Armchair, living room tomb) *56*
Poltrona di Paglia (Straw Armchair) *42*, 255
Poltronova 39
Pomodoro, Giò 95
Ponti, Gio 8, 13, 19, 21, 36, 40, 44, 65, *71, 83–84, 86, 123*, 135, 185, 255
Ponti, Lisa Licitra 83, 85–87
pop 69, 131, 161, 188, 189
Porro *238*
Portaluppi, Piero 14, 18
Portoghesi, Paolo 91, 98, 159, 185
post-avant-garde 38
postmodernism 44, 69, 83, 85, 91, 92, 98–99, 114, 159, 218
post-Radical design 65, 66
Prandi, Lidia (wife) 17, *20, 42*, 46
progressivism 7, 8, 14, 19, 83
Propp, Vladimir, *Morphology of the Folktale* 167
Proust, Marcel, *In Search of Lost Time* 14, 18, 65, 66, 245
Proust armchair 65–66, *67*, 77, 83, 135, 188, 218, 220, 246, 248
Proust laminate 77, 162, 168, *173, 182*
Proust pattern 77, *173, 182, 198–99*, 245, 255
public transport 46; *see also* Hannover Bus Station; Milan Metro Station; Naples Metro Stations
Puppa, Daniela 38, 87, 91, 118
Purini, Franco 251

Q

Quali Cose Siamo (The Things That We Are, exh., 2010) 252–54
Quartiere Maghetti, Lugano 219

R

Radical architecture 36–43, 163
Radical design 35–44, 96, 98, 113, 114, 118, 185, 246, 254
Radice, Barbara 46, 87, 88, 91, 116
Raggi, Franco 38, 46, 47, 65, 87, 91, 92, 118
Ramun 255, *268–69*
Rashid, Karim 186, *209*
Rationalism 19, 69, 114, 133
Rawsthorn, Alice 254
RDE 116
Re Nudo magazine 47
ready-mades 66
realism 46, 185
Redesign del Movimento Moderno (Redesign of the Modern Movement) chair series 65, *71–75*, 91, 131
Renaissance 161
Renault *Super 5* decoration 135, *154*
Repubblica newspaper 249
'Research on Environment' project 133
Restany, Pierre 8, 83, 84, 87, 135, 162
Ricci, Leonardo 36
Riccio, Gianluca 255
Rietveld, Gerrit 65, *72*, 163
Rinaldi, Rosa Maria 87, 94, 116
robotics 85
Rogers, Ernesto 18–19, 21, 35, 116
Roman antiquity 161, 188
romanticism 14
Rome Prize 161
Rosica, Arianna 255
Rosselli, Alberto 38
Rossi, Aldo 18, 85, *86*, 91, 98, 159, *160*, 163
Autobiografia Scientifica (A Scientific Autobiography) 220
Rota, Italo 251
Rotella, Mimmo 186, 189
Ruggeri, Cinzia 135

S

Sabrina armchair 131, *144*
Salone Internazionale del Mobile, Milan 47
Sangregorio, Giancarlo 23
Santachiara, Denis 186
Sapper, Richard 96
Sargenti, Anna 186
Sargiani, Franco 95
Savinio, Alberto 17–18, 255
Autoritratto in forma di Gufo 16
L'Annunciazione (The Annunciation) *10*, 17
Savioli, Leonardo 36
Scheggi, Paolo 21, 23
Scott Brown, Denise 159–62, *160*
Scully, Vincent 161
sculpture 138, 188, 220, 248
Sedia (Chair) *56*
Sedia 'Elevazione' oppure 'Erezione' ('Elevation' or 'Erection' chair) *52*
Sedia grano (Grain chair) *60*
Sedia terra (Earth chair) *58*
Segoni, Roberto 46
Sejima, Kazuyo *250*, 251
Seoul Design Fair, *La Punta* pavilion (2010) *221*, 222, *230–31*

INDEX

Serafini, Luigi 186
Severini, Gino 188
Shakespeare & Company 116
Sichterman, Jan Albert 163
Sieger family castle, Schloss Harkotten *205*
Signac, Paul 66, 255
Signs of Life: Symbols in the American City (exh., 1976) 161
Silva, Egidio 186
Simmel, Georg 113
Sironi, Mario 17, 188
Slide *265*
SMH Italy 188, 189
social realism 162
social-democratic ideals 19, 35, 44, 85, 162, 188, 249
Società Artistie Designer (SAD), Zurich 138
Song, Bang-ung 255
Sottsass, Ettore 7, 36, 38, 39, 43–44, 46, 47, 65, 66, *67*, 69, 85, 88, 91, 95–96, 99, 118, 134, 163, *164*, 188, *191*, *217*, 223
Sottsass's Scrap-Book 44, *45*
South Korea 162, *191*, 222–23, *229*, 240–41, 254
  La Punta pavilion, Seoul Design Fair (2010) *221*, 222, *230–31*
Soviet Constructivism 69
Soviet era 167, 216
Sowden, George 186
Spalletti, Ettore 186
Spaziale table and chairs 66
SPC Group *212*
Speciale gallery, Bari 119
Speer, Albert 83
Spot the Dot wristwatch *198–99*
La Stanza del Secolo (The Room of the Century) 65, 66
Starck, Philippe 167, 168
Steinberg, Saul 13
Steiner, Rudolf 13, 21
Stella, Frank 167, *169*
Stella (Star) sculpture *205*
Stelline chair *150–51*
Stölzl, Gunta 131
Strada, Nanni 40
Strada che si avvolge (Winding road) *28*
Le Strutture Tremano (The Structures Tremble) table 66
Studio Alchimia 14, 39, 65, 66–69, *67*, 83, 85, 87, 88, 91, 94, 114, 118, 119, 133, 135, 159, 163, 165, 189, 215
  Bau-Haus I collection 66, *68*, 69, 114
  Fast Design collection *120*
  Galla Placidia pattern 99, 188
  Tender Architecture 118, *125*, 222
  'Universal Museum' model 139
Studio Job 188
Studio Temp 234–235
Stuttgarter Bank mural, Stuttgart *204*
Sudjic, Deyan 218
Suncheon Bay National Garden, South Korea 223, *240–41*
Superego *264*
  La Superficie Modificante (The Modifying Surface, exh.) 1980) 88, 94
Superstudio 36, 38, 39, 40, 43
Suprematism 248
Supreme skateboard *263*
Sussman, Deborah 135
Svincolo floor lamp 66
Swarovski 185, 246, *256*
Swatch 134, *182*, 186, 188–90, *191*, *195–99*
  Lab *191*, 199
  Lots of Dots wristwatch *182*, 188
Swatch Art Clock Towers, Atlanta Olympics (1996) 189–90
Swatch Emotion, World Trade Center Singapore (exh., 1994) 189, *194–95*
symbolism 161, 162, 185, 255
Szeemann, Harald 83

T

Tarshito (Nicola Strippoli) 119
Tatafiore, Ernesto 186
Tateishi, Kōichi (Tiger) 99, *108*
  portrait of Mendini *86*
Tavolino da salotto (Drawing room table) 39, *61*
Tavolo dolmen (Dolmen table) *56*
Tavolo e sedia capitonné (Upholstered table and chair) *54*
Tavolo preghiera (Prayer table) *54*
Tavolo voragine (Chasm table) *54*
Taylor, Lisa 96
Tea & Coffee Towers (exh., 2002) 218–19, *221*, *236–37*
Tea & Coffee Piazza programme 80, 94, 97, 98–99, *106*, 113, 159
Tebe door handle 185
Telegrammi al Designer (Telegrams to the Designer) 215
Tender Architecture installation 118, *125*, 222
Teodoro, Franco 131
Termini Station, Rome 219
Terragni, Giuseppe 133
Tête Géant (Giant Head) sculpture *261*
Thonet no. 14 chair 65, *73*

Three sculpture *264*
Thun, Matteo 189
Tigerman, Stanley 98
Tompkins, Doug 135
Toraldo di Francia, Cristiano 36, 40
Torre Panoramica (Panoramic Tower), Suncheon Bay National Garden 223, *241*
Torre Paradiso (Paradise Tower), Hiroshima 185, *192–93*, 246
Torre Velasca, Milan 19, 21
Transavanguardia 138, 188
Tre Primitivi QFWFQ storage unit *267*
Triennale di Milano
  (1933) 13
  (1980) 96–98
  (1985) *117*, 119
  (1986) *67*
  (2011) 185
  Pulviscoli (Particles, 2019) 220, 246
  Incheon headquarters 222, *228*
  Quali Cose Siamo (The Things That We Are, 2010) 252–54
Trinks, Dagmar 185
Türler 135, *149*
Tusquets, Òscar 88, 98, 186
Tutta office chair *237*

U

UFO 36, 65
'Universal Museum' model 139
Università Iuav di Venezia (IUAV) 159
Université Libre de Bruxelles project 35, *48*
Untitled paintings 138, *141–43*
Untitled sketches *24*, *62*, *78*, *103–4*, *152*
urban planning 19, 159, 186, 249, 254
Urbolante: Ricognizione sul paesaggio (Urbolante: Landscape reconnaissance) *50*
Urquiola, Patricia 188
utopianism 8, 13, 19, 35, 40, 43, 44, 46, 83, 113, 159, 167, 186, 249, 252, 254

V

Valcarenghi, Andrea 47
Valigia per ultimo viaggio (Suitcase for the last journey) 39, 40, *61*
Vasi di Manici 120
Vasi Utopici 227
Venere door handles 185, *200*
Venice Architecture Biennale 23, 88, 91
  Ponte dell'Accademia (1985) 159, *170*
  Stanza Banale (Banal Room, 1980) *90*, 92
  Tea & Coffee Towers (2002) 218–19, *221*, *236–37*
Venini 248, *256–61*
  Achernar Murano glass pendant *258*
  Galassia (Galaxy) series 248
  Guerrier de Verre sculpture/earrings 248, *261*
Venturi, Robert 7, 98, 160, 163, *164*, 216, *225*
  Complexity and Contradiction in Architecture 159, 161
  decorated sheds 161–62, 222, 223
  Learning from Las Vegas (with Scott Brown and Izenour) 159–62, *160*
Vergine, Lea 46
Vietnam war 39
Viganò, Vittoriano 21
Visage Archaïque (Archaic Face) sculpture *261*
Vodoz, Jacqueline 188
Vossaert, Gerda 165

W

Wanders, Marcel 188
Wenders, Wim *250*, 251
Wilde, Oscar 252
Wilson, Bob 8
World War II 18, 43, 83
  post- 19–23
Wunderkammer Design (exh., 2011) 253

Y

Yamashita, Kazumasa 98

Z

Zabro collection *128*, *132*, 133–34, *147*, 154
Zanotta, Aurelio 7, 91, 131, *132*, 133
Zanotta 7, 44, 88, 91, 94, 114, 131–34, 135, 138
Zabro collection *128*, *132*, 133–34, *146–47*, 154
Zanuso, Marco 19, 35, 38, 47, 131
Zerodisegno 114
Zeus 138
Zevi, Bruno 136
Zona sofa 133–34

ACKNOWLEDGEMENTS

Every book is a long and deeply personal journey through time and space for its author. But when the journey involves a person with whom one has shared decades of cultural work, time, space and sentiment can blur – even as we strive to preserve memories and affections against the looming threat of oblivion.

My first thanks go to Fulvia and Elisa Mendini, Alessandro's daughters and spiritual heirs, for their gracious and enthusiastic support in allowing this book to be published and for generously opening up the vast archives of the studio, of which they are the curators. They helped uncover rare or previously unseen materials, added vital clarifications on well-known events, and did so through heartfelt conversations. There were emotional moments, at least on my part, upon seeing in them Alessandro's intelligence, irony, resilience, as well as his characteristic restraint. Equally invaluable were the memories of Lidia Prandi, based on her diaries and personal recollections from family gatherings and professional settings.

Another central role in this publication was played by Beatrice Felis, who was Alessandro's assistant for nearly as long as anyone can remember. Without her and our intense and focused working sessions, it would have been impossible to meticulously reconstruct the events and circumstances recounted here – from the main text to the richly detailed captions, which could easily fill another small book of their own. Thank you, Bea.

My grateful thoughts also go to Phaidon Press, to Joe Pickard for his attentive care as editor, and especially to associate publisher Emilia Terragni. Since my first idea for the book, Emilia believed in this complex project and has been of great help to me through our seminal discussions and her advice on content, along the 'long and winding road' to final publication.

I extend heartfelt gratitude to architect Franco Raggi for his reconstructions, both verbal and through documents, of the long and significant years of collaboration with Alessandro on magazines and exhibitions, from Radical *Casabella* to *L'Oggetto Banale* for the Venice Biennale in 1980. I'm also grateful to photographer Santi Caleca, whose archive contains even more images and memories than could be included here, bearing testimony to a long, joyful collaboration with Mendini, his producers and collectors.

Special thanks to Alberto Alessi for the insights he shared over numerous conversations held before and during the work on this book. These dialogues revealed a profound alignment between the design and existential visions of the entrepreneur and the architect, which led Mendini to inspire all of Alessi's cultural and industrial strategies, ultimately shaping both the private living spaces of Alberto himself and the public dimensions of his communications and business. Thank you also to Piero and Rossella Bisazza, among the main supporters of the ideas and works that brought Alessandro's colourful and visionary utopias to life.

I am also grateful for conversations with Gabi Faeh, particularly about the history of Studio Alchimia, and thank her and our daughter Lunella for their unwavering support during this complex editorial venture.

In no particular order, I also wish to thank filmmaker Ester Tatangelo, photographers Carlo Lavatori, Matteo Cirenei, Donato Di Bello, Salvatore Licitra and Mario Ermoli – personal friends and collaborators who have always been ready for a conversation and to share images that proved invaluable for more than one book.

A heartfelt memory goes to the late Renato Pedio – scholarly poet and editor in chief of *L'architettura* magazine – and the brilliant industrialist Aurelio Zanotta, who were both friends and companions of Alessandro Mendini. Like him, they taught me much about the culture of industry and design, as well as the principles of professional and existential integrity.

Finally, my deepest thanks go, naturally, to Alessandro Mendini himself, the most generous intellectual in the history of contemporary Italian design, for the opportunities he provided and shared in this singular professional and cultural journey. He created the monumental body of work this book seeks, in part, to portray, and for those who knew him well, he evokes Jorge Luis Borges' parable:

A man sets out to draw the world. As the years go by, he peoples a space with images of provinces, kingdoms, mountains, bays, ships, islands, fishes, rooms, instruments, stars, horses and individuals. A short time before he dies, he discovers that this patient labyrinth of lines traces the image of his own face.
  Jorge Luis Borges, *El Hacedor* (The Maker), 1960

Stefano Casciani
November 4, 2024

Stefano Casciani
Born in Rome in 1955, designer, writer and artist Stefano Casciani started his career at the age of 24 as freelance editor of *Domus* Magazine, when he was invited to join the team by Mendini. Since then, he has developed a special interest in the connections between the arts, design and architecture – through publications, exhibitions, books, magazines and commercial projects. Internationally acknowledged as one of the most important disseminators of design culture, he has received important awards such as the Compasso d'Oro 2001 for the RAI program *Lezioni di Design*. He was the long-standing deputy editor of *Domus* magazine from 2000 to 2010, and co-editor in chief alongside Alessandro Mendini (*La Nuova Utopia* series, 2010/11). In 2012 he founded the magazine *disegno. la nuova cultura industriale*, as publisher and editor in chief. Some of his projects and objects are in private and public collections (Musèe des Arts Decoratifs, Ghent; Wolfsonian-FIU, Miami; ADI Design Museum, Milan). He has written and curated more than 40 books, including recent titles about Massimiliano Fuksas, Thom Mayne and Gio Ponti. Casciani is particularly proud of his large mosaic *ENJOY (Y)OUR LIFE* produced by Bisazza for Milan's Montenapoleone metro station.

Phaidon Press Limited
2 Cooperage Yard
London E15 2QR

Phaidon Press Inc.
111 Broadway
New York, NY 10006

phaidon.com

First published 2025
© 2025 Phaidon Press Limited
Text © 2025 Stefano Casciani
Images courtesy Alessandro Mendini Archive
© 2025 Elisa and Fulvia Mendini

ISBN 978 1 83866 867 9

A CIP catalogue record for this book is available from the British Library and the Library of Congress.

All rights reserved. No part of this publication may be reproduced, stored in a retrieval system or transmitted, in any form or by any means, electronic, mechanical, photocopying, recording or otherwise, without the written permission of Phaidon Press Limited.

Commissioning Editor: Emilia Terragni
Executive Editor: Joe Pickard
Production Controller: Zuzana Cimalova
Graphic Design: La Tigre

Printed in China

Cover images:

Front: Gorilla beringei beringei – Akeley African Hall, postcard from American Museum of Natural History shop in New York, halo drawn in pen by Mendini, 1972, Alessandro Mendini Archive

Back: *Proust* armchair drawing by Alessandro Mendini, Alessandro Mendini Archive